EVERYTHING BITES, SCRATCHES AND STINGS

A Thousand Days in the West African Bush

Preface

I traveled throughout West Africa during the early nineteen seventies, capturing reptiles and amphibians for export to Europe for various pet shops. My colleague, Karl Bischof, was a knowledgeable herpetologist who knew what animals to collect, their identities, natures and location. This astonishing adventure required living in the bush isolated from Western civilization and sometimes remote from all human habitation. It was a life of utter self-reliance, subsisting very much as the Africans themselves did, while camping in the wilds. Thus we were able to experience and come to respect the essential Africa in a direct, authentic way and not merely from the remote perspective of the tourist or privileged class. It is for this reason that, forty years later, I have returned to my original, unembellished account written between 1971 and 1974 adding merely a few helpful details in terms of history or politics and improving the writing. I hope this narrative of my travels will inspire other young adventurers and even assist them in their planning and explorations.

The cover photograph was taken on the day that we arrived back in Austria after three years in Africa, July, 1974. Julian Hamer on the left, Karl Bischof on the right. The vehicle is the small Citroen 2CV van that we drove back across the Sahara Desert.

This book is dedicated to my beautiful wife, Ellen, for her support and for editing the manuscript. Further, I dedicate it to Karl Bischof who was the real hero of this narrative.

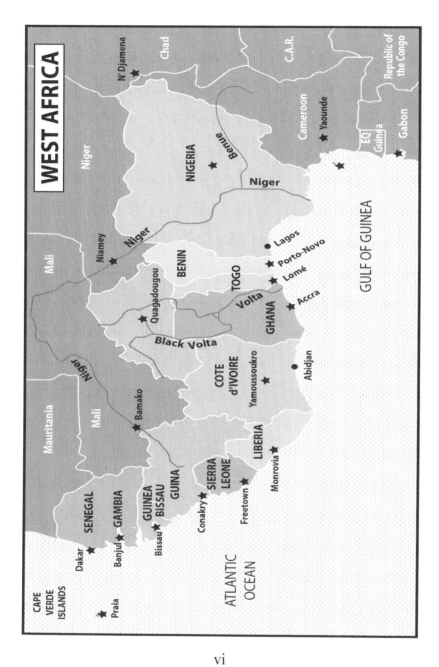

WEST AFRICA

CAPE
VERDE
ISLANDS

★ Praia

ATLANTIC
OCEAN

Dakar ★

SENEGAL

Banjul ★ GAMBIA

Bissau ★ GUINEA
BISSAU

GUINA

Conakry ★

SIERRA
LEONE

Freetown ★

LIBERIA

Monrovia ★

Mauritania

Mali

Niger

Bamako ★

Mali

Ouagadougou ★

Black Volta

COTE
d'IVOIRE

Yamoussoukro ★

Abidjan ●

BENIN

TOGO

Volta

GHANA

Accra ★

Lomé ★

Porto-Novo ★

Lagos ●

Niger

Niamey ★

Niger

Mali

Niger

NIGERIA

Benue

N'Djamena ★

Chad

GULF OF GUINEA

Cameroon

Yaounde ★

C.A.R.

EQ
Guinea

Gabon ★

Republic of
the Congo

★

vi

EVERYTHING BITES, SCRATCHES AND STINGS

A Thousand Days in the West African Bush

1. SENEGAL
Reptile Catching in the Desert du Ferlo

The cargo ship "Django" trembled a little as it turned. It trembled just enough to wake both of us up. We stumbled to the porthole and looked out, shoreward, across the dark sea. There was a slight early morning mist hovering over the surface, hiding the waves. Part of the horizon was brightening slightly, showing a little of the outline of the landscape. Before us were the flashing lighthouse lights on the silhouetted island of Goreé, the infamous former slave station of West Africa. Deeper through the darkness and mist, we could see the red and green lights of the harbor, the harbor of Dakar.

We had only been four days at sea but had waited over a month in Morocco for a ship. For us it was an exciting and elated feeling as the vessel passed the island and entered into the harbor. The first main step had been taken, we had managed the first stage of our journey according to plan.

Karl and I had met in Innsbruck, Austria in 1970, just a year and a half earlier. Karl was originally from Styria, Austria while I was born in the U.K. We quickly became good buddies and somehow hatched the adventurous idea of traveling to Africa to catch animals for pet shops. Although entirely self-taught, Karl had a great deal of zoological knowledge and skill, particularly pertaining to reptiles and amphibians. It was those creatures and perhaps tropical fish that we planned to export in order to finance our travels.

Both now very much awake, we hurried down to get breakfast over with, the last meal on the ship. The French steward, Jean, was also glad to be in port and was singing.

As we came out on deck afterwards, things were already on the move. The sun had risen up over the horizon spreading its warmth, telling us we were in the tropics. There was a great deal of activity onboard: lots of new and grinning faces. The heavy iron hatches had already been removed from the hold and our cargo van looked remarkably clean in the early morning sunshine. An army of Senegalese dock workers were down there laughing and springing about. They fixed rubber-bound beams under the van's chassis and tied

1

everything, we hoped firmly, with extra rope. The captain of the Django was also already on deck keeping a watchful eye on things.

The intention seemed to be to hoist the van out of the hold onto the quay with the ship's crane, usually just used for unloading bananas, and it didn't look at all strong enough for our heavy van. We told the captain the weight of the van, but he said the crane was strong enough and he was prepared to take the risk. We were not at all sure, but the maneuver was already under way.

The two men operating the crane seemed to be concentrating on everything except the job at hand. One of them was cleaning his teeth with a piece of stick and the other was laughing and joking with one of his friends.

Cries of glee and other noises usually heard only when watching fireworks announced that the van was already in the air. The hoist swung dangerously from side to side, grating at its pivot. The van, rocking in the air, jerked threateningly and a group of Africans ran quickly out of the way.

The captain shouted "slowly" and we echoed "slowly" but much louder than an echo should be. The van swung over the side of the ship and was speedily lowered down onto the quay; it bounced a little and then came to rest.

We bolted for the gangway and within seconds were on the quay examining the van for damage. Hardly a mark, just one small dent where the ropes had been and a door that didn't open quite as well as it once had. Nothing serious; we were more than a little relieved.

We went back on board to say "cheerio" to the captain, who said "goodbye" in German and English for the benefit of both of us.

The Commandant had by this time also appeared on deck and we said our farewells to him too, as we had eaten most of our meals with him throughout the journey. He apparently didn't find Africa at all exciting, having been waiting for the custom's officials to arrive since the ship had come into port several hours earlier. "In Africa," he said, "they say Tuesday and come on Friday!"

We left him to wait alone and went down onto the quay again, this time fully enjoying the feeling of being on the African mainland. There was still a crowd of workers around the van, peering in at the windows and looking at themselves in the driving mirrors. I climbed inside to drive into the cool shadow of the warehouse wall and understood from the banging and shouting outside that certain people wanted to ride with me. I drove the few yards alone into the shade, got out, and was greeted by disappointed faces on all sides.

We made our way to the harbor gates and inquired as to where we could find the touring club of Senegal. With vague information, we strolled leisurely in the approximate direction. We were astonished and impressed; all around were happy, laughing people.

Young souvenir sellers followed us a considerable distance along the street, trying to convince us that aluminum was silver. Unfortunately for them, we had already learned to say "no" in Morocco and were soon left in peace.

It was providential that we had traveled slowly down through Europe and spent several weeks in Morocco before arriving in Senegal. We later met many individuals who had arrived in West Africa by plane and did not have the advantage of our gradual transition. They were a naive and easy prey to all kinds of trouble, in particular thieves and official corruption.

We reached the town center, roughly where the touring club was supposed to be and, after a few inquiries, found it. Before we had passed through the door, we were greeted in a loud, friendly manner by a young but very heavy woman. We later learned that there was considerable status in having a large wife. The husbands seemed quite proud of the fact that they had attained a certain outwards status of affluence as demonstrated by a well-fed wife. Our new friend proved to be very efficient, despite her size, and in no time at all the formalities were over and we received our "Carnet de Passage," the document necessary for the temporary importation of vehicles.

We had not known about the Carnet nor that we would be charged harbor fees for the unloading of the van. These things took some time to sort out but, in the meantime, we made a new friend. We were still parked within the harbor compound when an African boy came up to us and enthusiastically presented us with a bowl full of sardines.

"Plenty, plenty fish", he kept saying over and over again. We accepted his gift and cooked them over our kerosene burner. They were tasty but full of bones. The young boy had wandered off without even sharing the meal but he turned up again later and assured us that the next day he would return again with, "Plenty, plenty fish".

Experiences like these, while at first amusing, made us also a little suspicious. But over time, we came to recognize the conventions. While the boy never asked us for money, it is nevertheless a significant African courtesy to offer something in return for a gift. This is what the young fellow was after and no doubt his approach had worked before. The idea is to give something and the recipient is then obligated to reciprocate. If he had tried to sell the fish we probably would not have bought them.

With our Canet de Passage, we left the town center and made our way back to the harbor to collect our van. After shaking hands with practically anybody and almost everybody, we drove off on our way. We never saw the boy with the fish again.

We followed the coast road away from Dakar as far as the airport, then, leaving the beautiful blue sea behind us, we cut inland and took the main route leading north towards St. Louis.

St. Louis was the original capital of the French colony of Senegal dating from the seventeenth century. It was a particularly intriguing choice for us not only because of the historical significance of the city itself but also the St Louis region seemed an easily accessible area of the Sahel zone, as it was our intention to remain primarily in the bush. From an ecological point of view, Karl thought that this might be a good place to pitch camp and start collecting our first consignment of reptiles for export.

The road was newly surfaced, straight and free of traffic. Both sides were lined with tall, golden savanna grasses and among them occasionally stood an enormous, stocky, monkey-bread or baobab tree, its short, twisted branches tipped with oval pods about half the size of a rugby ball, olive green and furry.

It had become very hot indeed, being early afternoon, but with the wind blowing through the open windows the temperature inside the van was quite comfortable.

After journeying a few hours, we decided to give the engine a rest and make some tea for ourselves. We slowed down and drove onto a stony pathway at the side of the road.

As the kettle began to boil, we heard a loud rustling in the tall grass behind us. Turning around, we saw the flat, dark head of a monkey peering through the grass. It became startled at our sudden movement and darted out across the road in front of the van. We quickly gave chase, wanting to get a better look at it, but it had already disappeared out of sight. We wandered about a bit in the grass, but nothing moved so we went back to make our tea. As we crossed the road, we saw the rest of the company. They were Patas monkeys, (Erythrocebus patas) at least twenty of them. The first one had been a big male while the rest included his harem and their young. The animal has a beautiful, orange-brown furry back and white underparts and a long, paint brush-tipped tail. A few of the company were climbing about on a fallen monkey-bread tree and hadn't yet noticed us. Suddenly, the whole group was in panic; a mother on the tree lifted her offspring in her arms and darted out of sight. Within a few seconds the whole group had vanished and we were left alone once more. We drank our tea quietly in the shade of the van, waiting for another display, but none came.

Underway again, we kept our eyes peeled, hoping to see something else of interest, but, apart from a snake wriggling its way across the road as fast as it could to safety, we saw nothing more.

We reached the outskirts of St. Louis by early evening and, after taking a quick glimpse of the town, we drove on once more into the sparsely populated countryside.

The landscape had changed altogether now. The tall savanna grass was replaced by acres and acres of swamps and short, wind-bent acacia had replaced the monkey-bread trees. The sun was setting. From somewhere, a few tattered clouds had appeared and kept changing position and color in keeping with the sunset.

We left the road and turned down a stony track. The way led away from the swamp area and we found ourselves in half-desert country, the sand tinged with orange from the setting sun. Along the track were a number of tall, very leafy trees and we decided to make our camp beneath one of them. We cooked our rice for supper and afterwards, as it was already quite dark, we decided to call it a day.

* * *

The next morning we were awakened by the singing, crying, wailing and whistling of dozens of different birds. The air was filled with their enchanting music. In our tree, a group of Red-billed Hornbills congregated and decided to make as much noise as possible to make sure we didn't oversleep.

The Hornbill (*Tockus erythrorhynchus*) is fascinating to watch. They begin to flap their wings excitedly as they call, building up vigorously to a crescendo of excitement. It is a very distinct bird-call and quite pleasing and in the context of the red sandy dunes dotted with acacia trees surrounded by a scattering of golden grasses and scrub it is unbelievably enchanting.

The female Hornbill lays her eggs in the hollow of a tree while, for safety, the male cements her in with mud and droppings. When the eggs hatch, the mother hammers her way out of the nest after which the pair rebuild the wall, leaving only a small opening through which they can feed the chicks. When the young are sufficiently grown they, in turn, break out to win their freedom and catch their own food.

We looked around at the morning panorama. Stretching out on all sides, sand, low dunes, slightly rippled and covered scantily with small thorn bushes, scrubs and, occasionally, some trees like the one under which we were camped.

Our first visitor that day arrived while we were still eating breakfast. He was driving his herd of goats to find pasture and had to come close by our camp. He was just a young boy, maybe twelve; he came up to us, touched his forehead and his heart in greeting and squatted down on the sand by our table. He wore a ragged shirt and typical Arabic baggy trousers and, of course, no shoes. He didn't say a word, just seemed content to sit there a while until he noticed his goats had begun to wander away on their own and then he sprang to his feet and started rounding them up by throwing stones at them and making a loud, clicking noise in the back of his throat which the goats seemed to understand, as they went in the direction he wanted. There wasn't very

6

much at all for the goats to eat on the ground, so they stood on their hind legs and tore down the one or two low hanging branches from the surrounding trees.

We spent most of the day wandering from one part of our patch of the desert to another. The thorns in the sand were very sharp and painful, strong enough to pierce even the soles of our shoes and I wondered why the young shepherd boy's feet were not all torn to shreds.

We were looking for lizards, one in particular, a skink that had a spade-like snout and lived somewhat like a mole burrowing in the sand. We found several holes nearby, but, although we dug them out and followed the tunnels a long way, we found nothing. Several times we caught a glimpse of something racing away from us into the bushes for cover, but the heat had made them faster while slowing us down and we were unable to catch anything. We panted here and there, our throats parched, the sun beating down on us. Now and then we saw tracks in the sand where the lizards had been, but we didn't try to follow them. It had already become far too hot, so we decided to rest a while beneath a shady tree. From a few yards away, we could see that it was full with agama lizards, but as we approached they all took cover. Karl recognized them as *Agama agama savattieri*. They run around the back of a tree trunk to hide in the same way that squirrels do. Karl became very adept at guessing where they were on the other side of a tree and catching them with his hand without actually seeing them.

After our rest, we made our way back towards our camp where we carefully laid some traps in the middle of a warren of skink tunnels. As we were preparing the last one, something wriggled underneath Karl's hand and he snatched at it. Of all things, he had caught the very skink we had been searching for the whole day long, here, just a short distance from camp.

* * *

Each sunset was always worth waiting for. There weren't a great many trees but quite a few scraggly thorn bushes and tufts of dried up grass spreading out all over the sea of sand. When evening came, there was often a gentle breeze, lightly blowing a little of the sand from the tops of the dunes into the air. The wind didn't whistle but arrived only gradually with the darkness, then disappeared again before daybreak.

Throughout the entire day there might not have been a cloud in the sky, but just before sunset one or two would appear as if from nowhere just to add an extra touch of wonder to the panorama. Before the sun actually set, the sky around it was yellow or perhaps faint orange. As it slowly went down, the one or two clouds reflected a little of that color as the sun itself turned gradually red. The larger trees, like the one which sheltered us and our van from the direct heat during the day, at evening became silhouetted against the horizon, standing quite alone high above all the bushes and plants. With the sun behind them, the spaces between the leaves and branches could be seen, giving the tree an X-ray look: strange, slowly waving skeletons standing about on the sand dunes. When the sun was finally gone, the whole sky, even to the opposite horizon, was splashed with rapidly changing shades of red. And what had been blue changed to turquoise, then pink, to red, to crimson. The cloud formations reflected the color-scape, different hues and tones steadily fading until darkness finally triumphed.

* * *

Mercifully, late one afternoon, some days later a pleasant wind sprung up and the air cooled slightly, so I decided to take the opportunity to leave the deep shade of our tree and take a walk among the sand dunes.

As usual, as I went my heels sank back into the sand, making the going difficult and soon very tiring, so that after just a few hundred yards I thought I had walked miles. Our camp was already out of sight, somewhere behind all of that sand, hidden away.

I brushed away the sharp thorns and sat myself down on the side of a dune a little in the shade of some skeleton bushes. The breeze was making miniature whirlwinds of sand and blowing them about among the dunes. From where I sat, I could look down over the landscape of scrub and thorny undergrowth to the one or two greener bushes that had been torn to pieces by goats. Somewhere much further away I noticed, out of the corner of my eye, a much darker shape moving about in a thicket of thorns. The first dark shape was followed by four other, smaller ones, each coming cautiously out of cover. They stopped, waited, sniffed the air, waited a little longer, then thinking the coast was clear, moved on towards the dune where I was sitting. I didn't have the binoculars with me, so at first I couldn't see clearly what they were. But as they came on, closer and closer and quite unaware that they were being observed, I recognized a mother and four baby warthogs!

Fortunately the wind was blowing against me and, although they stopped and raised their enormous heads in the air every few minutes because of their poor eyesight, they didn't detect me. In any case, I froze to stone and didn't make a sound. The ugly menage went around each of the bushes, munching away at the leaves and, after each mouthful, they waited, listening carefully to make sure there was no danger and then carried on once more with their meal. They came so close I could see their great, fleshy faces and the mother's bristly mane and her four large tusks curving upward over her snout. In the bushes, just a stone's throw away, they found a hoard of nearly ripe paprika-like fruits which they tore down from the stems and greedily chewed up.

Slowly but surely they made their way from one plant to another, still sniffing and listening until they moved off into the distance, just as the sun was starting to redden and begin to sink over the horizon. Then all at once they were gone and I was alone once more in the descending dusk.

* * *

The young native boys were very curious to see what we were like and what we were up to and often spent the best part of a day at our camp, just sitting on the sand and watching. They soon noticed our interest in reptiles and saw how, day after day, our cages became fuller. It had to happen; the day came when one of the little boys caught a lizard himself and brought it to us; unfortunately it was dead. We did our level best to dissuade them from catching any more and showed them that the animals we had caught were all alive and healthy.

The following morning, the same boy came back and, a wide grin across his face, handed us a piece of screwed up newspaper with something inside that wanted to get out and was madly scratching about. We cautiously opened the bundle and peered inside and found half a dozen coal-black dung beetles. Unfortunately for the boy, I knew exactly where it was he had found them and could have easily collected another twenty myself. There was a deep trench just a few hundred yards away from our camp which must, at one time, have been used for military exercises but had become a trap for beetles like these. They would tumble down the steep sides and find no way out. We thanked him and said unfortunately we had no use for his beetles, but he wasn't particularly deterred and sat himself down on the sand among his friends.

These goat herders did not appear to speak French and they generally seemed taciturn even when talking among themselves. When we needed to explain something it was through the sign language of hands and feet. Otherwise they just sat and watched silently for hours.

In the morning of that day, I occupied myself making an apparatus for catching snakes. It was like a hand at the end of a pole: two curved forks covered with plastic tubing that closed in on one another when the rope was pulled. In the meantime, Karl had gone off to see if he could catch some more lizards and, when I was nearly finished with the new device, he returned from his hunt. He had found a snake skin, quite a long one, but we weren't sure what it was. He had managed to catch one or two colorful lizards as well.

In the afternoon the persistent animal catcher came back and proudly presented us with a dirty old polyethylene bag bound tightly with a piece of thin, twisted rag. This time we really had to laugh; finally he had managed to catch a large, healthy lizard of the type we were after. Obviously he had developed a technique. We gave him a large, clean bag made of cloth to put the lizards in the next time and, of course, a reward for his trouble.

About midmorning of the next day, our visitors were, as usual, spread about the place, sitting in groups wherever there was shade, when suddenly they all sprang to their feet and started yelling and

10

shouting in their Wolof language, pointing to the cages. We didn't understand a word they were saying, of course, so we went to have a look to see what was up. A snake, green-brown and yellow underneath, had squeezed its way between the cage netting and was looking hungrily at our lizards. Our approach and the shouting and yelling from the boys startled it and it started to make an agitated retreat. I ran to fetch the new catching claw and Karl grabbed a towel. The snake was already out of the cage and the boys were running around it, frightening it with sticks. I thrust the claw at it and pulled the rope tightly, but only caught a pile of sticks and leaves. I tried again and this time gripped it in mid-body. It wriggled and writhed and tried its hardest to get away, but the plastic-bound prongs held it tightly. Karl threw his towel over its head and, in its rage, the snake bit deeply into the cloth. The rest was easy. It was an olive green sand or grass snake about four feet long (Psammophis sibilans), our first snake of many!

Karl was an extremely knowledgeable herpetologist. In 1970, he worked at a pet shop in Frankfurt am Main that later became one of our customers. At this time, we had already planned to travel to Africa and we were both working hard to earn as much money as possible in preparation for our adventure. I was in England, studying French, while also working as a hotel waiter. We saved every penny we could towards our expedition.

While in Frankfurt, Karl met the director of the Senkenberg Museum, Professor Robert Mertens. The elderly professor instructed Karl how to collect and preserve reptiles in alcohol and also gave him a copy of his book on the reptiles of Namibia, Southwest Africa. Ironically, in 1975, Professor Mertens died of a snake bite while feeding a poisonous bird snake.

The grass snake that we had just caught, like the bird snake that killed Professor Mertens, was back-fanged. It was far less dangerous than the cobras or vipers that we caught later but still needed to be treated with respect. I was never very comfortable with poisonous creatures and much preferred lizards, turtles and frogs. But Karl was utterly fearless.

The boys calmed down and resumed their former positions while staring open mouthed, dumbfounded as Karl confidently examined his catch.

In due course our lizard catcher turned up with his bag full of lizards, but, as soon as he saw the snake, he kept his distance and threw his bag over to us.

The difficulty was less catching the animals and more a problem of feeding them. We had a large cloth net that we used to catch flies and other insects but, as the reptile collection increased, this proved to be inadequate. We had noticed a market in St. Louis, along the banks of the river Senegal. There was a powerful stench of dried fish and piles of refuse everywhere. We set off for the city to buy a few supplies and to see if we could also net a substantial quantity of flies. Sure enough! I have never seen such swarms and we soon netted plenty to feed our hungry creatures.

After several weeks exploring the St. Louis region, we decided to leave and head south. There were maybe just two more weeks until Christmas and we wanted to celebrate in Gambia, mainly because it was cheaper than Senegal. We had already collected all the animals we needed for our first consignment to send to Europe, so we decided to leave the Desert du Ferlo and return to Dakar, first to the airport and then off to Gambia for Christmas.

2. GAMBIA
Abuko Nature Reserve

On the map Gambia looks like a tiny, crooked wedge in the side of the vast continent of Africa. Scarcely one hundred and fifty miles long and not very wide, it edges its way into the heart of Senegal. Its source in the highlands of Guinea, the Gambia River meanders its way through eastern Senegal, opening out as a broad river flowing down the center of Gambia itself. Upriver both banks are lined with dense mangroves, the breeding and hiding places for crocodiles and the muddy, slow flowing water, a paradise for hippos. As the river flows down to the coast, it becomes wider and its wildlife more scarce.

Gambia was the last of the British colonies in Africa to receive independence, in 1965. Since then it has led a moderately peaceful but relatively poor existence. The men are mainly groundnut farmers and their wives grow rice and a few vegetables.

We arrived at the border on the twenty-third of December, 1971 late in the afternoon, intending to enjoy Christmas in an English-speaking country. At Kaolack, we had missed the road we had intended to follow and ended up instead crossing the border more than a hundred miles up-river, away from the capital. We drove up to the police station, parked the van, walked up the steps and into the little office. On the whitewashed walls were pinned one or two old, faded wanted posters, a few public notices and, in a prominent position, a framed photograph of the Queen Elizabeth of England and the Duke of Edinburgh. The air was comfortably cool due to a large fan on the ceiling whirring slowly round and round. Behind the heavy wooden counter on the floor against the wall was a heavily chained gun rack with five or six old British army 303s. The policeman on duty was dealing with a couple of French tourists who had arrived without visas, so we had a couple of minutes to wait and sat down on a wooden bench by the door.

Evening was drawing on. Outside a few cars drove past packed tightly with people and with the roof racks piled high with boxes and bundles. Mosquitoes decided it was time to come out and eat people and I squashed one which was in the process of boring a hole into my arm.

The policeman was ready, the French tourists having been allowed to continue their journey despite not having visas - probably the Christmas spirit. We presented our passports and, everything in order, said "goodbye" and continued on our way.

A little distance from the police station at Farafenni was a garage; we drove onto the forecourt to tank up. Nobody was in sight; the office was open but we could see no one. We called out a few times then, from behind a tree, sitting in a deck chair, answered a very large African lady who called out in a deep, sonorous voice:

"Sorry, no more petrol, after Christmas maybe."

The tank was nearly empty, but it was only a couple of miles more until the ferry station; maybe we could buy petrol at the other side. We drove the two miles along a very good, recently surfaced road and parked our van in a queue behind four or five other cars and a lorry.

It was becoming dark as we looked out across the wide, muddy river, its banks draped in a tangle of dense mangroves, its surface swirling slightly, as it wound off out of sight down towards the sea. The air was filled with the sound of night birds calling out to one another from the trees and of chirping crickets and buzzing mosquitoes.

Slapping our arms and the backs of our necks, hoping to diminish the mosquito population as much as possible, we made our way to the pay office to buy our ferry tickets.

The office was very small, scarcely room for more than two people at a time and with three people already inside. We called to the man, over the heads of the other two, that we wanted a ticket for the ferry and he called back that it would cost one pound. We reached past the other people to give him his money and he reached back to us to give us the ticket. A policeman on duty outside told us that there was a garage on the far side of the river, about five miles down the road, and that they stay open most of the night so we would be able to tank up there. We thanked him but knew that Africans always like to offer good news even if it is untrue. We hoped we had enough petrol to get us that far and that it was indeed open.

On both sides of the road, leading down to the water's edge, standing side by side, were numerous little stalls neatly arranged with various items from chocolate to baby powder, many with English trade names and, from somewhere behind one of the stalls, we heard a tiny transistor radio playing a Christmas carol: "Oh Come All Ye Faithful," and, for just a moment, I forgot that we were in Africa.

The arrival of the ferry interrupted all other activities. It came splashing up to the shore puffing smoke from its tall chimney in all directions and filling the air with the thudding of its engines. It was very rusty and old and not very large; we wondered if there would be enough room for the half dozen cars and the big lorry all at once.

The ramp was let down onto the concrete slipway with a bang and, one by one, the cars drove off the ferry, up the steep slope and off into the distance. As the last car disappeared, the first one in our queue started its engine and drove up onto the ferry to park in the corner at the far end. Before long it was our turn and we parked ourselves closely behind the big lorry.

Up with the ramp, the ferry blew its whistle and chugged off across the river. We got out of the van and went to the side to see if we could maybe spot a crocodile. Although we kept our eyes peeled throughout the trip, we saw no sign. The crocodiles were staying discretely out of sight.

We reached the opposite bank, the ramp was steeper and half underwater on this side and, when it was our turn to drive down, the number plate scraped harshly on the concrete. We drove on, hoping we would be able to reach the garage before we ran out of petrol completely. The well-kept road was lined on both sides by tall palm trees and the beginnings of dense forest undergrowth showing up in the headlights looked most sinister.

After scarcely ten minutes of driving we arrived at the garage, which was really a bar with a petrol pump outside. We tanked up, paid in dollars and carried on along the riverside road towards the Gambian capital, Bathurst, or Banjul as it has since been renamed.

It was very late as we neared the capital. We wanted to take a quick glimpse of the city itself to satisfy our curiosity and then we would quickly find somewhere to camp for the night. The streets were well lit, but it was difficult to make out which was the main one and where the town center actually was. Bathurst seemed to consist of just four or five broad, parallel roads and that was all. We stayed just long enough to get a rough impression of what the capital was like and then began our search for a suitable place to spend the night.

We had learned from experience not to be fussy when looking for somewhere to camp when it is late, otherwise we would find ourselves driving around until morning. After traveling a little way out of the town, we decided to stop at the next reasonable place we saw, which turned out to be a parking spot a few miles back along the South Bank Road, the route we had just taken. We turned off the road; it seemed a good place, everything was quite peaceful. We cooked a light meal and then crawled to safety under our mosquito nets, out of reach of those dreadful insects.

The next morning we awoke quite early, not because we wanted to but due to the noise of the arrival of a lorry drawing up beside our van. If we were not properly awake, the sound of laughter soon made sure that we were. We looked out to see who our new and rather unwelcome neighbors were. Suddenly there was the sound of gallons of water being emptied out. Apparently we should have been a little more fussy the previous night in choosing somewhere to camp; this was the sewage emptying station. We didn't share the amusement of the workmen at all and, as quickly as we could, we backed the van out and headed off towards the ocean where the air was sweeter smelling.

We made our breakfast of rice pudding and tea to the sound of ocean waves rolling against the shore, of monkeys springing from tree to tree, of the early morning bird chorus and lizards scampering up and down the hollow-sounding bark. Quite a contrast to our previous camp.

We weren't the only ones enjoying this glorious stretch of beach. Further away down the tree-lined shore was another Volkswagen van and a small French car. As yet there was no sign of activity in their camp, although the sun was already shining brightly.

It was time to test the inviting Gambia sea water. We splashed through the waves, enjoying the shock of the cool water and then swam further out to where it was deeper. We swam for over an hour and finally came out onto the shore again opposite a large hotel where people were sitting outside under umbrellas, eating their breakfasts. We made use of the outdoor shower there and then started on our way back along the shore to the van. We decided to come and visit the hotel again one evening and have a celebratory Christmas drink.

As we arrived back at our van, we were visited by a girl from the other camp whom we didn't recognize at first but then realized that we had met two months earlier in Tan Tan in southern Morocco. They had crossed the desert down to Senegal with their Volkswagen van and Citroen "deux chevaux" while we had made the trip by ship. The sand had completely ruined one of the engines and they had had to buy a new one. Apart from that, they had endured numerous tire punctures along the way and had ruined the shock absorbers on both vehicles. And they had been robbed. The Mauritanian Arabs had shadowed them and managed, amongst other items, to steal their shovels which made it difficult and extremely tiresome whenever they got stuck in the sand. Now they were short of money and would only be able to make part of their intended journey as far as the Ivory Coast. So it seemed we had made the right decision to go by ship.

We had also been robbed but in Morocco while we were collecting sea anemones at the coast. We had a camping pad on the roof of our vehicle that was flapping in the light breeze as we meanwhile drank tea inside. All at once the noise stopped and we imagined that the wind had blown the pad away. We both got out and searched around, never more than a short distance from the van. When we returned someone had been in the van and stolen a watch and Karl's radio. It must have all happen within a minute.

There was a small village close by and Karl went over to see if he could somehow track the stuff. He approached someone who was lurking around and the man just snarled at him. Karl was convinced that he was our thief but there was nothing we could do about it except to learn never again to leave the our van unlocked or any of our belongings unattended.

We decided to move our camp near Bathurst for somewhere a little more isolated further down the beach and, when evening came, we

17

cooked our Christmas dinner by the light of the paraffin lamp under the starlit sky, beneath the palm trees. After the meal, we smoked African tobacco from the Saint Louis market and drank numerous bottles of beer until finally we couldn't keep our eyes open any more and each of us slept outside where he was despite the mosquitoes.

The next morning we awoke late, feeling rather unsteady and covered with insect bites. We drank black coffee and then went for a swim in the sea to see if that would help. A few of the guests from the hotel had found their way to our part of the beach and one little old lady in a bikini started talking to us in Swedish. We understood a little of what she was saying because of the similarity of some words in German and Swedish, and she told us how she had found a scorpion in her bedroom and about a python that had been found on the beach in front of the hotel. Before we parted she invited us to visit her in the hotel that evening and meet her husband and daughter.

On the way back from the beach, along the dusty path leading to our camp, a beautiful red snake was lazily sunning itself and shot off into the bushes as we startled it by our approach. We searched high and low but it had simply disappeared into thin air.

Evening came and we drove back in the direction of Bathurst to the hotel. As we parked the van, an African youth with a small, pointed beard and wearing a gaily colored pajama suit came over to us and introduced himself as Kintaboy, telling us he would show us around the town, to the best bars and to the brothels. We told him we didn't like him and that he had better disappear fast, which he did.

The Africans that we enjoyed the most were frequently the farmers and the fishermen. We met wonderful people out in the bush, in little villages far away from the cities or in isolated coastal areas. Apart from corrupt officials who tried to intimidate and pressure us for a bribe, the very worst were the slick city youths with their wheedling and cajoling who tried every devious scheme to rip off naive tourists. But the men and women who worked the land or toiled fishing all day, although they didn't have much themselves were always hospitable and gracious. They didn't resort to deception or crime in order to make a living.

At the hotel most of the guests were still in the restaurant having dinner and we couldn't see the little old lady anywhere. We sat down at a table and ordered a cold refreshing beer. Before we had been there very long, a tall blond woman came up to the table and said, "Hello." Following closely behind her was the old lady and her husband. The daughter spoke very good English and introduced herself as Barbara. Barbara suggested we go to a club that she had visited a couple of times in Bathurst. Her parents were content to stay in and rest at the hotel so the three of us drove into Bathurst to visit Joe's Pub.

Joe was a true Irishman in every sense of the word. He hadn't been long in Gambia, about five weeks. His pub was the roofed-over courtyard of a hotel in the middle of the town. On all the walls were scribbled slogans, most of them with double meanings. Joe was a very short man with bushy hair and a young face. Barbara told us that he suffered from malaria and didn't play his guitar every evening, but this evening he did, and very well, too. He was a very good entertainer and created a lively atmosphere in the room. Everyone seemed to be enjoying themselves; the place was packed.

As the evening wore on, Joe became a little drunk and stopped singing and switched on a tape recorder instead. Most of the people left and we found ourselves sitting among a group of eight or nine, mostly from Sweden. There was a man called Leif, a travel courier who kept buying drinks for everyone, a bubbly girl named Sunbeam, a British engineer, Joe, of course, and a handful of other people.

The engineer was sober and told me a lot about Gambia, in particular about another Englishman called Mr. Eddie Brewer, who had established a wildlife park a few years before in 1967 with his daughter, Stella Marsden. Apart from that, Mr. Brewer worked for the Gambian government as a game officer.

Time flew by, the party really started to liven up. Leif emptied his gin and tonic on Joe's head and Joe, in his turn, thinking it a shame to waste good gin, emptied his tonic over Leif. Everyone laughed, so Joe and Leif showered the rest of us with everything they could find. Sunbeam became drenched and her mascara ran down her face. Everyone found it amusing except Joe, who still thought it a shame to waste good gin.

Later we left Joe's Pub and drove Barbara back to her hotel. As we said goodbye, we noticed that she was a little drunk, too. We went back to camp to sleep the few hours left until morning.

* * *

Of course, wherever there are tourists there are bound to be African souvenir sellers and that part of the beach in front of the hotel was no exception. It was swarming with them, all trying to coax the guests into buying anything, from African costumes and masks to strange wooden carvings of animal gods with long horns, big pointed breasts, short stubby legs and prominent buttocks, and some people had other things to offer.

I was sitting on the sand leaning against the stump of a coconut palm after having enjoyed a long, refreshing swim in the cool water when a young African girl came walking slowly down the beach with a pile of gaily colored shirts balanced on top of her head. Unfortunately, she spotted me and came to try her luck. She called "hello," dumped her pile on the ground in front of me and stayed leaning over while sorting through the shirts until she found one which she thought suited me. Her black hair was tied in tiny braided rows over her head and she had some red cream smeared over her cheeks which made her look like a puppet.

She threw a shirt over my chest to see if it would fit and then stood back to admire it.

"Nice shirt for you, good price!" But she saw the way I looked at it and, always smiling, she sorted through her pile to find another.

"Here are for you!" she said, chuckling as she took the first one away and covered me with the second to check for size.

"Look," I said, and showed her my own shirt lying on the sand beside me, "I have one already, better than yours," and smiled back at her.

"Mmm," she remarked, "and what 'bout me, you want love me?" She was still leaning over her pile, one hand on one knee and the other dangling and her mouth hung wide open grinning, showing her pink gums and all her shiny white teeth.

20

She was certainly more interesting than her shirts but also more expensive and I wanted to stay healthy.

"No thanks, no shirt, no love and no business today!"

"You don't want love me?" she asked again, "I love you!" But she had already noticed that there would be no sale and looked the other way as she said it, already disinterested. She piled her shirts back together and lifted them up onto her head. Smiling, she said "goodbye" and slowly wandered off again in search of a better customer.

Back at camp, Karl told me that an old watchman had paid him a visit from a nearby peanut roasting factory but had soon gone again as Karl began hacking away at the undergrowth searching for snakes. That morning he had seen two but had been unable to catch them, although he had given chase and had searched high and low after they had disappeared in the bushes.

We decided to leave the Bathurst area entirely and head off into the bush somewhere, our Christmas festivities being over until the next year. Away from the townspeople and the tourists to the wilds for peace and quiet and to put together another shipment of reptiles.

We took the main road away from Bathurst, the only road from Bathurst for that matter, and drove on our way to visit Mr. Brewer and see his game reserve; afterwards we planned to search for a good spot to make our camp.

As we drove past the peanut roasting factory, we were hailed to stop by the old night watchman who had visited Karl earlier. He asked if we were going to Serekunda, which we were of course, so he climbed into the van with a battered old suitcase and a bundle of God knows what. Just then a man called over to us from the factory,

"Hey, hello, you taking my friend with you, that very nice, thank you, thank you, wait, I fetch you some peanuts, do you like 'em? Give me a bag!"

We gave him a bag and followed him into the factory, where there was a lorry emptying its load of several tons of unshelled peanuts down a chute. The man caught them in handfuls as they fell and filled up the bag.

"Here you are," he said, handing us the bag, "Have good, good time in our country."

21

We all shook hands warmly and then went back to the van, where our passenger was waiting. The watchman enjoyed the trip immensely and, hardly saying a word the whole time, he just concentrated on the journey. We left him at his home and continued on to visit Mr. Brewer at the Abuko Nature Reserve.

We turned off into the yard at the reserve, where it was pleasantly cool, the whole area surrounded by tall, shady trees.

There was a narrow wooden bridge over the river made loosely of logs so that they rattled as we crossed. Behind was a waterfall in the midst of dense jungle growth, a mixture of beautiful shades of green and the silver, sparkling, splashing water. On the other side of the bridge, the river broadened and twisted off out of sight. Along the edges were hundreds of pure white waterlilies, open and half-open, and all sorts of reeds and green water-weed. It was really an enchanting place.

On the far bank was an attractively built rest house made out of bamboo and palm branches, but, as we had only just begun the walk, we didn't feel much like a rest. We carried on along the winding path around the bushes and among the trees. Unfortunately, there were lots of other visitors that day and all the animals had been frightened away out of sight. Before long we came to the middle of the forest, to another rest house, not quite as attractive as the first but more welcome. All around the building were animal compounds with wild cats, antelopes, and hyenas. In one large compound were half a dozen chimpanzees. We paid for our ticket and chatted for a while to the attendant. Mr. Brewer would arrive at about six when he had finished work. He would come feed the chimpanzees.

Sure enough, at six o'clock sharp, he arrived. A man in his late forties, Mr. Brewer had lived in Africa for over ten years, and this wildlife park had been his dream for a long time. He was a fairly short man, rather stockily built, and very friendly and polite. He had already heard that we were coming to visit him from a police sergeant who had given us directions on the way there. He took us around and proudly showed his animal family, in particular the chimpanzees, whom he was clearly very fond of. Mr. Brewer suggested that if his captive male chimpanzees were allowed unrestricted contact with females then they were less likely to become aggressive as they matured. I remembered having seen isolated male zoo chimps in Europe that were terrifying for their violence. One had a car tire that it threw against the bars of its cage with tremendous force and then, tiring of that, it began to assault its companion with horrifying screams and uncontrolled violence.

Mr. Brewers' animals seemed calm and content and a baby chimp eagerly reached up and hitched a ride on Karl's back as we walked about the compound.

Mr. Brewer told us how, earlier, before he had opened the park, he had kept a collection of snakes and then later let them all loose on the grounds. One in particular was a python that was over twelve feet long. Most of his snakes, he said, he had caught near a village called Mandinari, and we resolved to make our camp in the very same place. Mr. Brewer showed us the path leading back another way to the rest house, along which we might spot the couple of green mambas that he knew lived in the forest. In the rest house itself there were two telescopes and, if we were lucky, we might see some crocodiles in the river. He told us that a Swedish friend of his had once seen a python crossing the river where it was caught and eaten in midstream by a crocodile. That was something quite unique that might not be seen again even if a person lived in Africa for fifty years.

On the way through the forest, we were accompanied by a very tame antelope, but, apart from that and a few monkeys, we didn't see any other animals at all, nor did we see any crocodiles in the river.

It was beginning to become dark as we left the park, so we decided to head straight away for Mandinari and find somewhere to camp.

3. MANDINARI
Too Many Cobras by far

Our camp was about three quarters of a mile from the Gambia River bank. The area was called Kunkoojan, which means *far away* in the Mandingo language. The nearest village was Mandinari, and the forest in which we actually had our camp was called Kutayba Forest, but nobody seemed to know what that meant so I suspected that it was the Mandingo word for *forest*. Parts of the forest were impenetrable, a tangle of twisting vines and dense undergrowth. At high tide, the area by the river became a mass of small islands where anyone who didn't know their way about could easily find themselves trapped. All over the place were crocodile and monitor lizard burrows. In the trees, the Red Colobus monkeys showed off their gymnastic skills. Once a group of them overdid things a little and brought the huge branch of a tree crashing down. They all fled screaming and yelling in panic. The monkeys were very beautifully colored. The male had a beautiful, bright red, furry back with black arms and white furry underparts. His tail was red with a white paintbrush-tip. As with many dimorphic animal species, his mate had duller colors than he, mainly green with white underparts. One of the hunters we met while we were exploring the forest had a stuffed male monkey on his farm and we were able to examine it closely.

On arriving back at camp at mid-day, after we had been there maybe a week, I met Karl just heading out. He said he was going to see about a snake that a farmer had disturbed in the bushes somewhere, and off he went with the catching claw and a sack over his shoulder, followed closely by a group of Mandingo boys who seemed to be his permanent shadow.

Ten minutes later, a small boy came running at full speed around the corner into the camp. He blurted out that Karl had seen the snake and needed gloves, binoculars and more string. I gave him what he had asked for and off he went again at full speed, back the way he had come. A few minutes later, Karl, himself, appeared and said that it was sunglasses he had wanted. The snake was a very large cobra that had managed to work itself out of the very powerful grip of the catching claw. It was now cornered in a hole and Karl was concerned that it might spit venom. Karl needed the sunglasses because if the venom were to reach his eyes it could blind him. He ran off again, out of sight, and I wondered what the devil we were going to do with a spitting cobra if he caught it.

As time passed, Karl came back with quite an interesting story to tell. The snake had been driven into a shallow burrow by the farmers where they kept guard while a boy had run to fetch Karl. When he arrived, he teased the snake until it came out of the hole and then he gripped it near the head with our catching apparatus. But it had shown such strength, so suddenly, that it caught Karl off guard and managed to writhe its way out of the grip of the claw. It made straight for the long grass and wound off out of sight. Karl caught up with it and tried to grip it again, but only succeeded in making it angrier. It raised itself up on its tail and opened its hood, swaying menacingly. The head becomes about three times as broad when the hood is open and this one, standing on its tail, was at least three feet high. Anyone seeing such an angry monster before him is well advised to get quickly out of the way. Karl threw the sack over its head and attempted to pin it to the ground with a forked stick, but the snake retreated into the long grass again. It was then that Karl sent the little boy off to collect the things and eventually returned himself. On his return, the snake had hidden itself in another hole and had its tail showing. Karl tried again, this time wearing the sunglasses as a precaution against spitting. By now all of his trusty, snake-hunting companions had taken flight, which was, of course, the prudent thing to do.

While I did not like the snake catching aspect of our enterprise and gladly left it to Karl, I had once been convinced by some farmers that they knew of a python hole. It was under a fallen tree. With the two farmers as guides, we set off into the forest. As we approached the place, the men were suddenly nowhere to be seen. As it happened, there wasn't a snake in the hole, although it did look as if there should have been. It seemed like an ideal python cave. I looked around to see where the farmers had hidden themselves and there they were high up in a nearby tree. They didn't mind leading me through the bush but they had no intention of taking part in any snake catching.

The same thing had happened to Karl, suddenly not a soul in sight. Karl was wondering whether it was even worth trying to catch this snake as our customers in Europe were not interested in poisonous cobras although they occasionally bought one or two other venomous species from us. But there wasn't very much we could do with a cobra even if Karl caught it. Nevertheless, he decided to make just one last attempt. One violent tug of the tail and the animal's head came gliding out. It raised itself up angrily and turned on Karl before he'd hardly had a chance to get a proper grip on the pole. It showed another feat of strength and freed itself from the catching claw. It hovered for a moment menacingly but did not attack, instead it preferred to make its escape. Karl was a little relieved that it had gone and decided to catch some lizards instead. His followers reappeared now that the danger was over. After he had finished his story, we both agreed that the next time someone came and told us about a cobra, we would say we weren't interested.

Later in the afternoon some small boys appeared and asked if the lizard they had brought the previous day had lived. Their methods of catching were terribly brutal. They had managed to find a beautiful orange and blue male agama, but they had knocked it out of a tree with sticks. It was now dead, of course, a great shame. Karl resolved that if they insisted on bringing lizards, then he would go with them and show them the proper way to catch them. He wandered off down the path with his little band tagging along behind him.

Maybe ten minutes later a strongly built African came into the camp in a great hurry, his face running with sweat. There were still one or two small boys around the camp and one of them translated what the man had to say. Eagerly, the man blurted out his story and the small boy passed the message on to me.

This man, together with a couple of other farmers, had trapped a snake inside its hole with stones and earth and one of them remained at the sight making sure that it didn't escape.

It was remarkable how enthusiastic the local people became when they realized that we were collecting reptiles and amphibians. Perhaps it had something to do with Mr. Brewers earlier snake catching expeditions in the area. The little boys turned up with lizards or perhaps a turtle but snake sightings were high on their list because they justifiably loathed them. The danger of a lethal snake bite was both real and constant in Mandinari. Along the banks of the Gambia river, it seemed that snakes were everywhere.

I told the man, through the interpreter, that I couldn't leave the camp unattended and suggested that we go when Karl returned in maybe half an hour. He wasn't in the least bit happy with that idea and pointed out that the hole was quite a long way away and that it would soon be dark. I reluctantly agreed to go with him.

I piled most of the things into the van and one of the boys who we had grown to trust said he would stay and keep an eye on the camp until Karl came back. As an afterthought, I asked the man if he knew what type of snake it was and he replied, "Beeda." I didn't have to wait for a translation for that word. I knew exactly what it meant; it was a cobra!

I was very curious to see a cobra at close quarters and, although we had agreed not to bother with cobras in the future, I decided I would go this time, if only to have a look.

It was well over a mile and a half to the man's farm, first through a dense part of the forest, then a long way down a dusty path and eventually around the rice fields to a tall tree, at the base of which was the hole. At first we were just the farmer and myself, tramping across the fields, but nearly everyone we saw wanted to see the fun and soon we were a group of about ten.

The tree was large but old and rotten. Among the protruding roots was a hole wedged tightly with pieces of wood and stones. The man who was keeping guard spoke French and told me that the snake was still inside. He had blocked up all the other tunnels, too, just in case the snake should find another way out.

They unblocked the hole and scraped the loose earth out with their machetes. I looked cautiously down into the deep tunnel. It was far too dark to make out anything, every shadow and every little stone looked like the head or body of a snake. One of the men gave me his machete and I started widening the entrance. The soil was full of stones and roots and somebody went off to fetch a small garden pick that one of the women in the rice fields was using. I dug for a while and then a farmer took over from me and started hacking away furiously. All at once, under the loose soil from the fallen roof, I saw about six inches of shiny black tail. I told the man to stop digging and bent down to look into the hole. The rest of the body was out of sight, deeper down in the tunnel. I gripped the tail firmly and gave it a couple of short, violent tugs just as Karl had described with the one that he had been trying to catch. But the cobra didn't come out. The men continued widening the hole as I prepared the catching claw and net ready for use. Then, suddenly, one of the men cut through the snake's tail and, half a second later, the snake came gliding swiftly out of the hole. At first I thought the man had made a mistake and that it wasn't a cobra after all. But as it rose up into the air and opened out its hood, there was no doubt about it.

For just a very short second we all stood there dumbfounded, the snake swaying slightly, standing three feet high on its tail in front of us. Suddenly all the men shot off in terror and the women in the fields picked up their skirts in their hands and fled screaming, out of sight. One of the men had even taken my sunglasses with him, wearing them on his head.

I picked up the catching claw and thrust it against the hooded neck and pulled the cord as tightly as possible. For a moment, I had it under my control, but then, of all things, the cord unraveled and the snake eased easily out of the grip and rose even higher; I really thought it was about to attack. I stumbled a few hasty steps backwards, trying to keep out of spitting range and, at the same time, not daring to look away. Then I felt a pole on the ground under my feet, picked it up, gripped it in both hands and brought it down on the snake's back with all the force I could muster. But the pole broke into three pieces and I only succeeded in making the cobra madder. It was at that moment that I felt a very cold and sharp shiver down my spine and I believed the snake would now make its attack. Instead, just as Karl had experienced, it preferred to get away while it had a chance and, still standing on its tail, it made off into the grass. A machete lay beside the hole and I ran back to fetch it. The snake was heading towards a well at the edge of the rice field as I sliced through its body with one blow and, with a second, I cut off the head, and a third time I cut deeply into

29

its back.

I experienced a feeling of ecstasy, a deep sigh of relief now that danger was past. I looked at the three pieces of snake at my feet, lying there, wriggling a little as the last of the blood oozed out, and I noticed that I was covered with sweat and that my hands were shaking.

I threw the pieces, one by one, unceremoniously, into the sack, which became stained straight away with bright red blotches. Slowly the men came back, one by one, smiling uncertainly and I began to laugh, mainly with relief. The women weren't as certain the danger was over and returned very cautiously with their fingers in their mouths, as though they had just done something very rude. The farmer reappeared and handed over my sunglasses, glad that I wasn't angry with him and the two of us led the band of merry men away from that wretched hole, around the rice fields, through that bit of jungle, and back to camp.

Karl appeared about twenty minutes later as I was busily filling my pipe for the second time. He came into camp hiding two small sacks behind his back and asked me to choose the one I wanted. I took the one on his left. Inside were two beautiful, full grown male agama lizards which he had caught while instructing his troupe of small boys. In the second sack were two giant dung beetles, both as large as a table tennis ball, coal black, dusty and bold, like two old German tanks - the bullies of the insect world.

I pointed to the blood stained sack lying in the dust with flies humming around it and told him that was his present.

At first he thought one of the farmers had brought it, so I slowly began to tell the whole story. He held up the largest piece and swore and asked again if it was really true. The men all began to laugh at his astonishment and finally he went to fetch a tape measure to see how long it was. Eight and a half feet, plus the couple of inches of tail it had lost at the beginning, that tiny piece that had driven it so wild.

I fetched a packet of cigarettes and gave them to the farmer who had led me to the snake hole, but he wasn't quite satisfied and wanted to have the skin as well. I ignored him; the skin was my souvenir! I shook his strong, muddy hand and off he went with his friends, all eager to be away from the forest before nightfall.

Karl and I discussed and chatted about the day's events, smoking our pipes and drinking tea by the light of the glowing log fire. It was not yet completely dark and the monkeys were still springing about up in the treetops, looking for somewhere to settle for the night. The rats and mice were scampering around in the tall grasses and not far away in the swamps, we could occasionally hear the whooping of hyenas.

After supper, we roasted a few peanuts in the fire and were feasting ourselves when a night visitor arrived. He was a hunter, one of the few people it seemed who was not afraid to go into the forest at night. He was a very strong man, indeed, with huge, broad shoulders and great, powerful hands. We couldn't see his face very clearly as it was already too dark, but we could see his shiny white teeth as he smiled by the light of our camp fire. He had a torch bound to his hat with string and, after drinking a cup of tea with us, he went off deeper into the forest among the tall trees and through the dense undergrowth towards the river, like a miner, with his lamp shining before him.

The next day one of the farmers came down the path on his way to work and stopped by to say hello. He was the father of the two small boys who were eager lizard catchers, but today he would have to work on his farm without their help because it was the first day of the new term at school. We decided to go along with him and film him as he harvested peanuts. We got our things together and locked up the van with everything else safely inside and set off in single file along the narrow path, the farmer leading the way. Although it was fairly early, it was already extremely hot and we kept to the shade whenever possible.

We made our way first through the bush and then across open land towards his farm. He certainly had a long way to go from the village each morning; we were soaked in sweat when we arrived. Unfortunately, the farm was very small and with him working alone there, just one man surrounded by heaps of dry peanuts, he didn't offer very good filming material. We stayed with him for a while, though, acknowledging his hard work in the hot sun and explained tactfully that we needed a few more people working together to make a good film. He understood perfectly and indicated another farm not far away. Before we left, he insisted we roast some peanuts with him and he

31

picked up huge handfuls of plants with the nuts dangling from the roots. He led the way to a cooler, shady spot among the trees, where he set fire to the dry peanut plants and turned them in the flames until they were all nicely browned. Then he took them in handfuls and let them fall through the air so the wind carried away the ashes. He filled up a large sack we had brought with us for catching lizards and then led us away to the other nearby farm.

The three men were hard at work amid piles of nuts, sorted and unsorted, and heaps of dried out straw. A wonderful chance to make a good film: three powerful men working in the heat of the day, on every horizon a beautiful display of tall palm trees, luscious jungle growth and above, the glorious blue sky.

All three were flattered to be visited and pleased to be filmed. One of them gave us a demonstration of the life cycle and harvesting, how the nuts were planted, later what the plants looked like and, finally, when they were thoroughly dry, the thrashing and sorting. It struck me that he may have been filmed before.

After the filming was over, we were ready to leave, but the men insisted we take a basket of nuts with us and they filled up the other two sacks we had brought for lizards. We told the men to come by our camp on their way home and we would give them some cigarettes for being so photogenic.

On the way back, we made a detour to where Karl had seen his cobra the previous day. We didn't want to try to catch it again, we just wanted a few more of the lizards like the ones he had found there the last time. Karl showed me the hole where the cobra had hidden itself and he groped about inside half-heartedly to see if it was at home. Fortunately, it was not.

The hole was at the base of a round-palm tree that had already been harvested of its fruits, some still lying uneaten but dried out on the ground around about. Each tree would have nine or ten clusters of huge coconut-sized fruits, looking like enormous bunches of grapes. Each cluster contained about twenty fruits. Inside were three segments filled with an almost transparent jelly that was practically tasteless but very thirst-quenching. If the fruits were too young, then there was only liquid inside; if they were too old, the insides were hard like wood. The ripe fruits were eaten by cutting off the top and pushing down inside each chamber with the thumb so that the pulp shot out.

On several occasions we had been with groups of young boys and farmers to cut down these "jalango" fruits. They bind together several long poles with strips of palm fiber, the ubiquitous equivalent of cord. The pole at the top is hooked so that it can be hung in among the palm branches. All the poles still had short branches to make climbing easier. This thirty or more foot long device is raised in the same way that we raise a ladder, with one end held down by the base of the tree and everybody walking toward it, raising the pole higher as they close in until, finally, when it is upright, it is lifted and hooked into the branches. The smallest of the group usually climbs up with a machete to cut down the fruit, while the others hold the pole firmly.

The first job is to quench the thirst. With their knives, they slice off the tops and a little of the sides, revealing the luscious white juicy centers. They had prepared a half dozen fruits for us, as their guests, and laid them at our feet for us to eat. But no sooner had we eaten one than they prepared another, so that when we had finished we still had six each to take back to camp.

When we arrived back at camp, we found the hunter from the previous evening waiting for us. He looked even bigger and stronger in the daylight and was a master of the language of hands and feet. He had heard that we had treated a carbuncle for a small boy and he had come to have a similar wound cured on his leg. We agreed to give him some ointment and a bandage, although he only had a small boil and nothing more serious. He was as pleased as punch and smiled from ear to ear as he groped about in his goat's skin bag and then handed us five huge, white roots which looked like parsnips. As he held them in his hands, he stopped smiling and adopted an expression of uncertainty. He was asking if that was enough payment. This fellow really was a master of language without words. It was more than enough, very kind of him indeed, but we didn't know what they were. He broke off a piece and offered it to us. It had the texture of a carrot but was sweet and had a milky juice. It was rather good. We all shook hands and the hunter went off still smiling, into the forest with his shotgun over his shoulder and the bandage already fallen around his ankle.

33

As I was sitting beneath a tree in the shadows, out of reach of the heat of the sun, I heard someone cycling up behind me. I turned around and recognized a schoolboy who had spent an evening with us a few days before and had told us about the devils and ghosts that live in the forest until, finally, he was almost too frightened to go home.

Over the handlebars, he had a huge basket piled high with small, green-brown fruits.

"Hello, there," he called as he leaned his bicycle against the tree and put the basket down carefully on the ground.

"What are you doing?"

I was sorting out some insects that I had collected that day, and I told him so.

"Ah ha," he commented, nodding his head sagely while thinking it a very strange and pointless thing to do.

"Do you want some?" indicating the fruits he had in the basket.

"Oh! That's very nice of you, thank you very much," not having a clue what they were or how to eat them.

"What?" he asked, not understanding.

I took my pipe out of my mouth and repeated what I had said and told him they looked very good, but that I didn't know what they were.

"They're good, yes, look, you eat 'em like this" and he pushed away the outer soft shell with his thumb, revealing a green, pasty substance inside. In the middle was a large nut covered with a mesh of thick, long, white hairs. He wedged the whole thing into his mouth and sucked at it with great difficulty because it filled his mouth. Finally, he spat out the remains.

Very interesting, I thought.

"Fine, they look good, I'll take one for myself and one for Karl." Then, I again took my pipe out of my mouth and repeated what I had said.

"Add," he said.

I took two for each of us.

"Take three," he said.

I did and thanked him for his kindness and off he cycled,

trying to wave back but nearly losing his balance, he rang the bell instead.

The day came swiftly to an end and we in turn ended ours, as usual, roasting peanuts by the campfire which had become almost a tradition as they were in such abundance and farmers kept giving us more.

We were barely up the next morning when the hunter came into the camp, still with his ragged bandage that had now rolled itself around his ankle like a bracelet. It occurred to me that he was wearing it like a grisgris or charm. Behind him scampered a group of small boys who quickly made themselves at home, perching on anything available around the camp.

The hunter was clearly very pleased with himself about something and greeted us warmly. He opened the old skin bag that hung over his shoulder and drew out a large, fat bush fowl, waving it in the air, very happy with his night's work.

Karl quietly asked one of the small boys who was perched on a water canister out of sight of the hunter what the normal price for the bird was.

Equally quietly, the boy said, "one and six."

"Two shillings," said the hunter, trying to look honest but only succeeding in looking more guilty.

We examined the bird carefully. It was really a good size and was neatly shot in the backside.

"We'll give you one and six," we told him.

He seemed very happy with this price and handed over the bird, which Karl began to pluck while it was still fairly warm.

After I had rearranged the hunter's bandage and covered his boil with some more ointment, he let me examine his shotgun and equipment. It was a very old muzzle loading gun with a precaution cap. Part of it he had made himself because the original pieces had become broken over the years. It really belonged in a museum. He used coarse black powder which he kept in a powder horn. He had a few steel ball bearings and a rag bag full of little lumps of iron, which he said he had cut from an old saucepan to use as shot.

After the hunter had left, one of the farmers came to visit us.

He had been working in the field not far from where I had killed the cobra a few days before and he wanted to see what animals we had already collected from the area. We hadn't very much of a variety, but he seemed quite impressed and told us that he knew a place where there were "big, big lizards!" They were easy to catch because they lived in holes in the mud by the river. I agreed to go with him. He led the way through part of the forest that was unknown to me and quite dense, like jungle, until we finally came out by the riverside, an area swarming with mosquitoes, even though it was daytime. In the stinking mud, I recognized the prints from hyenas, wild pigs and small forest cats. Here and there in the swamp, under bushes and among the protruding roots of trees, we found large, deep holes and one of these he started to dig out with his machete. He cut away the whole roof, revealing a long, damp tunnel, but there was nothing inside. I began on another one, much deeper, which went down and down and opened out into a small pond under the earth. I prodded about in the water with my machete, but, again, found nothing.

I told the farmer that I would go back and fetch a shovel so that we could dig the holes out properly and he pointed out the direction I should follow. Every bush and tree looked alike and, if it hadn't been for the undergrowth that we had hacked and trampled flat and the branches we had cut down where they blocked our way, I may well have walked in circles for hours before finding my way back to camp in just twenty minutes. I fetched the shovel out of the back of the van and told Karl that we were digging out holes somewhere in a swamp on the riverbank, but as yet we hadn't found anything. I then made my way back through the forest to the swamp. The farmer was nowhere to be seen and I assumed he had lost interest and gone off home. I carried on digging by myself for a while, but the mosquitoes became such a nuisance that I decided to get out of there. One or two landmarks were beginning to become familiar to me and I found my way back much more easily than the first time. Just a few hundred yards before our camp I met the farmer, who was on his way back to the swamp to fetch me and tell me that he had already found a lizard. He said that he had carried on digging out another hole and discovered a giant lizard inside. We returned to camp together, where he had left the lizard with Karl. There, in the lower compartment of a large cage, was a young crocodile, a yard long. Now we certainly had an interesting pet for our collection!

* * *

There were always hosts of interesting and colorful birds flying about in the trees by our camp but, during the last couple of days, we noticed we had some new visitors; vultures were circling in the sky. At first we hadn't paid any particular attention to them. Then one evening our large savanna monitor (*Varanus exanthematicus*) started behaving very unusually. Instead of hunting about the cage, catching the bats hanging from the netting or lying in a bowl of water as he often did when he was too hot, he stood with his eyes closed, his body curled and his head pointing upwards into the corner of the cage. Occasionally, he flicked his blue tongue, but half-heartedly. From his closed eyes trickled a little stream of water; as if he was crying but in fact he was dying!

We poured some more water into the bowl, filling it to the brim and laid the creature in it and placed the cage under the shade of some bushes. He didn't splash about or try to hide himself underwater as he often would in the past, but just lay there with his head over the rim, looking very miserable and without any of his old spirit.

The monitor had been with us for quite a while, ever since Karl had dug it out of a hole in the Desert du Ferlo in northern Senegal. All the people had gathered around from the village to watch what would happen. It had made its home just a few feet from the village well and many of the women were afraid to fetch water. Karl had hauled it out of the hole by the tail; it had hissed and thrashed, twisted and writhed, but was unable to reach Karl's hand or body being held high in the air at arm's length. Then into the sack and off back to camp. A little boy had cried in horror when he saw the thing and had hidden himself behind his mother.

Back at camp, we had made a harness for the monitor out of plastic-covered cable, which was attached to a long cord and then to a stake in the sand in order to allow a little freedom and allow it to catch some of its own food. Straight away it tried to hide behind a thorn bush, but had left its tail sticking out. As time went by, it became a little more used to us until, eventually, we could handle it readily without being snapped at or whipped by its powerful tail. Later, we had provided a very roomy cage where it could roam about and hiss at everyone if they came too near. In fact, the four foot long lizard became very useful to us; visitors to our camp had seen it and the word had spread about that we allowed it to prowl about at night on a harness; no one came near after dark.

His diet varied from grasshoppers, which he took from the hand, to baby mice and, in the last couple of days, he had the good fortune to feed himself on bats, which we had found in a hollow tree not far from camp. There was still one left in the cage and it seemed likely that it would be given its freedom.

We felt very sorry for the monitor, lying there with tear-filled eyes, but there was little we could do.

Early the next morning we didn't have to look into the cage to know what had happened. The company of vultures was no longer circling overhead but had settled in the trees around about. The monitor was dead and they were waiting to eat the carcass.

The poor fellow was now lying on the floor of his cage, his tail in the water, his body twisted and hard. The bat was flapping against the netting, wanting to get out, so we opened the door and it fluttered off into the forest.

We looked at the monitor in this pitiful state for a few minutes, both said what a shame it was, and then we resolved to skin it.

The vultures seemed to be growing in number the whole time. Soon the trees were full of them and they stared at us viciously and jealously as we poked about with the insides, trying to determine the cause of death. Karl cut deeper into the head section and we saw what the trouble had been. A huge growth had developed over the nasal passages and eaten into the brain behind the eyes. Some time or other, one of the villages had probably hit it across the head and caused an internal infection; it seemed very unlikely that he had been left untouched the whole time, living right there by their community water hole.

We attached the meat to a stake in the tall grass and Karl hid himself in the bushes, concealed with blankets, waiting with the cine-camera for the ugly friends to come down and feast. One after another, as they were sure it was safe, the vultures swooped down and tore savagely at the carcass, looking about the whole time to make sure no one was coming. Suddenly something did disturbed their feast and they all became alert, looking around with scraps of bloody meat still hanging from their cruel beaks. Somebody was coming down the path on a bicycle. One of the vultures panicked and flew off; the panic spread and suddenly there were no more vultures left. While most of them circled overhead, a few remained in the highest trees, twisting their naked heads trying to get a better view of the intruder.

The visitor hopped off his bicycle and pushed it into the camp, calling out "Hello" as he came. Seeing that this man was here to stay, most of the vultures left altogether; off to find some other bones to pick. Fortunately, we had already shot enough film and we came out of our hiding places to greet whoever it was who had arrived.

He was a fairly old man with a slightly withered hand. He had brought us a bowl of peanuts as payment for some snake skins we had given him a few days before. He was a very pleasant fellow and, although he only spoke a few words of English, we all seemed to understand one another. He was very interested in the monitor skin, salted and drying, pinned to a board lying in the sun, still with little pieces of meat attached to it and he kept running his fingers over it. Then he asked us what we had done with the insides and we realized why he was looking open-mouthed, so longingly at the skin. We teased him a little, pretending we hadn't understood and then I wandered off and fetched what the vultures had left and wrapped it up in a sheet of paper. As I came back, I could almost see his mouth watering. We told him he must cook it very thoroughly because the animal had been ill and the remains had been lying in the grass. He promised to bring us some more peanuts as payment, but we said that that wasn't necessary and that it was a present. As he was thanking us for the fourth or fifth time, a small boy came along the path and into camp carrying a pile of logs on his head. The old man introduced the boy as his son, which made us rather pleased that we hadn't charged him for the meat, because we knew the boy's family was too poor to send him to school. In order to attend school a boy must have a white shirt and this the family could not afford.

Before they left, I asked the old man what it was he had done with the snake skins. He raised his shirt and tucked it in his armpit and indicated that he had laid the skins over his kidneys to cure kidney pains. Then they left us, the old man carefully carrying his meat and pushing his bike and the boy following behind with his load of wood.

* * *

As we got up at first light, cleaned up our camp a bit and started preparing the breakfast, a couple of farmers came strolling down the path and called over to us. We called back the same "G'morning," and they came over to warm themselves by the fire; the air was still damp and cool. The rice was cooking and Karl was stirring it while I was busily cutting up the tobacco leaves which we had bought in Bathurst.

One of the men wore an old military great coat and a sun helmet and spoke very fluent English. It seemed he had been in the British Royal Air Force during the war and had taken the coat with him when he left. He didn't say where he had gotten the sun helmet. His friend kept in the conversation by nodding in agreement or saying "yes" or "no" from time to time, whichever was appropriate. As I stuffed some freshly cut tobacco leaves into my pipe, I looked up and saw that both men had suddenly produced their own, empty of course! I should have known better! I offered them the tobacco and they both eagerly filled their pipes and then left us to eat our breakfast.

In the forest clearing where we were camped were a number of towering palm trees that bore the palm seed clusters from which red oil is obtained. The clusters had already been harvested from our trees by the farmers and a few enormous palm branches were laying about, brown and dried out like parchment so that they rattled in the wind.

Before long, other people came down the path, five or six men on bicycles. Fortunately, we had already finished our breakfast and we concealed our tobacco. They all rang their bells as they approached the

40

camp and the leader cycled towards us with the others following closely behind. He was a very short man but extremely strong with very broad shoulders. He had a rope made out of palm fibers slung over his shoulder and, with this, he explained he could climb up the palm trees to cut down the fruits.

His name was Jung Kassama. He was a jovial, friendly man and the second person that day who spoke very fluent English. He said he lived in the nearby village, Mandinari, and worked in Bathurst for the Public Works Department. He had a very good job as planner for minor projects in the town.

The men were eager to be on their way, but we managed to persuade them to give us a demonstration of their climbing skills before they left.

The leader took his rope and looped it around his body and the trunk of the tree and tied the two ends tightly together with a special knot. Then he leaned back in the rope and started walking up the tree, jerking the rope a little higher after each step. He reached the top in no time at all and came down as swiftly as he had gone up. I asked if I could try and attempted to do exactly as he had but unfortunately my shoes slipped on the bark and, after only three paces, I had to come down again. Karl decided to try it too, but without shoes. The Africans' feet are tough like leather from walking barefoot since childhood but a European's remain soft and tender. Karl soon came down again with grazed and scratched soles.

"Good," said Jung Kassama, getting on his bike and grinning all over his face, "I'll come and see you again on our way back."

Off went the group again, wildly ringing their bells all the way down the path.

In due course, Jung did come back and spend some time with us while his friends cycled back to the village with huge clusters of palm nuts draped over their handlebars.

Jung let his bike fall into the grass and came over to us, grinning widely showing all his fine, white teeth.

We chatted for a while and, as usual, the topic of snakes fascinated him the most. The cobra skin was pinned out on the same board with the monitor, both covered with salt and drying in the sun.

Jung looked curiously at the skins and poked them distastefully with his finger.

"Is the meat edible?" he asked, not looking around.

"Yes," I said. "A man in the village ate the monitor and we ate the cobra ourselves with some rice"

"Isn't it poisonous?"

"Nothing has happened yet, Jung, we're waiting to find out. It tastes like chicken."

He turned around and looked at me, unbelievingly and sideways, then he glanced at the snake skin one last time and came away thoughtfully.

"I know a place where you can find plenty of snakes," he said. "I'll show you this afternoon, if you like."

"OK. Why not?" I did not want any more snake experiences for a while but thought it would be interesting to explore the forest in other areas and also visit the village itself. Jung was delighted.

"Good, I'll see you later after lunch. I'll come here. Goodbye," he said as he hopped onto his bike and cycled off at top speed.

By and by, he turned up again and we left the camp, he pushing his bike and I with the catching claw and a sack slung over my shoulder just in case.

During the course of our conversation, as we followed the path between the tall trees and the high, golden grasses towards his village, I happened to mention that one of the local boys had told me about the devils that lived in the forest and had managed to scare himself in the telling.

"It is no laughing matter! The devils," he said, "are everywhere. In the trees in the forest, in the houses, in the villages; they are everywhere!" He seemed to enjoy this subject a great deal and became increasingly enthusiastic.

"For example, all along the roadway here are dead people, both good and bad. The bad ones we call the devils. They live the same as we, everywhere, but we can't see them ourselves, only magicians can see them. These are men who can talk with the dead and they come here at night sometimes, in groups, but I've never seen what they do myself.

42

It's something to do with medicine. There is a man who lives in a village not far from here who can mend bones within a couple of days. In the hospital, when they can't do anything, they cut the limb off, but this man can always mend them. The government even offered him a job in the hospital and a new house to live in, but he refused."

"What about the Juju. Who makes those charms?" I had noticed that everyone wore amulets.

"Oh yes! But I have that knowledge, too. My father passed the secrets on to me and I wrote them all down in a book. I have them at home, I'll will show you when we arrive. There is even a Juju against snake bites. Look, I'll show you what it looks like."

He gave me his bicycle to hold and bent down and thoughtfully traced a pattern in the sand.

"That's interesting," I said, "and what do you do with that now?"

"That has to be written on a piece of paper and tied tightly in a leather pouch or in a goat's horn, then it is worn on the body and no snake can bite. Or, you can wash the ink off the paper and wash yourself with it and then you are protected as well."

Clearly, he was very serious.

"There is another one you can put on your lorry (he meant our van) to protect your things against thieves. When the thief takes something, then he becomes very ill and slowly dies. And in the war, all the soldiers were afraid of the Mandingo people because they couldn't be killed. All the Mandingos came back alive; the bullets just couldn't harm them. If you shoot a gun at someone wearing the right Juju, then just water comes out instead of bullets, and you can try to cut him with a knife and the blade will just bend or break."

We had arrived at his house. He unlocked the padlock on the door and carried his bike inside. We went into the second room and I sat down on a chair made out of palm. He gave me an orange to eat and one for himself and then showed me his book of Juju charms which was a school exercise book filled from cover to cover with strange diagrams and instructions written in Arabic. I thumbed through the book, while he explained some of the preparations: how people can turn themselves into animals and what they have to do to

43

turn back again; the ways of killing one's enemies and so on until, at last, the conversation exhausted itself and we left the house and set off, as originally intended, to see if we could find some snakes.

We went down a narrow pathway lined on both sides by banana plantations all the way from the village to the riverbank. Jung led me into the swamps and pointed out the places where he thought the snakes lived: a fallen hollow tree, a termite pyramid riddled with holes, a gaping hole in the side of a bank, and so on.

Soon we were deep in the forest, where the air was stickier and where very little sunlight shone through the dense canopy. Jung showed me the footprints from crocodiles and the holes in which he thought they lived. We went on for a while in comparative silence and then, suddenly, he stopped dead in his tracks.

"D'you see it?" he screamed in a whisper.

"What did you see?" I asked, pushing past his frozen figure.

"A snake, it's gone into that bush there. D'you hear it?" Something squeaked. "D'you hear that?"

It squeaked again. "D'you hear it?"

"Yes," I said, and put my heavy boot down into the grass beneath the bush from where the noise was coming. I pushed some more grass out of the way and the thing squeaked again and so did Jung.

"D'you hear it?" and each time it squeaked he asked the same question. Finally, I told him I couldn't follow the noise properly if he kept talking, but he didn't stay quiet very long before he began again, asking me if I could see or hear whatever it was that was squeaking and I realized that Jung was scared stiff. Finally I felt something wriggle a little under my boot and I pressed down harder and pushed the grass away with the catching claw. There, pinned under my foot, was a big, fat, black rat and it was squeaking furiously. Jung looked enormously relieved.

We carried on again in silence until Jung found something else to say.

"There is a monster-sized snake that lives here somewhere in the forest; we call it the "Nin-ki-nang-do." It has hair on its head and if you look at it you might die of fright. It comes out in the rainy season and eats the dogs and often sheep as well."

Eventually we came out of the forest and made our way across the peanut farms and finally back to camp. Jung and I roasted and ate a few peanuts and then he decided it was time to be off home before darkness came. He cycled away, smiling all over his face.

While his tall stories seemed quaint and his Juju charms appeared merely as harmless native superstition, it also struck me from my conversations with my new friend that the African people live daily in the midst of very profound dangers. Everything seems to bite, poison or make a person sick. Their folk knowledge of medicinal herbs and barks, muddled with animistic notions were scarcely effective against life threatening tropical diseases but, in spite of that, they were all that they had. These people were enormously vulnerable. Jung's belief in menacing devils around almost every corner seemed somehow entirely justified.

* * *

The next morning when we awoke we found the door of the cage open and the crocodile no longer there; it had probably made off back to the swamps to its hole and we thought that it was maybe better that way. He was too large to export and we did not want to have to feed him. But it was strange. The wire that bound the cage door closed was unraveled and we wondered if someone in the night had perhaps taken the crocodile for the value of its skin.

The day passed by uneventfully and soon evening was drawing near. The farmers and their wives and children were returning past our camp on their way home after the day's work in the fields.

A few Mandingo boys were amusing themselves, singing and talking on our tape recorder, for which privilege they had to gather firewood and fetch water from a well behind our camp in the forest.

Throughout the day, a large tree by our camp had been making loud, cracking noises as if it were about to break in the middle.

One of the older boys, whose father had a large tomato farm, came up the path carrying a huge bowl of tomatoes on his head. He was a particularly friendly fellow and came over to us to say hello. He

45

placed his bowl of tomatoes underneath the huge tree. We chatted for a while about this and that and he started spinning more yarns about the devils who live in the bushes. The same stories that had scared him so much on an earlier occasion. He couldn't understand how on Earth we could choose to stay in the forest at night. We didn't tell him that the evening in the forest was the most peaceful time of the whole day, the only time when we had no visitors. Our friend said that he had seen the devils himself on one or two occasions when going home late, after dark, from the fields. We tried to persuade him to draw a picture of one, but he refused. Yet it later occurred to me that he may not have meant anything supernatural at all but could have been talking about hyenas which are sometimes described as devils, while the name is not literally meant to imply anything unearthly. He just did not know the English word for hyena.

As we stood there talking, the tree let out another terrific groan and the boy became very worried about his tomatoes lying in the shade of its great branches. Nevertheless, he wasn't going to rescue them; he was afraid the tree would fall on top of him. I couldn't see any immediate danger, the tree having been making similar noises the whole day long, so I went to fetch his tomatoes for him. The bowl was certainly very heavy and I was astounded at the thought of him carrying such a weight on his head. As soon as I was out of the danger zone, the tree let out its final cracking moan and down it came with great force, smashing its own branches to splinters against the ground as it fell. It made a terrific thud that shook the ground on which we stood and set the birds and monkeys screaming.

Everyone heaved a sigh of relief, in particular the tomato farmer's son, and they all began to laugh, except us. Our cages had been within the reach of some of the branches and were now nowhere to be seen. Most of the animals we had so far collected from Gambia were inside. We ran over to where they had been and searched them out from underneath the branches. Fortunately, they were strongly built and had missed the full force and were all intact, so now we could laugh as well. Our lizards were safe and so were the tomatoes.

We decided to celebrate the jungle devils being apparently on our side and somebody went to fetch some peanuts while the rest of us piled logs onto the camp fire until we had a great bonfire.

It was our last evening in Gambia and a very wonderful climax to an extremely enjoyable and fascinating stay.

Darkness came and our friends left, perhaps sorry to say goodbye; we certainly were, but we were off to see other places and had other people to meet in different countries. But we were sure that it wouldn't be the last time that laughter would echo around our camp wherever it might be.

4. ÎLE AUX SERPENTS

We were waiting, camped on the beach a few miles from where John the hermit lived, hoping that the sea would soon become calmer. Everything, everywhere was shrouded in mist and a sort of clammy haze gave the nearby huts along the shore the look of an African ghost town. The breakers sprayed, rushed, thundered continually. Wedged forever tight among the rocks was part of an old wreck. Just the wet, rusty hull gaped out from under the swirling, surfy waters. Not very much left, but still determined somehow to withstand the merciless thrashing of the Atlantic.

John the hermit lived in a shelter built of smooth rocks that he had gathered from the beach. With driftwood and twisted branches, he had fashioned the flat roof and covered it with more rocks. His house was perhaps ten feet long but only just high enough for him to crawl inside.

We were searching for somewhere suitable to camp so that we could safely leave the van while we crossed over to the island. John was a strange old Senegalese but he seemed kindly enough and, while definitely eccentric, he did not seem to be entirely crazy. We had told John of our plan because the island was visible from his house. He had enthusiastically volunteered his services as guide and cook so that we could spend several nights on the island. But this location was definitely not a good place to leave our things although John assured us that it was quite safe. He had never had any trouble with thieves albeit he did confess that he kept a pistol in his shelter.

We had ourselves witnessed a thief at work on a parked car. He had been hanging around all day and had even spoken with us while he no doubt assessed if we were worth stealing from. He produced a length of stiff wire from his robes and was busy forcing the door of a Peugeot. He did not seem to care if we saw him or not but was intent on helping himself to the couple of packs of cigarettes that lay on the passenger seat. We chased him away but it was farcical. He pretended to beg for mercy. He wasn't afraid of us and just wandered off to find something else to steal, mocking us as he went.

The sea seemed to be becoming rougher instead of calmer. If

49

the bad weather was here to stay, then we would have to postpone our visit to the island and we were unsure if we would have another chance to return to Dakar. The island was interesting but we wanted to continue on to Mali and the next leg of our journey. In any case, we had been across to the island once already, before we had left Senegal to spend Christmas in Gambia. The sea had been calmer then, but, even so, the waves around the Île aux Serpents had been wild enough to turn us and our equipment out into the water and literally throw us and our rubber boat up onto the stony beach. We had lost our camera.

The island interested us for two reasons. First, it had become separated from the Senegal mainland by a volcanic disturbance a long time ago and we thought there might perhaps be some interesting animal varieties there; the second reason was its name, "Île aux Serpents," the island of snakes!

The island, south-west of Dakar, was scarcely one and a half miles long and maybe just three quarters of a mile wide at the most. Very close by was another island, "Ile de Madeleine." Together they are called the Madeleines and since 1976 they have become a national park, the smallest in the world.

That first time, before Christmas, we had spent a few hours on the island and discovered that it was indeed a paradise for snakes and lizards. We had made our way down the cliff-side to the boat as evening was rapidly drawing on. Although the beach where we had landed seemed to be the best place for casting off again, it was nevertheless very tricky. The rocky headland sloped gently away from the island, becoming narrower all the time, until, at one point, it disappeared into the sea. At that place the waves beating from both sides of the island, which lay parallel to the mainland coast, met, pounding into each other with a roar of thunder and forcing a spray of surf shooting high into the air. We had climbed into the boat at the furthest point around the headland where the shore discontinues and the island becomes invincible, protected by its sheer, towering cliffs. Frantically pushing with the paddles against protruding rocks, forcing the craft forward despite the coming waves, and then paddling wildly, we had managed to maneuver our rubber canoe past one treacherous rock, narrowly avoiding the next, being thrown the whole time off course by the waves, until eventually we managed to get beyond the island, from where we paddled at full speed away out to sea.

During Karl's military service, which is compulsory in Austria for all young men, he had trained extensively at water maneuvers on the waterways of Austria. His unit had become quite skillful so that they competed against other teams in terms of speed and expertise in crewing a boat full of soldiers, punting flat bottomed landing craft across raging rivers.

I am certain that Karl saved our lives that afternoon. I had virtually no skill with water craft and the wind was blowing the canoe all over the ocean. It was Karl who saw what to do, took charge and kept us from being capsized in the violence and confusion off the treacherous rocky foreland of the island of snakes. I just paddled with all my strength.

At a reasonable distance, we made a wide curve and returned to the west of the island some way out to sea. Even so, we narrowly missed being swept back by the powerful wind into the concussion of waves where the receding tide and the violent ocean met off the island shoreline. To make matters even worse, the tide was against us and we had to keep up a hard, steady pace fighting the whole time against the undertow that was savagely trying to drag us out further and further from the shore.

The return journey took twice as long as the journey out to the island and we landed on the sandy beach in darkness, both of us drenched and aching, while a cold night wind blew, cutting into our weary bodies.

Now we were waiting on the same beach for the mist to clear. Our original plan had been to camp on the island and spend a week which would give us plenty of time to examine everything of interest. We had intended to take John the hermit with us until we discovered that he was not only a bit mad but also that he took drugs. We gave up that idea as it seemed to needlessly stack the odds further against us and we decided instead to make one or two day trips.

The next morning was a little better. The mist had cleared and the sea seemed quite calm. As soon as we were both awake, we packed all our things into the van and drove down the coast road to the beach where the fishing boats were.

We parked and wandered down onto the sand. A few men were painting and repairing their boats and others were mending holes in their nets. But we were too late; the majority of the fishermen were already out at sea, out of sight. We had hoped to be able to persuade one of them who would be going close to the island to drop us off there and pick us up again later on his return, which would have saved us having to use the rubber boat again.

A man was busy attaching floats and weights to his new net and we decided to ask him how much he would charge us.

No luck, he only spoke Wolof.

Further along the beach, we spotted a policeman on duty and we went to ask him if he would translate for us. He seemed very pleased to be able to help and we approached the fisherman for the second time.

The sun was already high in the sky and began to warm our backs.

The policeman entered into a lengthy conversation with the man and finally turned around to us and told us the price was $3,000 fr, which is about five pounds! We asked if that was the price to fetch us in the evening as well and he replied that it was but it was still far too expensive for us. The policeman said that the price was fair but it was self-evident whose side he was on. We offered the man 1,000 fr., but were, of course, refused.

We thanked the policeman and he carried on with whatever it was he was doing before and the fisherman returned to his work.

"The sea does look much calmer," we said to one another, "much calmer than yesterday."

We decided to risk it with the rubber canoe.

A few fishermen and an ever present group of young boys followed us back to the van, curious to see what we would do next, whether or not we would pay the ridiculous price. As they saw us pull out the rubber boat, their curiosity intensified. We pumped and pumped and the boat grew and grew, as did the crowd of spectators. We packed a few basic items which we thought we might need in case of emergency into polyethylene bags: a torch, starting pistol, matches, etc. Then, with the van securely locked up, we hoisted the boat onto our shoulders and carried it down to the beach, our hoard of excited spectators swarming behind us, eager to see us get turned over into the waves or whatever it was they expected. Our starting place was a calm bay, and we had no trouble at all as we paddled off, out towards the open sea and our island.

52

After about twenty minutes, the sea became quite a bit rougher, after forty, treacherous! It was high tide around the island and our previous landing spot was submerged beneath the waves, leaving just sheer cliffs all around. We paddled on, our bones and muscles aching as we fought against the various and numerous currents determined to throw us against the cliff wall.

Beyond the island the waves now covered the rocks that on our last visit had barred the entrance to a small cove. If the water was deep enough, we might be able to make a very nice landing there.

We paddled on gingerly into the bay, looking carefully ahead and underneath us for any sharp rocks that might be hiding just below the surface. Fortunately, the water was crystal clear. The way through was very narrow indeed, but the pointed rocks were covered by about two feet of water, so we were lucky. Once in the cove itself, it was easy and we paddled gently up onto the sandy shore. No trouble!

We pulled the boat out of the water, rather pleased with our achievement and even more pleased to be able to rest at last. As we laid the boat down on a boulder, we heard a loud hissing noise. The side chamber had been punctured by the sharp corner of the basalt rock - a hole the size of a thumb!

So we had managed the crossing, despite the rough sea, with great success and now something like this had to happen. We were stranded!

I decided to try to attract the attention of one of the fishermen offshore to see if it would be possible for him to collect us from the island on his way home.

I saw one boat north of the island and made my way, slipping about on the wet rocks, to a small peninsular to see if I could attract his attention. As I reached a position where I thought he could see me better, I spotted a man fishing from the rocks below. Apparently we weren't completely alone on the island after all.

I climbed down to him to explain the situation, but could hardly hear my own voice above the concussion of the waves and had to shout. He said that it was a friend of his who was fishing in the boat and that he would be fetching him from the island later and we could go back with them. Excellent! We had several hours more to see what we could catch on the island afterwards, we were sure of a safe ride to the mainland.

We spent a long time catching geckos that hid themselves in deep crevices in the rocky cliffs around the island. They were larger than the same type on the mainland and much more ferocious, biting at the cloth sack which we put them in and putting up quite a fight.

We found two dead snakes and saw three live ones during the course of our stay, but unfortunately we had no opportunity to catch them. There were too many places for them to hide.

Mid-afternoon I went back to the canoe to roll it up and pack our things together to be ready when the fishing boat arrived. As I was nearly finished, the fisherman came and told me that his friend was due at any time and that I'd better fetch the other fellow.

Karl had gone to see what the cliffs were like on the other side of the island, but I couldn't see him anywhere. I shouted and shouted and cursed, but heard not the faintest reply. The boat had already arrived and the men were impatient to be away, wanting to get their fish to market as quickly as possible. A half hour passed, but still we couldn't find him. My throat was burning with too much shouting. We loaded the things into the fishing boat and hoped that Karl would soon return, but still he did not!

The two fishermen couldn't wait any longer, we would circle the island once and, if we didn't spot Karl, then we would both have to stay there.

Already the other fishing boats, which had earlier dotted the horizon, were on their way back to sell their fish. If we couldn't find Karl, it would mean we would be spending the night there. At night, it would become cold, damp and windy, and we had no protection from the elements. We would have to keep a fire going all the time to stay warm.

We pushed the boat away from the rocks and chugged out to the open sea. The tide was going out and the rocks were now dangerously close to the surface. The waves were riding even higher than before and a powerful wind was blowing around the island. Around we went, just once, riding up and down over the high waves. One fisherman stood by the rudder and the other and I bailed out almost continuously.

We arrived back at the bay, but it was impossible to enter. The jagged rocks were showing their sharp edges above the surface. Karl was

54

there on the beach, a dead seagull in one hand and a bag full of geckos in the other. He had to clamber over the slippery rocks to reach the boat.

The two men were in good spirits again, glad at last to be able to get going and relieved that things had turned out well.

Soon we were back on the mainland helping to haul the boat up onto the shore. For dinner, we ate the seagull.

* * *

Part of the next day was spent repairing the hole in the boat. Karl wanted to visit the island just once more to see if he could catch some snakes. The rubber boat, however, looked decidedly unsafe, even with the hole well patched up. It had been badly scratched in several places on the underside and we both knew that if it hit a rock just once it would burst.

Nevertheless, Karl was adamant and was prepared to take the risk; he would go alone to make just one last visit. With less weight, the boat should manage the journey a lot easier and, from the peninsula along the shoreline, I would keep watch through the binoculars until I was sure he was safely there and, if he got into difficulties, then I would pay for a fishing boat to go to the rescue.

The next day was gloriously warm. The white crested waves rolled over the jagged rocks of the shoreline then, seeming to gain courage, threw themselves with all their might against the beach. We were camped much further down the beach than previously, mainly to keep as far away as possible from the beggars, thieves, and scroungers who were constantly on the prowl nearer the town.

After breakfast, we drove back towards the fishing bay where we had left for the island previously. Karl decided to start off from the side of the peninsula from where I would be watching through binoculars.

I busied myself pumping up the boat while he collected the things he needed for the journey and tied them all tightly in polyethylene bags.

The first stage of the journey was easy; the wind whipping around the cove, the boat was blown like a feather out towards the open sea. I could see through the binoculars that he only had to paddle very gently to keep up a good speed.

The fishing boats were already dotted about among the waves, some near the island and some just tiny points on the horizon.

Everything seemed to be going very well indeed. In no time, he was halfway there, then three quarters, and then fast approaching the island itself. I could see the waves around the island rising and falling and I could well imagine what it must be like between the two islands with waves charging irregularly against one another. It was very difficult to keep the boat in sight. Without the binoculars, I could see absolutely nothing and with them I could only make out a tiny red spot where the boat was when it reached the crest of a wave; sometimes I could see the silvery flash of the wet paddles caught by the sunlight. Fortunately, there were several large fishing boats in the area laying nets, so, if he did get into difficulty, they would be there to help.

Somewhere between the two islands I lost sight of him completely, the waves were too high and they hid everything. I waited a while, scanning the gap until I saw a fishing boat passing through. Then I knew he must have made it or have been rescued. The boat passed by the island and continued on its way out to sea. Evidently he had arrived!

The day passed fairly quickly and, towards mid-afternoon, I took my place again on the peninsular and scanned the island. This time I used my telescope, which was much more powerful than the binoculars. On the island itself, I could see no sign of movement and no boat was coming through the gap. I turned my attention to the sea around the island. Already the fishermen were on their way back with the day's catch, each eager to arrive back first at the market. One in particular was now on its way, riding over the waves between the two islands. Just for a moment, I thought I saw something red coming around the rocky coast close behind it. I zoomed in on it with the telescope. Could I make out the long shape of the canoe now and then as it rose and fell among the waves? As the boat came away from the island, I saw that it was indeed the canoe, being towed by the fishermen.

My eyes were beginning to ache. The sun was glaring down onto the waves around the island and the water reflected the light back to me, like a dazzling mirror. I threw everything into the van and locked it up.

As the fishermen came racing into the bay with the lone canoeist in tow, I was on the shore waiting. The large boat ran aground and one of the fishermen cut the tow rope and Karl paddled in under his own steam. The fishermen were the same ones who had brought us back the last time and seemed to be getting used to this sort of thing. I helped Karl carry the boat up to the van and then we returned to give the fishermen a couple of packs of cigarettes that were the standard currency and acceptable manner of saying thanks. We loaded everything into the van and he told me about his adventurous day.

The journey to the island had gone well due to the strong wind behind him, until he had tried to paddle between the two islands. Then the waves had come in such a manner that they spun him around and he had only just missed being capsized by another wave that caught him side on. Behind the island, the water was too low for him to cross the rocks, barring the entrance to the cove. He had to clamber out at the base of the cliff onto a narrow ledge and struggle with the boat into the bay.

Once on the island, all had gone well until around midday, when he heard a gunshot. He had thought that he was alone on the island. He made his way down to the beach and found two boys using his net to catch fish in the lagoon. They had arrived with three men who were fishing from the coast. Karl wasn't particularly disturbed until he found that all his things had been gone through. The sacks had all been untied and even his food lay half eaten, scattered about on the sand. The starting pistol had been used; that had been the gunshot he had heard. He went to the two boys and whipped the net away from them. Karl was particularly annoyed that the food had been eaten, or rather wasted, because, not having caught any snakes, he had intended to spend the night on the island. He asked the boys which of them had eaten the food; both of course denied it. But he shouted at them so furiously that at last one of them blurted out that the other had done it and Karl gave him an almighty swipe that sent him falling back down the wet rocks, almost into the lagoon.

The mood of the island expedition completely spoiled, Karl decided to pack his things together and return to the mainland. It was high tide as he paddled over the treacherous rocks out to sea.

The waves were higher, the wind was stronger and against him. It was all he could do to prevent the boat from being thrashed against the rocks. His progress was nil. He struggled about for a long time, being thrown here and there, becoming wetter and the boat continually filling with water. Things looked very bad indeed and he decided to try to get back to the island and perhaps call to a passing fisherman. As he began to turn, a fishing boat came around the back of the island. He recognized the men from the last time and they, of course, recognized him. He threw them his line and they towed him to safety.

* * *

Before we left Senegal for Mali, we made a new camp further away from the city but still on the coast near the site of an old World War 2 bunker. The concrete platform above had once hosted heavy guns that pointed seaward to protect Dakar during the years between 1940 and 1942, when Senegal was aligned with the French Vichy government.

Beneath the old gun placements, the bunker consisted of a row of rooms that had once accommodated both soldiers and munitions. But the place was infested with fleas and any further exploration was out of the question when we realized that we were being eaten alive. Even though Karl managed to catch a few geckos as they scurried along the underground walls in the darkness, the flea-bites made the experience throughly miserable and hardly worthwhile.

Behind the bunker was a compound where an African man lived with his family. The man was a lighthouse keeper. He and his much younger wife had two small children, one of whom was called Marguerite. She was a lovely child and, with her little brother, she frequently visited our camp on the beach and soon we became friends with her parents as well. Apparently, two other European tourists had camped in the same location the previous year but one of the men had developed an ulcerated leg and had died. I had seen these ulcers in Gambia. These were horrible infectious wounds that never seemed to heal. A (women) had arrived at our camp one morning while on the way to work in the fields. She had a nasty hole in her upper arm. She asked for some medicine as Africans often did and we gave her a penicillin powder. With her thumbnail, she scooped the infection out herself and applied the penicillin. We gave her a large band-aid and told her to see a doctor. But Gambia, before it

58

became a tourist destination, was one of the poorest countries in the world. It seemed unlikely that she would go to hospital unless the wound deteriorated severely and she became really ill. But perhaps the powder did do the trick!

Marguerite had heard the Beatles' song *"Hey Jude"* and greatly enjoyed the melody. But she sang it over and over, just as it sounded to her and it was very funny: *Hey Jude, ye nanky bay* … Her little brother would chime in whenever he felt confident.

Her other favorite song began, *Li la, Senegal est nearho* … I asked her what *nearho* meant and she replied in French, "Pas, pas bon", *not, not bad*, which is to say, "Good!"

Our new neighbor had a much older son who was a professor at the University of Dakar. The lighthouse keeper insisted that we drive with him to the school and that we all meet. We bundled the old man in the back of the van and set off. The University is very impressive and we met the lighthouse keeper's son in the library. He was a very intelligent and cordial man, tall and handsome as the Senegalese often are. He invited us to his home. He, too, was very interested in zoology and, in particular, marine life. Beneath his house he had build a concrete tank in which he was breeding sea snails. We talked further and recognized a fellow entrepreneur. He exported the snails to Europe for fish aquariums.

The old lighthouse keeper examined a few snails in his palm and scoffed. It was beyond his comprehension that anyone would want to keep such foolish things. What use were they?

The next day we drove back into Dakar. We were waiting for our mail to arrive poste restante at the Dakar Post Office before the next leg of our journey could begin. In Austria, Karl's father would forward our mail with the payments we received from our customers. We had to anticipate the country and city where we would next be so that he could address the mail to that particular post office. This was unpredictable and often required a long wait for our funds to arrive from Europe as well as frequent visits into town and the disappointment of discovering that we had no mail. But these forced delays allowed us to explore a particular location more thoroughly than we would have otherwise and even to get to know the Africans who lived there and to make friends. It provided essential insights into the culture through direct experience over an extended time that could never have been achieved had we traveled, for example, as conventional tourists.

Late one afternoon our lighthouse keeper received some visitors and he sent Marguerite down to our camp to fetch us. They were several of his brothers or cousins. The distinction was not always clear. One of them was smoking a pipe and I offered to share my tobacco and he reciprocated. His was uncured and green. He called it *saha tabac* and it seemed to be a herbal smoking mixture very alike to tobacco but much milder. We stood smoking, looking out to sea and only occasionally speaking softly, consumed by the magnificence of the evening.

A few days later the mail arrived and we made ready for the next stage of our journey, bidding our new friends farewell and thanking them for the warmness of their hospitality. Karl and I had bought some head-scarfs and some other trinkets in Austria that we thought would make great gifts and serve as currency in Africa. However, the days of trading with beads was clearly over. We gave one of the scarfs to Marguerite's mother but she was not impressed and passed it on to her daughter to wear. Marguerite was sad to see us go. I shall always remember her delightful rendition of the Beatles' song. I wonder if she ever learned the real words.

5. MALI BY TRAIN

For the last eighty miles of the journey from Dakar to Tambacounda, we had to drive along a dusty, rugged track. When the going was good, we could drive at about twenty-five miles an hour, but that was seldom possible. Some of the time the road was so deeply furrowed that we had to stay in first gear and drive around the enormous potholes. Sometimes other vehicles would race past us over the washboard bumps at full speed, churning up dense clouds of red dust in the process. The dust seemed to hang in the air for a long time and we could scarcely see the road ahead of us. The bushes and dry grass along the track were all colored red. Our van was very heavily laden, making it quite impossible for us to drive at any speed over the bad patches. From time to time, without warning, we suddenly found ourselves entering a rough area and the van shook and everything inside rattled and banged; we thought it was breaking apart.

Nevertheless, towards midday, we arrived at Tambacounda, after a grueling journey lasting a day and a half. It was a very quiet rural town with hardly any traffic and very little activity. We found the railway station right in the center, next to a hotel. Inside, the ticket office was closed but we found someone in another office who said he could speak French. He was a little man dressed in an oily coverall, like a mechanic. It was hard to understand him; he seemed to be speaking a mixture of his African language and French and he gave us answers to our questions but not to the ones we had asked. We wanted to know where we could buy tickets for the van, ourselves, what it would cost, and when the train would be leaving. He told us that Bamako was a long way away and that the journey was very expensive.

Fortunately, before long, somebody else turned up and said that he was a representative for the touring club of Senegal and he would help us to arrange matters. He was a smartly dressed, young African who spoke not only French but English and German as well. He told us that he had studied in Germany for two years, but he didn't say what it was he had studied. He led us off to the goods department, to an office that was in fact a fenced-off corner of a storage shed. Inside were two men sitting at their desks, quietly chatting to one another with apparently nothing to

61

do. The representative spoke to them in French and one of them started to fill out a form which he then gave us to sign. We looked at it carefully and noticed that it was divided into two halves, the cost of the journey as far as the Mali frontier and an additional figure that would have to be paid in Bamako on our arrival for the other part of the journey through Mali. That seemed quite reasonable, but we were expected to pay another 2,000 francs for loading the van and fixing it to the platform with cable and we knew they were trying to make extra money on the side. After considerable negotiation, they finally agreed to accept 1,000. We were quite accustomed to the flexible pricing and horse trading.

We drove our van around the back and into the goods' yard and up over a ramp onto a flat-bed railroad car in a siding. The two men from the office set about fastening the van with cable. Soon the vehicle was secured and we climbed up on the flat-bed to await the arrival of the train.

Before long we had several visitors. A large group of young boys besieged our siding and one of them started yelling, "Pig! Pig! Pig!". We had found that when kids become belligerent like this, it was best to do as their own parents and elders did. Without warning, I gave the boy a swat and they scattered in all directions and we were left in peace. Later, Karl and I reflected upon the incident and we realized the boy was yelling "Bic" not pig. He was demanding we give him a ball point pen.

We had seen a couple of American travelers in the station yard, a man and a woman in their twenties. Now they turned up again and joined us on our freight car. We did not care for them at all. They were scroungers, going from place to place, cadging their meals and freeloading wherever possible. The man stood up and urinated over the side of the car like some vagrant and we were inclined to slap him across the side of the head, too.

Fortunately, our train arrived. The Americans disappeared and our car was hitched on and pulled out of the siding. It was already dark when someone came and checked our tickets and, a few minutes later, we were on our way.

Our van had two removable bunk beds inside that ran down the center between rows of cabinets in which we stored all our gear. We also had a mountaineer's tent that we had bought from a mountain climber in Austria. It had an extra heavy ground sheet and a fly that kept it both dry in rainy weather and cool in the heat. When we made camp, we pitched the tent, but when traveling, we often just slept in the van. We slept fairly well despite the rough ride and, in the morning we woke up to find ourselves already over the border. A customs official came and took our passports and, at a town called Kayes, we had to register at the police station. Kayes might have been an interesting town and region to explore but we had to get back to the train or be left behind.

We enjoyed the journey immensely, sitting on the freight car or on the roof of the truck watching the changing countryside, speeding past mountains, villages, forests, and rivers. So many striking colors: the red, sandy slopes and rocks, the green trees and tall grass, the housetops made of golden straw, and the glorious, blue, cloudless sky. It struck me that this was the perfect way to see the countryside. Just a couple of miles from one of the little stations, we saw a whole troop of baboons on the move, going off down into a valley, at least thirty of them. We managed to take quite a few good shots with the cine camera from the moving train.

At several stations we caused a stir. It seemed that white men were quite a rarity in many of the out-of-the-way places and crowds of people came to look at us, keeping their distance, staring at us and very quietly whispering to one another.

The journey lasted two and a half days and we awoke one morning in a station and all was quiet. The train had gone and we were left in a siding. We had arrived; we were in Bamako.

We got up, didn't bother about breakfast but went about settling all the necessary formalities so that we could drive out of the station. We found the customs office and the station master and made arrangements to get our van unloaded from the flat car.

Along another siding there was another Volkswagen van, like our own but with side panel windows and also on a flat-bed. As a diesel engine started shunting us here and there to bring us to a ramp so that we could drive off, a woman came over to talk to us. She was an American teacher, about thirty years old, and traveling alone around West Africa. Although she spoke very pleasantly with us, she was clearly upset about something and couldn't wait to leave Mali and reach Upper Volta, where she had some friends waiting for her. She had been in the siding for two days already and was hoping to be able to leave that day. Finally, we discovered the cause of the trouble. The young man we had met in Tambacounda who had claimed to represent the Senegal Touring Club had helped her settle her affairs at the station. He assured her that there was nothing more to pay in Mali and now, suddenly, she was presented with a bill for the second half of the journey from the border. Also, the representative had charged her for his services and she had paid 3,000 francs to have her van loaded onto the truck. Now, on top of all that, the workmen in the goods' yard had told her that she had to pay a further fee for unloading. Our journey had only lasted a couple of days, but her truck had been shunted onto a siding somewhere along the way and she had had to wait a week there until the next train came past. During the night, someone had stolen some of her things which she had left outside on the station platform, and now, with these further shenanigans at the Bamako station, she was thoroughly disgusted. I thought how hard it must be to travel as a woman alone in Africa.

Our truck was by the ramp and the workmen came to cut the cable so we could drive off. One of them then asked us to pay a fee of 1,000 francs for the unloading but, as he couldn't give us a receipt or a ticket, we refused to pay and drove on our way. We were glad to see the American woman also being shunted towards the ramp as we left the station and hoped she would not be ripped off yet again.

We wanted to take a good look at Mali's river and forest life and headed north-west towards a river called Baoulé in a forested area in the direction of a place called Fana, about eighty miles from Bamako. As we left the city, I noticed the American lady teacher driving along in her Volkswagen and I was glad that she could now continue her journey, hopefully without any more mishaps.

Somewhere along the main road we were supposed to turn off down a track leading directly to the river, but we had great difficulty in finding it. We drove down one trail which, after a couple of miles, only led to a village and no further. We had to go back to the main road and start again. The second track we followed did in fact lead to the river, but it wasn't the one marked on the map. It was very, very hot and dusty. The temperature in the van, even with the windows open and the air blowing through, was 110° F.

The way became rougher, sometimes with giant termite pyramids blocking the access so that we had to drive off the road into the dry grass and maneuver around them. The dust cloud behind the van was so intense that we couldn't see a thing behind us when we turned to looked back.

Eventually we came to a wooden bridge that spanned a dried-out river bed, but the termites had eaten away three quarters of it and it looked very precarious. A person just walking across the bridge would have brought it down. Although the banks were steep, we decided to drive down and cross the riverbed itself, which we managed fairly easily because the surface was sun-baked mud and very hard.

After just a few hundred yards more, we came to yet another bridge, but this time the river had stagnant, muddy water in it. The termites hadn't done such a thorough job on the timbers and we drove across it at full speed and winced as we heard it creaking under the weight of the van; fortunately it held but I did wonder about the return journey.

The track seemed to be endless. On the way, we met two men who were driving a small herd of cows back the way that we had just come and we asked them if they understood French, to which they both replied enthusiastically, "Oui, oui," but then proceeded to converse in their own language. However, we managed to understand that there was, in fact, a forest by a river just a short distance further. We were only a few miles away.

This was the Koulikoro region of western Mali. The river is a tributary of the Bani that eventually meanders its way down to the Ivory Coast. We soon came into view of its broad expanse. The water was a steely blue, dotted here and there with fishing boats and men throwing their casting nets in a graceful fan across the sparkling surface. It was spanned by a very modern iron bridge and lined on both sides by luscious green forest vegetation. We stopped in the middle and looked down at another group of fishermen below us, spanning their nets across the river from bank to bank. Others were punting on the slow flowing, shallow water in dugout canoes. A picturesque village continued up along the bank.

We drove some distance following the river and decided to make our camp right in the middle of the forest where it was much cooler.

The next morning we each made excursions by ourselves. I went a long way up the river bank. My journey was fairly uneventful, apart from being awestruck at the sight of so many different, beautiful and colorful birds, both on the small, sandy islands in the river and in the forest itself. On the way back, I noticed a patch of darker green among the bushes and creepers. Through the binoculars, I recognized it as a baboon; he was staring straight back at me. We stayed there for a while, looking curiously at one another, until he finally became agitated and decided that maybe it would be wiser if he left.

When I arrived back, it was nearly midday and once more very hot. But, in spite of the heat, Karl was eager to explore the area, too. We thought it better if one of us always stayed at camp just to make sure nobody became too interested in our belongings. As yet we hadn't gotten to know the people of the region at all and we didn't know what they were like or what they were likely to do.

Maybe an hour before sunset Karl returned and we cooked our evening meal as he told me what he had seen during his walk. He had crossed the river to the opposite bank where he had met a group of small boys who were fishing from a dugout canoe. They had taken him with them a long way down river to where some men were fishing with nets. The nets were round, about five yards in diameter and weighted all around the edge. They were thrown in such a manner that they spread out and then fell into the water, trapping the fish underneath. One of the men had dived down to collect the trapped fish and brought them back to the boat. While Karl was there, he saw them catch some really large fish.

On the way back up the river, he had seen a huge snake, completely black, curled upon the bank, but the boys had been too afraid to go near so Karl had to content himself with just watching it.

The day had gone by very quickly and we were once again enjoying the cool evening sitting by our log fire. We could hear voices carried by the light wind from the village not far from the iron bridge. People were talking and sometimes laughing, the noise echoing enchantingly around the forest and off the surface of the water.

The next day came and, once again, we both made visits to the wilder parts of the area. Karl went off first this time and came back a couple of hours later. He had been a long way further than previously

66

and had heard a terrific noise in the forest. Some men going past in their boats had seen Karl and shouted a warning because there were gorillas in the forest! In French West Africa baboons are frequently called Gorillas. The main troop was some distance away, but one of them seemed to have been watching Karl and, as he approached, it went off on all fours to catch up with the others. He hadn't seen very clearly what animal it had been, but he assumed they were baboons. Of course there ·were no gorillas in West Africa until the great apes in the mountains of Cameroon.

In the afternoon I went exploring also, the same distance down the river as Karl, but on the opposite bank. I wanted to see what it was he had heard in the forest earlier that day. I scanned the opposite bank for a while and then noticed something moving deep in the bushes. A big baboon, dark olive green and powerful, was coming down out of the forest to the river. He looked around very cautiously and then stooped down to drink. He looked just like an enormous dog with a heavy, furry mane. Then, off he went up the bank again and sat himself down beneath a shady tree. I whistled to him and he looked across but didn't see me. I whistled again and he was joined by two of his friends who looked about them uneasily. Finally, they became unimpressed by my teasing and ignored me entirely, going about their own affairs, climbing around slowly among the bushes, looking for tasty things to eat.

I left them in peace and started on my way back to camp, but, on the way, I was met by yet another baboon who ran out of the bushes and climbed up a termite pyramid some distance away, where he could watch what I was doing in safety. I walked towards him very slowly. He became more and more agitated the nearer I came, until he couldn't stand it any longer and shot off somewhere behind the pyramid. I gave chase, but discreetly so that he couldn't see me and when I reached the place where he had been, I saw him again, sitting in a low tree, still keeping an eye on me. I continued towards him and, when he bolted off out of sight again, I broke into a run and quickly reached the tree where he had perched and, there among the tall dry grass a little ways away from the forest bordering the river bank, was the whole company. Big ones, small ones, mothers with their young, all peacefully wandering about. Some were eating the fruits on the bushes, others searching about in the grass for insects. In all I saw well over thirty animals, some of them magnificent, powerfully built creatures—the leaders of the group. One or two of them noticed my approach and climbed into the trees to try to get a better look at the intruder. I stayed half concealed behind the trunk, watching them through binoculars, but they had got wind of my presence. A few moved slowly off, out of sight into the long grass, a few more followed and then, all at once, the whole group began to panic and stampeded off out of sight and out of danger.

The first one I had come across was probably the look-out. Many mammals and birds do the same. One of the troop is somehow selected for guard duty and keeps watch while the remainder feed.

I went back down to the river bank to see if the other baboons were still there, but there was nothing, no movement in the trees, no noise, nothing to be seen. As I came away from the water's edge, I heard a loud rustling coming from somewhere behind a mound of earth. I moved very slowly and quietly, being careful not to tread on the dry twigs and leaves lying all around and, as I climbed the low hill and peered over the other side, I saw two small eyes peering back at me. It was a monitor lizard, in the same family as the one we had had in Gambia, but much more beautiful. This was a Nile Monitor, (*Varanus niloticus*). It was colored black with yellow along the body and a tinge of red. The head was gray, almost silver, with black stripes. We stared at each other maybe as long as ten seconds; he was as surprised as I was fascinated. I looked at him, trying to note as much detail as possible and he looked back, bewildered. He was a huge creature at least four feet long. Suddenly he unfroze and was off like a shot, galloping away into the bushes. Within a moment, he was gone without a trace.

These explorations allowed us to discover if there were suitable rocky outcrops or areas where we could set traps to catch small lizards or geckos and determine if it was worth returning at night and catching small reptiles by flashlight. In the heat of the day, it would be enormously unlikely to be fast enough to rope a monitor lizard unless it was somehow trapped in a burrow or cave.

I made my way back along the forest path towards our camp, keeping my eyes open, hoping to see some more interesting animals. Beneath a tall tree, I saw heaps of twigs scattered about and, looking up, I could hardly believe my eyes. There was a nest, about a yard and a half in diameter, made of sticks heaped together in a ring, so high up and of such a size that I was astounded! There was nothing moving in the tree or around the nest, so I assumed that it was deserted. But what creature could have made such an enormous eyrie? In 1977, it was discovered that chimpanzees inhabit certain isolated areas of Mali where there is a sufficiently dense forest canopy and adequate edible vegetation such as would flourish along a significant river. This discovery is founded upon the evidence of droppings and other signs but few, if any, sightings have actually occurred. My enormous nest may have been a chimpanzee structure and the fishermen warning Karl of gorillas may have been referring, not to baboons, but to chimpanzees. While western zoology did not know of Malian chimpanzees, the natives most certainly would have.

Then, as I was gaping up at the enormous nest, a beautiful butterfly floated down from above. It was the color of Autumn and the sunlight through the tree tops dappled its reds and golds. But the most striking thing of all was its size. It was as big as my whole hand. I have since looked at pictures and descriptions that might qualify my sighting of this gorgeous African insect but I have never found anything that even remotely resembled what I saw.

I carried on back to camp where I found Karl had built an armchair for himself out of logs. He had already prepared our evening meal of rice and vegetables and, after drinking a kettle full of boiled water, I told him all about the things I had seen during the afternoon.

We were fortunate in our choice of a camping spot. The forest endlessly followed the river and it was teeming with interesting creatures. But what fascinated Karl the most after his trip up the river in the boat was the skill of the casting net in the hands of the fishermen and we decided that, as soon as we could, we would buy one.

Unlike almost every other place where we camped we seldom had any visitors in the forest along the river. While we found this to be more typical of isolated rural parts, here it appeared that the Africans used the waterway to get about and did not venture into the forested area. I wonder, in retrospect, if it was a precaution because of the presence of chimpanzees that, in the wild, are enormously powerful animals and can become very violent. Unlike the baboon, the chimpanzee may not run away when encountered. In any case, the solitude was very pleasant for us. But before we left a few days later a Malian man came into the camp and greeted us courteously. He was of a different build than the tall Senegalese, but stocky and powerfully muscled. He carried a short handled ax that was club-shaped, heavy and rounded at the end where the steel head was wedge securely. He was on his way to chop fire wood. After a few uncomfortable moments while he collected his thoughts, he spread his palms in the gesture of despair and said one word, " Malade." And asked for something to make him strong, "Fort." Of course there was nothing we could do to help but Karl gave him a few malaria tablets and at least that cheered him up considerably. He thanked us gratefully and, smiling, he continued on his way.

While this was a fascinating area of the country, it was less than ideal for catching reptiles. Karl managed a few snakes but the habitat was not conducive for lizards. While, no doubt, there were turtles in the river that would interest us, we decided to research a different and more hilly location where the small animals might live in greater numbers in the rocky crevices and be easier for us to catch.

6. BALA
Mystic or Charlatan

About five miles west of Bamako, away in the hills, a shallow river begins as a spring, then twists and winds its way down through the valley, eventually flowing into the great Niger itself. On its way, the river irrigates a variety of crops from rice to bananas and eventually also a mango plantation where, beneath the shade of the tall, leafy trees, we had found an ideal spot to camp.

Cornered by the steep slopes of the valley, covered with red, stony soil on which hardly anything could grow, with the little river bubbling past and the trees with branches weighed down by the thousands of nearly ripe mangoes, the gaily colored birds happily singing and flying about made this place a paradise.

In the rainy season the little river would swell, overflow its banks and flood the whole area, making the narrow, dusty road an impassable swamp and hiding the few surrounding fields under water. Now the water level was so low that the little fish could find nowhere to hide and swam erratically, here and there, getting into each others' way.

In the far corner of the mango plantation, deep in the shadows of the leafiest trees, was a hut that was the home of Bala.

Shaking hands with Bala was a little odd. His right hand was slightly withered and the last two fingers were paralyzed in a half-closed position, (*Dupuytren's contracture*). It was like trying to shake hands with a bundle of sticks, the ends jabbing into your palm. When we first met, it was as if he peered at us over his pupils or through the whites of his eyes, and it was hard to tell if he was looking beyond, into the sky, or at the ground. In addition, his shoulders drooped, bending him forward and, to counteract this, he threw his head back so that his huge Adam's apple stuck out, making him seem even more misshapen.

He had no family, except for one son whom he had beaten so often that finally the boy had left home and nobody had seen him since.

Bala had been a woodsman as a young man, not after leaving school - he had had no education - but as soon as he had been able to handle an ax. That had kept him busy until an ice-making factory had opened and there he had found a job as watchman. That was thirty years

71

before, at the same time when the mangoes had been planted around the factory. Now the trees were enormous and bore so much fruit that the branches sagged under their weight and the factory was just a ruin, full of rusty machinery.

Bala was a Muslim and prayed several times a day, always at the same place, a few yards from where we were camped. He would stand there in his bare feet, facing away from us up into the sky, his faded green robe hanging over his bony figure like a sheet over a post. First he would begin muttering, then go down on his knees and touch the ground with his forehead a few times and finally finish by quietly wailing a strange prayer as he wandered away back to his hut.

When it was too hot, he wore a white robe, like an Arab and a small, white skull cap and he seemed to feel worthier like that and would stride about among the trees looking very important with his hands behind his back.

It was dressed in this fashion that he came to visit us one morning as we were cleaning up our camp and packing everything back into the van, preparing to leave to go to Bamako. We told him we would be back that afternoon and that we were only going to buy some food.

As I stood by the front of the van polishing the windscreen, he came over to me I thought to shake hands. Instead, he took my hand in his and started examining it very closely. For a moment, I stared at him in surprise, but then it struck me that he was reading my palm. Actually he was more interested in the tips of the fingers and the fingernails than the palms. He mumbled strangely in Bambara, which neither of us understood, then pushed my hand away and gripped hold of Karl's. He continued muttering and humming and then, all at once, he progressed to pidgin French and we could at least understand his meaning.

"Oooh! Monday!" he wailed, "Midday, no before midday, when the sun like now, like that," he pointed up towards the sun. "Be careful eh! Careful, midday, Monday, when the sun like that!"

We asked him what was supposed to happen on Monday, but he didn't understand us and just repeated what he had said before.

"Monday, when the sun like that be careful, eh!" his tone rising ominously and dramatically as he turned and strode away, head held high with marvelous effect and dignity. "Be careful eh!" he warned, wagging a

72

crooked index finger at us without looking back.

* * *

We could hardly wait for Monday but when it came, in spite of the suspense, we chose to clean up our gear and wash our clothes. We had thrown our blankets onto the roof of the van to air them a little and, as we were beginning our breakfast, we heard a loud tapping sound on top of the van. And then several taps more and a splash. It continued for a few moments and we went over to the van to see what it was. Karl climbed up onto the roof. There, all over the tarpaulin and over our blankets as well, the droppings of some animal up in the trees had fallen onto the roof of our van and splattered over all our things.

Despite the foul smell, we both had to laugh; it seemed the old fortune teller been right after all!

He was coming over to us just at that moment and heard us laughing. We showed him the mess the animal had made on the roof and he shared our amusement, although he didn't quite appreciate the significance of it. He had probably forgotten about "Monday, be careful eh!"

While he was there, he decided to read our palms and fingernails once again, but this time he studied them much longer. He told Karl that he would have one daughter when he got married and probably a second one, too. Years later Karl did indeed have two daughters but also one son.

He spent more time with me, probably trying to think up something good, then finally he made the shape of a gun with his fingers and boomed, "You die," and he made a sign as if cutting off his finger, "You dead, bang, bang, bang!"

Bala's palm readings, despite his attempt with us, were famed for their success. He was able to tell people the date and day of their birth, but that was easy because many West Africans were uncertain of when they were born and exactly how old they were.

He was also a doctor and made his own medicines out of roots, bark, and plants, which he collected from around about the place and cooked over a fire in a large, round, blackened pot - a cauldron. He had his own method of sterilizing wounds: with glowing cinders from the fire.

73

He seemed to think that without pain there was no cure and the louder his patients screamed the more chance they had of recovery. He was treating a middle aged man by this method one morning and had left his medicine simmering over the fire unattended. I walked quietly round about through the trees until I saw him looking the other way, then I quickly crossed the path between his part of the plantation and ours and reached the hut where he lived and behind which he was curing his patient. His brew was a dark brown, murky tea with bits of wood and leaves floating about in it. I had brought the camera with me as a precaution, which was as well because Bala caught me leaning over his cauldron. I smiled at him and told him that I'd been searching for him to take his photograph, a souvenir for us, and that seemed to be the right excuse; it flattered him.

Every day, without fail, a very special patient arrived in her pale blue sports car. She was a middle aged French woman who taught languages at a school in Bamako. She was under treatment! She spoke Bambara but was nevertheless always accompanied by another teacher from the school, a tall, lean African man. We spoke with her several times and she seemed very impressed indeed with Bala.

Bala had enormous influence on the local people also and he had numerous visitors the whole day long, asking advice, having their fortunes told or collecting medicine from him. He had made a few quite spectacular cures which had made him famous.

The story goes, a farmer had had an enemy who was constantly looking for an opportunity to kill him and one day succeeded in giving him poison. The sick man came to Bala almost on all fours. He had a terrible pain in his stomach which was puffed out like a balloon. Bala made him a medicine out of bark, roots, and the legs of a turtle. Within a short time, snakes started leaving the sick man's body and his pain became less and less until it disappeared completely. When we heard this tale we imagined that the man may perhaps have been suffering from tapeworms and that Bala's potion had effectively destroyed them.

Another story tells of a woman who came to Bala in great distress because she had been married for such a long time and yet bore no children. Thanks to Bala's medicine, she had a son.

Bala was famous for his medicines; no one knew so many as Bala. But it wasn't only for that reason that people respected him; he was

74

something of a double agent! By day he prayed to Allah and at night he was said to talk with the devil! It was unwise for the natives to disrespect Bala.

In one of the sheds by the factory, there lived an old woman who was under treatment from Bala. In return, she kept house for him and cooked his meals. They lived on what Bala's patients gave to him. He never charged anything but left it up to the person to give something reasonable.

Bala seldom went anywhere very far. He just strolled about within the couple of acres around the factory, singing or talking to himself. He could speak very little French. When he ran out of words, he would abruptly continue a conversation in Bambara. One day we brought a huge log back with us from the river bank, planning to cut it up for firewood. Bala was wandering around the compound as usual and came into our camp, mumbling to himself and then he suddenly caught sight of the log. He let out a squeak of surprise and made his eyes quite large and white. He chuckled a little in an embarrassed fashion, looking about him. Then, suddenly he caught sight of the log for the second time and let out another loud squeak, as if he hadn't see the log the first time at all. I think he was impressed that we had dragged the huge thing all the way from the river.

He pondered it at great length and then turned to us. To Karl, he said, "Julujan" and, to me, he gave the name, "Doudda".

How the presence of the huge log inspired this name-giving honor, I shall never know.

* * *

I knew a dozen words of Arabic. I could greet someone and ask them how they were and, after a few more remarks, I ground to a halt and that was more or less the end of the conversation.

One morning, a Malian man came by our camp. He was dressed in long robes and carried a kettle as many Muslims do because they wash before they pray. I greeted him with my smattering of Arabic and he replied and we seemed to understand one another perfectly until I ran out of pleasantries. He returned again the following day and we repeated our formalities. The next time I was occupied with some task and Karl called over to me, " Hey, Sidi, your pal is here!" I looked up and there was my Muslim friend in his white robe beaconing to me. He had pages with prayers printed upon them in Arabic. With tremendous patience, he recited the verses and I dutifully repeated his words. He seemed delighted and asked me many things that I could neither understand nor answer.

The following day my new friend returned this time with a wedge of white soap. He indicated that we must wash at the waterfall near our camp before we said prayers. It was at that point that the penny dropped. He was endeavoring to convert me to Mohammedism. I politely declined and we each went our separate ways, one of us disappointed and the other very much relieved.

* * *

Shortly after breakfast the following morning, an old man came to visit us. He was still strong but bent and he carried an ax over his shoulder. He made a very friendly impression; he shook hands warmly, asked how things were going and sat himself down to have a chat with us. We offered him some tea that was left over from breakfast, which he accepted and quickly consumed. Then he saw that we had some rice left over and asked if he could have that, too. We agreed and he delightedly polished that off as well. When he had finished, he said "goodbye" and went on his way.

That evening he appeared again and said "hello" in a friendly manner, but this time we weren't at all sure about him. He asked if he could eat what was left over again, but there was nothing except tea, which we gave him, hoping he wasn't going to be there for every meal.

But breakfast time, the bad penny turned up again, and this time he annoyed us and we sent him away and told him to scrounge from someone else.

In spite of our unfriendliness, that evening he turned up again, pushing his bicycle. It was a really old one with no brakes, no rubber on the pedals, and only bald tires with gaping holes in them. He had cut up an old tire and put the pieces in between the holes and the tube to save him getting too many punctures. The back wheel had seized up and wouldn't turn at all. We gave him a wrench to use and told him to do it himself.

If anyone else had seen him working with that wrench, they would have done exactly the same as we did. We took it out of his hand, told him to sit down, and then mended it for him. The wheel had refused to turn because there were two ball bearings inside which were larger than the others.

As the job was nearly finished, a couple of very smartly dressed young Africans came walking down the path, one of them wheeling his moped. The old man called over to them to stop and went, almost bent double, running off through the trees to catch up with them. He chatted for a little while, said "goodbye" and then came slowly back to us. The bicycle was finished and the old man told us how grateful he was and, to our surprise, he reached over a neatly folded hundred franc note. One hundred Mali francs was very little for us, but a great deal for the old man who had had to beg for it from the two passersby. We refused and told him to sit down and eat with us, which he did but this time we didn't mind.

We ate so many unusual foods during our journey that were quite a new experience for the both of us. From tiny ocean crabs boiled in oil and eaten whole, snails, octopus, and snake meat, to some very dubious African dishes which baffled us completely. But there was one thing neither of us could stand and that was rice with stones in it. We had bought six pounds of just such a rice in the market and, although we had washed it before cooking, there were still always stones left in it. We decided to offer some to the old man the next time when he came by and, if he ate it, we would know for sure that he was really hungry. Sure enough, the next day the old man came to visit us at breakfast time. We cooked some of the rice and offered it to him. He sat himself down on the dry mango leaves and gratefully began his meal. It was quite clear that he had seldom in his lifetime eaten rice without stones in it. He knew exactly how to go about it. He poured water over it and washed it thoroughly through with his muddy hand, turning the water a dark brown. Sieving each mouthful this way, he managed to get through the whole meal, only occasionally having to spit out a stone. He said "thank you" enthusiastically several times and wished us a good day and went off to chop wood. What a useful demonstration. We had learned how to eat rice with stones in it.

That evening he didn't turn up until very late, when it was already dark. We had finished our meal but had kept some to one side for him. He came into the camp with a huge pile of logs which he had chopped for our fire. He ate his meal and then stayed chatting with us for a long time. He said his name was Niokolo-Koba which was also the name of the great game reserve in southeastern Senegal. He spoke quite fluent French because he had been a soldier in Indochina during the Second World War. It was this man who told us most of the stories about Bala. Before it became really late and too dark, he decided he had to go and set off down the road back to his village.

The next evening he brought us a squirrel that he had caught during the day but didn't stay to eat it with us. He just gave it to us and then left us in peace. He often brought us more logs for the fire and once he even brought us some lemons as a gift. He was very poor and frequently hungry and we realized that we had misjudged him. We began to look forward to his visits and thereafter enjoyed many a bowl of rice and stones in his company.

* * *

Despite the shade from the leafy mango trees under which we were camped, the temperature practically all day long stayed at about 112°F and at night dropped to only 105°F. If there was any wind during the day, then it was hot air in the form of a whirlwind caused by cars and lorries passing down the road. The gusts often came with considerable force and brought with them clouds of dust as they spun their way through our camp and off down the valley.

Out in the direct heat of the sun, particularly at about midday, the heat was almost unbearable. Neither of us could stay out of the shade for very long; the sun whipped down on us, leaving us drenched in sweat, with throbbing heads and throats as dry as cardboard. Sometimes we came back from exploring the surrounding district feeling quite dizzy. We estimated the temperature in the sunlight to be 150°F, and on the sides of the rocky hills even hotter. The only creatures capable of enduring it appeared to be insects, in particular, cicadas whose song became louder with the heat and seemed at times to be coming from inside our heads.

Nevertheless, it was necessary to go off despite the heat to catch reptiles. We had scraped and saved enough money in Europe to cover the first few months of our journey, but, for the rest of the trip, we had to live on the money we earned by exporting animals. In Senegal, we had sent away two consignments containing various and interesting creatures, some of which were quite valuable and earned us a good income.

This area around the river, among the hills, seemed to be rather good and, as far as fish were concerned, we thought we had found a gold mine. The little river was crowded with colorful fish, ideal for a fresh water aquarium.

After our evening meal, when it was really dark, we took our nets and buckets and wandered up and down the river bank, the powerful beam of a lamp run from the van's battery, which we carried between us, showing the way.

At first all went very well. We hauled the fish out one after another, filling first one bucket then the other. But stumbling about in the mud and water with the heavy car battery was very tiring and, after an hour or two, it became torturous, like a prisoner with a ball and chain secured to his ankle.

We kept the fish in a ten gallon bucket and a large tub, both covered with mesh and, on their sides, immersed in the stream. Night after night we waded about up river and down, bringing back more and more of those beautiful fish.

Then one morning we noticed little white spots appearing on the fins of some of them. That was bad, but fortunately curable and we poured some medicine into the water and the white spots seemed to disappear.

It seemed that we had been too lucky in finding the river so full of such wonderful fish and slowly our good fortune turned sour. We noticed tiny worms living under the scales of the fish. We tried to treat that as well, but without success. A few days passed and the fins of all the fish were becoming ragged and frayed.

There were too many of them living too close together. The parasites were leaving one fish infested and going on to the next. We sorted them out, throwing the really sick ones back or killing them and spread the fish out into more containers so that they were less crowded. But it was no use, every day there were more and more dead ones.

A week earlier we had booked a passage at the airport for an eighty pound consignment of fish that would have been in three boxes. The airport agent had sent four telexes to Paris to secure connections to Germany for live animals that had to be kept warm, at a temperature of about eighty degrees. Now we had just a few left and they were sick.

We drove around Bamako trying to buy a special medicine called "Typoflavine," but of course nobody had heard of it. We even visited the Bamako zoo where we were astonished to discover dead animals in the enclosures until we realized that they were food for larger predators. It occured to us that some of the caged animals would be sure to go missing from time to time and end up as dinner for an African. Mali was an extremely poor country and here was all this food walking about!

Finally we ended up in a veterinary school that was run by the French. We found the professor in charge and told him about the fish and asked if he had the medicine. He had never heard of Typoflavine either, but he let us search through his medicine cupboard. But it wasn't there! The doctor was a very kind man and wanted to help, although he wasn't very well up on fish parasites. He gave us three flasks of white powder that he thought might do some good.

We went back to camp and gave a bucket of fish the full treatment straight away.

By evening, there was little change apart from a few more corpses floating on the surface. The flight was due for the next day at seven in the morning; we had one chance; to spend the night catching fresh fish and send them to Germany the next day with instructions to our customer to give them a bath of Typoflavine on arrival.

We went further downstream than we had been before and far upstream, where the river narrowed. The mosquitoes haunted the banks in such numbers that we thought if they were all to bite at once they might well eat us alive. If that wasn't enough, they were attracted by the powerful light I was carrying and the buzzing they made about my head overwhelmed the sound of the gurgling water.

As we plodded along the marshy banks, unintentionally

disturbing the frogs and toads as we went by and watching their hind legs disappear as they sprang into the water, we became more and more certain that we would not be sending any fish, anywhere the next day. They were all diseased. Some of them were completely blind with white, empty eyes; others had pieces of their fins eaten away and had holes in their backs made by worms. We decided not to send them.

The next morning, as it was just beginning to become light, we drove to the Bamako airport with our modest box of reptiles. At six, we arrived and explained to the company representative the reason we only had eight pounds and not ten times that much; he was as disappointed as we were. We returned to camp crest fallen and determined to explore a better location.

7. UPPER VOLTA
Wiley Python and the Baboon Hunt

After a two-day long journey, we arrived in Ouagadougou, the capital of Upper Volta. Upper Volta has since been renamed Burkina Faso which means *land of upright people* in a combination of the Mòoré and Diola languages.

The road, since we had left Mali territory behind us, had become very rough indeed and the van was covered with the same red dust that we had experienced on the way to Tambacounda. Both inside and out, fine powder seemed to have found its way into every crack and corner.

We had stopped briefly in Bobo-Dioulasso in order to change some money at the bank which was just closing when we arrived. A French bank clerk took pity on us and let us in. "We are closed really you know. I am changing your money only out of kindness," he explained, magnanimously.

In Ouagadougou, we explored a little of the city, filled our water canisters at a public pump but quickly decided to head out of town and find a place as far away as possible from the ubiquitous cadgers and moochers. We had learned to avoid large towns and much preferred the countryside of small, traditional hamlets and trustworthy farmers.

Fortunately the road leading south from Ouagadougou soon became newly surfaced, wide and, apart from one or two overloaded trucks delivering goods from Ghana, donkey carts piled high with logs to sell in the city and the occasional African on his wobbly bicycle, it was mostly deserted of traffic.

At first it proved difficult to simply drive off the road and find somewhere to camp; the entire countryside was covered everywhere with clusters of straw roofed, clay houses, the same color as the sandy, dry earth, and each group was encircled by an outer wall. Thousands of little fortresses dotted the whole landscape. Most of the population of Burkina Faso is settled in the South of the country.

At last, about thirty miles or so away from the city, we turned off down a dusty track leading alongside a lake. It was mid-afternoon and extremely hot, despite the constant breeze blowing through the van windows and even the muddy water in the lake looked inviting. But, valuing our health more than a swim, we drove on away from the little villages and clusters of houses to a spot where we found ourselves quite alone.

The whole area was flat: a tan colored, sandy soil covered sparsely with dry yellow grass and dotted with big trees, small trees and thorny bushes and, abruptly, a lone granite hill. We drove around it and found a worked-out quarry on the other side, a huge gaping hole in the side of the slope and scattered everywhere were tons of rusty, old machinery lying about in pieces as if someone had simply forgotten they were there. Further around the hill we came to a group of round, thatched houses made of stone with whitewashed walls, all quite empty but still in good condition. In front of one of them was a huge, leafy tree under whose shade we decided to make our camp, at last out of the scorching heat of the sun. As we got out and stretched back to normal, we noticed long, green pods hanging in clusters from the tree. We picked a couple and broke them open, but inside were just small seeds in a white paste with a terrible taste. We started a fire and boiled some water to make tea.

As the second kettle of water began to boil on the log fire, someone came cycling slowly up to us on a rattling old bicycle. He called out "Hello" and he threw his bicycle onto the ground and came over to shake hands. His hand was flat, broad, and strong like a spade and the lines and creases of his palm were accentuated with dirt. We had met our first farmer. He told us that his brother, the watchman of the houses behind our camp, was in Ouagadougou that day but he would return later in the evening. Although he was a very powerfully built fellow, he did everything in slow motion. He even talked slowly, as if half in a dream, as many rural people seem to do and was satisfied with every answer we gave him, even if he hadn't understood what we had said. It was not the conversation that mattered. He was evaluating us.

We came to understand the significance of this initial interchange and often observed a similar cautious affability between rural Africans when they met one another in the fields or along the country paths. Their greetings were elaborate and intricate. At first I found it strange when they asked each other after their health, the well-being of the farm, the wives and children and it seemed amusing. Later, I realized how essential cordiality was to survival. One failed crop might mean destitution to these small farmers. The community of others was an essential safeguard. Who knows when misfortune might strike and they might need the provision and security of one another.

Similarly, everybody always greeted the stranger, including white travelers like us, arriving suddenly out of the blue and, even though we incited particular suspicion, nevertheless the newcomer was always cordially received.

He saw the beans that we had picked from the tree, lying broken upon the ground.

"You know this?" he asked very slowly. "Rhooda, they're very good but they are not ripe yet, we pick them in winter, they are good!"

Some of the beans, high up in the tree, were in fact already ripe, but we didn't have to climb up. Our friend said he would bring us some from home and off he went, very slowly and unsteadily on his rattling bicycle.

Before he returned, the watchman himself appeared cycling down the track on his more modern machine, which he threw on the ground just as his brother had done. Like his brother, too, he was very powerfully built but much shorter. He wore a woolen helmet with a hole in it just for his nose and eyes and a plaid jacket like that of an American lumberjack. He jumped from his bicycle as if it were a horse, walked over to us like John Wayne and confidently stretched out his muscular hand in greeting. "Hello, Bernhard the name!" We all shook hands and he told us how glad he was we were there and even more pleased that we would be staying a while. He told us that he had had such a lot of trouble with thieves. I asked him what there was to steal and he groped in his pocket for a bunch of keys and then led me to one of the houses. Most of the windows had been wedged with thorn bushes where netting had once been and, inside, the doors were all missing.

"Wood is very expensive here," he told us. He asked which of the houses we wanted to live in, we could choose whichever we wanted. These were dwellings used by the foreman who ran the quarry and for road building supervisors from the city. We were astonished but delighted. We picked the one in front of which we were already parked and he opened up the door. The termites had eaten away most of the

85

frame and he warned us not to open and shut it too often.

Bernhard had bought himself a hen and was eager to get home to cook it, and, without further ado, he said "goodbye" and cycled off at top speed and left us wondering if it was really true that we had been given a house to live in.

Abel, the watchman's brother returned the next day with the Rhooda beans and slowly showed us how they should be broken open and how the yellow, crunchy insides should be eaten. They certainly were good and, as soon as we got to know our way around, we found the trees with the ripe ones and didn't have to rely on him any more.

The area was particularly good for snakes and, during the first couple of weeks, we found altogether six different species, from the harmless snake-eating file snake to the rhombic night adder and the highly dangerous puff adder. But the one that interested us most of all lived high upon the rocky hill in a deep, narrow cave. It wasn't the same knoll that was near our camp but a second, much larger hill, over a mile away. Karl had been there one morning catching lizards and had approached the cave from above with the wind against him and there he saw it luxuriously sunning itself in front of the cave—a large rock python! He had clambered down as quickly as possible in the hope of catching her, but it had swiftly returned to the depths and safety of the cavern.

On a second visit, he found a freshly shed skin by the entrance, measuring eleven and a half feet long, which made him even more determined to catch it. The whole afternoon he was occupied drilling, sawing and hammering, building a sturdy trap. I went off to visit Abel to see if I could buy a chicken for bait and spent what seemed like hours, at first, meandering around the issue and eventually haggling with him before I finally received the animal and handed over the money.

Karl wasn't quite finished with the trap that day and so he decided to attach the hen on a cord to a peg in the ground in front of the cave. He would then wait above until the python showed itself; it should be very hungry after having shed its skin.

Abel had a small brother who had followed me back from the farm and kept well behind most of the time, until finally he had plucked up enough courage to catch up and hand over a small turtle he had found. Unfortunately, it wasn't very healthy, the shell was very soft like wet cardboard. The boy was deaf and everyone thought that he was daft because he couldn't speak properly. I showed him what was wrong with his turtle and gave him a mango from Mali to encourage him to bring some more, healthier ones. Back at camp, I gave him an animal book to look at and he spent an amusing afternoon laughing at the monkeys.

Evening came and twilight followed, but still Karl hadn't returned, so I decided to go and see what was up. I started off among the rocks and across the plowed fields to the second hill, seeing my way only by the light of the stars. Suddenly, I became aware that someone was following me. I couldn't see anyone, but I could hear dry grass rustling every now and then. I ducked behind a bush, out of sight, and waited very silently. Sure enough, someone had been following me; it was Abel's deaf brother. I signaled to him, trying not to shock him, and he caught up and we carried on together.

At the foot of the hill I called out and Karl answered. All was well, he would stay a while longer as the snake hadn't yet showed itself. I told him I would take the deaf boy back to his house and then come and keep watch too. Off we went again, back along the pathways among the rocks to the van. There, in the language of hands and feet, I explained to the boy that I was going back to the hill and he should go home. I gave him a couple of mangoes and went some of the way with him to the farm, then we parted company.

Back at the hill I called out, but there was no answer. I assumed Karl had gone back to camp and that we had passed each other in the darkness. I started back once again; by now it was almost pitch dark, some clouds had appeared and hidden the stars. I found a stick and tapped my way like a blind man, stumbling every now and then over the rocks. Then, on the way, I heard someone singing Austrian songs and there was, of course, no doubt as to who it was. Karl had already been back at camp and had now come to tell me just that. He hadn't seen the snake, but he would try again the next day with his trap.

Early the next morning, Karl was finishing off his trap, with the hen standing beside him looking very annoyed, when a group of boys came along with a small owl. They had caught it in some bushes at the base of the hill and had broken its wing in the process. We gave them two cigarettes for it, enough for them to let us have it but not enough for them to bother a second time.

The owl received first aid treatment and some raw goat's meat which it ate greedily from forceps. We made a pen for the creature in a corner of the house and there he considered himself king, strutting around with his bandaged wing like Long John Silver, swearing at everyone.

A little later, Abel came by on his bike with another hen, a red one. After interminably haggling over the price, we finally bought it and decided to use it as bait instead of the first one who we felt had endured enough already.

That afternoon, we laid the heavy trap across two poles and lugged it across the countryside towards the hill. The climb was steep and the day particularly hot. By the python cave we were glad to be finally rid of it. We set the trip mechanism, baited the trap with the live hen and made our way back to camp.

The whole day long we were tormented by flies. Flies that came in the thousands to drink our sweat as we cooked at 112°F even in the shade of the Rhooda tree. We were both relieved when a few clouds appeared and, from time to time, blocked off the terrific heat of the sun. But by evening, the whole sky had darkened over and become a purple gray, leaving just a little opening through which we could catch a last glimpse of the setting sun before it disappeared and night abruptly descended.

A light, damp wind had blown up from somewhere, cooling the air, warning us of the coming storm.

The flies had all vanished with the approach of night, leaving the space available for the mosquitoes. Fortunately, the wind whipped up and they were scattered, driven under cover, just this once leaving us in peace.

We stayed sitting outside, enjoying the one or two minutes we had left before the downpour was to begin. Opposite us, on the rocky hill, a few mother goats were scampering about trying to bring their families together under cover before the start of the deluge. The kids were bleating back from somewhere among the rocks, calling their mothers to come and fetch them.

First, far away on the horizon, the sky lit up in a flash, then another and another, then closer. Still quiet, just flares of light cutting the heavens and then all at once the first boom of thunder, so loud we could feel the ground shake. The lightning increased and the thunder roared in from all sides, making the earth and sky tremble, shaking the clouds so that they, at last, had to release their torrents of rain. The wind blew harder and faster, wailing in distress, trying to find refuge in any crack, beneath any beam, or through the partly open window of the hut in which we now sheltered.

Every second the vicious lightning bleached the landscape and silhouetted the rugged hill away in the distance, stark, wind whipped and thrashed by the torrential rain.

Straining my eyes, I thought I could still see an old nanny goat standing alone, crying out in dismay, calling for her kid, but unheard above the commotion of the storm. Once more the lightning cracked like a whip through the sky and, for a moment, it was as light as day but the goat was no longer anywhere to be seen.

From the conical straw roof of the dwelling, the rain poured down on all sides, spraying away from the walls as the screaming wind in its turn hurled the water back again.

Outside, the van was having a thorough scouring which would save us the trouble of washing it. But the storm was pummeling the tree above and sending leaves and twigs in every direction. Ripe and green Rhoodah pods covered the windshield. The great limbs above swayed back and forth menacingly.

This was an unusual storm that didn't belong to this time of year at all: the rainy season wasn't due to start for another month and a half. But at least the heavy rain would wash our human smell away from the trap and from the rocks around the python's cave. Tomorrow the weather would return to normal, with the temperature certain to be back up to 112°F once more.

We were horrified that we had left the little chicken up on the hill top during the violent storm and we were convinced that it could not survive such an assault. Perhaps the trap was destroyed and the hen had escaped. It was uncertain which of the experiences would be the worst, to be eaten by a python or drowned in the rain.

The early morning was still cool and it was comfortable to go about although the paths were very muddy and the terrain was strewn with debris. We hurried up to the python cave. To our surprise the hen was still in the trap and the python was presumably still in the cave. This seemed providential and we generously agreed to spare the chicken her plight as bait and abandoned the trap idea for the time being. We ate her for our dinner instead!

We decided to drive to the city to see if we had any letters and to buy some provisions. As we prepared to leave, a mouse ran out from under the driver's seat and hid itself away somewhere inside the van. We turned everything upside down but couldn't find it. We would set a trap for it that evening or else it would eat us out of house and home.

About ten miles along the road, in the direction of the capital, was a diversion along a muddy track full of rain-filled holes from the storm the previous night. We kept up an even speed to prevent the wheels skidding in the mud. Then, as we drove out of one deep puddle, we heard a loud crack, like breaking iron, from somewhere underneath the van. We drove to a dry spot and got out to look for damage, but couldn't find a thing wrong. We carried on cautiously, but suddenly heard another loud crack and the whole of the rear of the van sank down. We were right in the middle of a muddy stretch, leaving scarcely enough room for other vehicles to pass. We still couldn't see exactly what the trouble was, one side of the van had sunk down deeply in the mud with the wheel wedged tightly against the chassis. We filled up part of the hole with stones and then laid a board across them. We jacked up the van and then saw the trouble. One of the spring arms had broken and the shock absorber had snapped off entirely. And, just at that moment, it started to rain.

In the distance we could see tractors and trucks working along a stretch of the main road. This was a section of the main artery leading south into Ghana that was still being leveled and paved. We decided to go across and ask if someone with a front loader could lift us out of the mud onto the grass verge at the side of the road. We walked across to the site in the drizzling rain, plodding through the mud until we spotted the man in charge. He was a French engineer. We told him of our plight and explained that we just needed help to get clear of the road so that we could repair the damage. He was very sympathetic and told us that a tractor would be coming down that road later in the day and we could ask the driver for help.

It always surprised me when I spoke in French and was readily understood. I wondered about the grammar and troubled that I might not be explaining myself adequately. Karl was of a completely different temperament. He had enormous confidence and, with just a few words and avoiding grammar entirely, he was impressively fluent. Before our arrival in West Africa he did not know French at all but soon picked up words here and there and quickly was able to use them to good effect.

We returned to our van and fixed ropes securely to the chassis and waited. Sure enough, about mid-afternoon, a tractor trundled and screeched down the road. But it was a bulldozer without a shovel. Nevertheless, the driver kindly agreed to help us and we bound the ropes securely to the hydraulics. Without any effort, the machine raised the rear of the van several feet into the air where it alarmingly swayed back and forth and from side to side, threatening to come crashing down at any moment. The ropes were rubbing against the metal, nothing looked safe. Nevertheless, we went ahead with the maneuver. Karl sat inside and steered and I kept an eye on the ropes and gave the driver directions. Then, suddenly, the ropes did slip and the van dropped down violently about a foot but held. The driver's vision was obscured but I waved to him to raise the hydraulics and he dragged us out of the mud to a dry spot beneath a tree. We gave him a packet of cigarettes and thanked him for his kind help.

An overloaded bus traveling by stopped so that the passengers and their livestock could watch the fun. Suddenly we heard a voice in German. A Swiss man riding on the bus had seen the whole thing. "Das war eine Wahnsinnsmanöver!" *That was an insane maneuver!* He yelled, waving enthusiastically.

As the onboard mechanic, I spent the next day dismantling the broken pieces of metal so that Karl could hitch a ride to the city to see if he could buy spare parts. Unfortunately, there were none that we needed to be found in the whole of Ouagadougou. If there had been Karl would certainly have found them. We had to have the old pieces welded, which proved to be expensive but unavoidable.

Money was becoming an increasing difficulty for us. We were exporting reptiles and amphibians but payment would only arrive sporadically. Karl's father in Austria acted as our agent and forwarded cash to whatever city, wherever next we planned to arrive. He also sent us his own camera after we lost ours in the ocean off the *Ile aux Serpent*, in Senegal. His generous help in this regard was both invaluable and indispensable but there were often long periods of time when we were quite broke. We were regularly having to revisit the various post offices to check if our money had arrived from Europe before we could continue on. To some extent, we were able to live off the land, particularly in a coastal area where there were fish, crabs or perhaps muscles and oysters. We ate a great many coconuts and caught small animals. In the markets we bought beans, rice or flour in bulk. Often onions or okra were very cheap. Sometimes we would buy a couple of legs of goat and a loaf French bread and enjoy a feast. We bought chicory instead of coffee. But the spartan diet had an increasingly strange effect upon us. We found ourselves constantly thinking about food and comparing recipes and different ways to cook the particular grain it was that, at that time, comprised our mono-diet. Yet, on the other hand, the rural African lived in a similarly frugal fashion and we felt we understood the native better by subsisting on comparable food to them. Other travelers in the bush, living comfortably, incited envy and inevitably a barrier to understanding was established through inequality. We lived similarly to them in many respects and, consequently, knew them better and on different terms because they knew to not expect constant largess.

Karl arrived back from Ouagadougou with the welded part. I had to borrow a couple of large wrenches from an African mechanic who maintained the road-making equipment. We had a complete tool kit and could repair anything that went wrong with the van but this job required some extra leverage to remove a couple of stubborn, rusty bolts. The next afternoon, as I was lying under the van covered in sweat and surrounded by parts of the suspension and struggling to replace the repaired part, the remaining hen suddenly started excitedly clucking and squawking. I crawled out to see what it was that was disturbing her. There she was pursuing the fat mouse stowaway from the van, pecking it in the backside as it fled. She was proving very useful. But I wondered where we had inadvertently picked up the mouse and what was its original country of origin.

When the repair job was completed, I went back to the road works to return the workman his tools. Upon my return to camp, Karl had something to show me.

"Look what the hen has done in the van!" he said and I thought that she had made a mess. But there on the floor, beneath the steering wheel, was a small white egg. She had probably laid it out of gratitude for not being used in the trap. She was definitely earning her keep.

From that day on the hen became an important member of the team, daily laying her egg in the usual place on the floor of the van. At night she slept on the roof on a specially prepared branch and each evening, when she was ready to go to sleep, she would begin her palaver, clucking around the vehicle impatiently until we helped her up onto the roof. There, sitting on her leafy branch, she cleaned her feathers and then settled down for the night oblivious that soon she would be needed as python bait once more.

* * *

The straw thatched house was a little too far away from the hill with the python cave, so we decided to make our camp more conveniently beneath a squat, leafy tree beside a dried up creek. We were determined to catch a python and we would probably be visiting the hill very often. If we had no luck with the trap, then Karl planned to crawl into the cave itself, which would mean dragging himself on his belly as the roof was very low.

In the meantime, I thought I would explore a possible water source for us by digging down into the dry creek bed. I made a huge hole and sure enough there was water there. I set up a simple filter to strain out the sand and successfully effected a supply of milky gray liquid that would at least be adequate for washing. I thought that if we were to boil it it may also be fine for drinking.

I attribute my first attack of dysentery to this hydro-scheme. In a very short time I was suffering from extremely unpleasant stomach cramps and, of course, the almost constant need to suddenly dash off into the bushes and relieve myself. We had some medicines and I took various remedies that alleviated the symptoms but only slowly did I regain my former fitness.

Karl checked his python trap regularly. The next day there was still nothing there except, of course, the hen, who was sitting quite happily in the cage without a care in the world. As soon as I could I accompanied Karl on his further exploration of the hill. We crossed over to the other side where the terrain was steeper and there Karl spotted yet another cave in the rock face but it looked very difficult to reach. We clambered and slid down over the baking hot rocks and, cut and bruised, dripping with sweat, we reached the gaping entrance to the cave. The tunnel twisted a way deeply into the hillside. Hanging from the roof were dozens of little black bats and hosts of geckos were crawling about the walls in the half darkness. The cave was putrid and stank of guano and the air was clammy and heavy. Then Karl found something by the entrance of the cave in the dry grass and dust. At first he called out that he had found another python skin, but, on closer examination, he saw that it was, in fact, a dead python, dried out and mummified. It was about four feet long but it had probably been considerably longer as some of it had already crumbled into dust. We turned it over and broke open the brittle skin. Inside, to our surprise, we found a dead hedgehog, a handful of prickles loosely held together by one or two last pieces of dry skin. The hedgehog was the snake's last meal and maybe the one that had killed it.

These rocks were infested with geckos. Karl developed an ingenious method to catch them from their hiding places in the crevices. He made a tiny noose of fine fishing line that he attached to a short stick. He used the tip of the stick to attract the gecko by touching the rock softly in front of its head. The gecko was deceived and, imagining it had a tasty fly within easy reach, it walked through the noose and Karl whisked it off the rock. It was easy to grip the lizard and transfer it into a cloth bag. Over the course of a few hours of this Karl caught eighty geckos while I only managed a quarter of that number.

The following morning we got up very early, before sunrise, locked up the van, put a snake in the tent to keep away intruders and set off for the python cave. If we hadn't caught anything in the trap, we were going to move it to the second cave where we had found the dead python.

We attained the top of the hill just as the sun was beginning to show itself over the horizon. We reached the cave; there was no snake in the trap and no hen either! Eaten, escaped, stolen, we had no idea. It was gone and we had to lug that heavy trap down the hillside again and back to camp.

That afternoon, as Karl and I busied ourselves photographing snakes and other reptiles, we suddenly became aware that the temperature had dropped very sharply. At the same moment a farmer frantically peddling by on his bicycle called over to us and pointed to the horizon. There was a dust storm approaching. The whole sky was rapidly darkening over and a huge volume of dust was whipping across the land, throwing everything into the air and becoming denser all the time.

Very hurriedly we threw everything into the van and closed all the windows. The tent was already swaying madly from side to side and the canvas was flapping wildly as if it would take off like a kite at any moment. First one string broke and then another and, as the wind ripped one of the pegs out of the ground, the whole thing fell onto its side. We weighed it down with heavy stones and logs and then ran for shelter ourselves inside the van. We had bought a new hen from a farmer for the eggs that she might lay and she had already scratched a hole for herself behind one of the wheels under the van and there she sat, with her eyes tightly closed, waiting for the storm to pass.

The stout trees boldly withstood the force of the wind, twisting and swaying, creaking and groaning. The little trees, however, spread out all over the landscape, were bent double, like so many old ladies and one of two of them were whipped out of the ground by the wind and carried off out of sight. The howling was unbearable, suddenly reaching a crescendo of fury that, even inside the van, made it was impossible to hear a word we said to one another, so we waited in silence until the storm would pass by.

By evening the wind had died down and we were able to raise the tent poles again. I started to cook our evening meal and Karl let out the one or two animals that we had already photographed. A frog headed straight for the hollow tree under which we camped and hopped inside to safety. But then there was a louder noise from within, as if the frog had disturbed a larger creature into movement. Karl peered through the opening with a flashlight and then called out excitedly, "Look there's a python in our tree!"

95

The snake was half-curled up in a corner of the hollow trunk out of reach and was looking very annoyed at Karl dazzling her with his torch. He prodded her with a stick, trying to provoke her to come out while I reluctantly kept guard on a second hole at the opposite side of the tree. But the snake chose another exit and climbed up inside the tree as quick as lightning. Karl climbed up almost as quickly and frightened the snake back down again. This time it made its exit by the unguarded hole and wound off surprisingly slowly across the dry earth towards the safety of a small thicket. Then, by the light of the lantern, we pinned it down, Karl subdued the biting end while I clung to the tail to stop it thrashing about. Our first python, about five feet long and very beautiful.

The African rock python, (*Python sebae*), can reach twenty feet in length. It is the largest snake in Africa. While nonvenomous, it constricts its prey and dislocates its jaw in order to swallow it whole. It then sleeps off its feast and it may be many weeks before it is ready again for its next meal.

* * *

Once again living in our round house, we were visited by Bernhard, the watchman, just as evening was approaching and we were about to begin our evening meal. We ate just twice each day. To have three meals interrupted our activities too much and we became used to a breakfast of rice since it would last the whole day and then, towards evening, we would cook an early dinner. We subsisted like this quite successfully. Karl had a small cook book that was written for the benefit of Austrian country folk. It was a compilation of traditional Austrian recipes. Published by the nuns of a convent in Styria, Austria, it also contained sensible domestic advice such as herbal remedies and other articles of a useful nature. From this little book, we were able to concoct some tasty meals using very ordinary and simple ingredients with the addition of perhaps a few herbs that we had brought with us all the way from Europe.

Bernhard came cycling up in his usual manner and stretched out his big hand in friendly greeting. He told us that he had seen a gorilla that morning on the second hill and he wanted to know if we would go and hunt it with him the next day. This was the hill where we had set the python trap and we had explored it extensively. We told him we didn't have a gun and he said he would organize that for us. He cycled off again and left us wondering what animal it was he had really seen as there were certainly no gorillas here. Whatever the creature was we assumed we would not even get close to it, let alone do it any harm.

Early the next morning a stranger came to our camp, said a very friendly hello, and presented us with a single barreled shotgun and two cartridges. Then he disappeared again. It seemed the hunt was on!

Maybe half an hour later Bernhard cycled into camp and asked if his friend had brought the weapon. Then off we went across the plain towards the hill, the three of us, Karl with the shotgun, Bernhard leading, and me, armed with a machete and the camera. We went along at a comfortable pace, glad that the sun was still low and that the sky was overcast.

We reached the large hill and scanned it through the binoculars. Then I spotted a large baboon right at the top, showing up as a dark silhouette with the dawn behind among the low trees and rocks. I shouted to Bernhard to look, but he was too late, the animal had already disappeared.

Bernhard and I went around the rock to the right and Karl, with the gun, to the left. As I began to climb the hill, Bernhard withdrew and went off at a trot to the next village. My side of the hill was the steepest and when I reached the top I was soaked in sweat and my head was throbbing from the steadily increasing heat. I met Karl and we checked with one another to find out if we had seen anything, but neither had. We scanned the plateau but there was no sign of the animal. We looked across to the second smaller hill nearer our camp and, there, in between the two hills, we saw the great beast of a baboon racing across the landscape on all fours. Some farmers working in the fields below raised the hue and cry, leaving their work and arming themselves with poles and picks. They went howling across the fields, giving chase to the baboon and wailing and screaming as the thrill of the hunt and blood lust infected them all. We bolted down the side of the hill, springing from rock to rock and sliding down the steep slope. We made the descent in record time, and then we ran at full speed towards the second hill from where all the noise was coming. As we went, we heard drumming coming from the village where Bernhard had gone. At first it was quite soft, just one or two drums, but, when an answering call came from a second village and then from a third, the drumming became louder and louder and wilder and wilder until the whole countryside was alerted and the air was filled with the frenzied pounding and we no longer knew from which direction it was coming.

The sun had broken through and was beating down on us, determined to slow us down. We reached the base of the first hill and asked the men who had given chase where the animal had gone. They pointed upwards and told us it had hidden itself somewhere in the rocks. We started climbing and Karl went around in one direction and I in the other as before. We were the only two on the hill; the villagers willingly kept watch below but were apprehensive to climb themselves, not only because of the baboon but because of the snakes as well. I discovered later that they traditionally feared the baboon not because of its aggression but because, in an attack, it was believed that a baboon would gnash at a man's genitals.

The baboon must have hidden itself among the boulders or in the crevasses and we each searched our half of the hill carefully, looking up into the trees, behind all the bushes, and in every small cave. About a half hour later, we met again and neither of us had seen a thing. Karl had sprung from one rock to another during his search and had landed on his chest. He had badly winded himself and had had to lie down a few minutes to get his breath back. As we were talking, the wailing started again and we knew that the baboon must be on the move. We bolted off down the hill once more and headed off in the direction of the commotion. Somehow along the way we lost each other and I was joined by a group of natives, but they weren't armed like farmers with picks this time but more like warriors with long iron spears and cruel-looking axes. At first we were just a handful, running across the land, but the group grew and grew until I found myself in the middle of a mob of wildly screaming, heavily armed tribesmen. I looked towards the hill and saw Karl coming from another direction, also accompanied by a couple of dozen spear-waving, howling villagers.

We reached the hill and, despite the terrific heat and being almost spent, we climbed up the steep rocky slope once again, Karl in one direction, I in another. This time a few of the Africans climbed also and we spread out over the top searching. Eventually, I met Karl as he circled the hill lower down and I went further around the summit. As I was moving about through the sun dried grasses, a startled hen flew into the air and, by the ring on its leg, I recognized it to be the one we had lost from the python trap. So she hadn't been eaten or stolen, she had escaped.

I forgot the hen as I heard the wailing, whooping below as the men circled around the base of the hill and, looking down, I could see that they now numbered well over a hundred. Then the screaming suddenly became high pitched with excitement and, from behind a boulder just a few yards in front of me, the baboon shot out of cover. It raced away on all fours and I gave chase, waving my machete in the air and calling out to anyone with a gun to shoot. The baboon feared the tribesmen below and would not descend but kept at the same level, racing around the whole plateau with me on its tail waving my machete like a lunatic. Suddenly there was a shot from below and I had to jump for cover. It seemed that Karl wasn't the only one with a shotgun. The baboon crossed the length of the plateau at top speed until it reached the other side of the hill, where it galloped down and made for the open countryside. We had given chase, it seemed, for dozens of miles and, despite the heat and despite exhaustion, the fever of the hunt carried us on. I reached the plain and asked the men where the animal had gone. Somebody said that it had climbed a tree and pointed in the direction and off I went again, with the mob running with me. Then, to our surprise, the baboon turned back and tried to reach the hill again, retreating in our direction. An old man with a percussion cap shotgun went down on one knee and took aim. I had to hold back for him to shoot before I could pass, but he waited and waited to be sure of a good shot until the baboon had almost passed us by and I shouted at him to shoot and "click," nothing happened! His old musket had misfired. I gave chase with my last ounce of strength and managed to gain on the very tired baboon before sending my machete hurling at him, giving him a haircut but not slowing him down in the slightest. At the same moment, Karl and his group came racing in from the other side and Karl fired and hit the baboon's hind leg. A second later, Bernhard ran in and brought the baboon to the ground with one blow of his pick. Then the other men closed in and each thrust his spear into the animal's body, so deep that Karl had to help one man cut his out of the carcass. Those armed with battle axes smashed the animal's jaws and skull, all of them wanting to make quite sure that it was dead and share in the victory.

The baboon was very old and very large indeed. We assumed it had been the leader of a troop but had been forced to leave by a younger, stronger male. We were awarded the skin, the head and all four feet because Karl had fired the shot that had brought it down. The meat was given to the villagers. We gave Bernhard the two hind feet as it had been he who had organized the whole thing.

Women with their babies came running over to us from the village, thanking us and asking us to touch their children. The drumming took on a new tone and a celebration started, the men hoisting the mutilated animal high in the air, chanting and screaming. We made our way back to the van with Bernhard and a few of the warriors and then, with both front doors of the van open, we drove off in high spirits to the office of the police commandant. The other men had tied the baboon's body to a bicycle for easy transportation and made their way across the fields, arriving only a few minutes after us.

The police commandant was the local authority although there exists a more ancient tribal structure with the Mogho Naba in Ouagadougou as its hereditary chief or king. Every Friday the leaders of the various Mossi kingdoms were required to attend court in full regalia, bowing low upon the ground, reaffirming their loyalty to the authority of the Mogho Naba. The Mogho Naba would then enact a ritual whereby a saddled horse would be brought to him. The traditional interpretation is that he was going to fetch his favorite wife who was visiting her father in the country.

While this seems quaint to Western culture, similar traditions of even less substance remain rife throughout Europe and are solemnly reenacted according to custom, centuries later. Before Parliament sits in London, the cellars are searched according to a four hundred year old tradition. This dates back to an attempt to blow up the Houses in the 1605 *Gunpowder Plot*. Similarly, a trumpeter upon St. Mary's Basilica,

100

Kraków, Poland interrupts his playing in mid-note to commemorate another herald who was shot in the throat while sounding the alarm in the 13th Century as the Mogul hoards attacked the city.

The Mossi ceremony does not last long and the Mogho Naba never speaks directly but always through the Widi Naba. This ritual serves to reestablish the authority of the dynasty. The homage and brief glimpse of the king sustains ancient allegiances.

As we spoke with the commandant and he awarded us the trophies and the baboon meat to the villagers, we became aware of a strange commotion outside. Thanking the policeman, we returned to where the villagers were gathered, still armed to the teeth with spear and ax. In their midst was Bernhard who was biting into his own hand as the tribesmen taunted him. They felt that Bernhard had made a deal with us and suspected they would receive nothing of the dead baboon. His own kinsmen turning upon him had the strange and profound effect of him paradoxically turning upon his own self. He was chewing into his own hand in submission to the group disdain. It was an extraordinary thing to observe. The threat of ostracism by his own community was a devastating concept and he would rather abandon himself that be shunned by them.

When the villagers realized that the meat was theirs all became right again in a moment and an unpleasant cloud was lifted. The celebrations began.

Later we followed with Bernhard to the village and drank "Dolo," which is milky colored beer made from millet and, as darkness approached, a much refreshed Bernhard cycled unsteadily down the track in the approximate direction of his own home.

That evening, under the guidance of his Austrian cookbook, Karl prepared a dish of the baboon's brains which we ate with boiled rice.

The events of the day were indelibly fixed in my mind. We had thrown ourselves wholeheartedly into an event of instinctive savagery without hesitation or even a second thought. We had glimpsed something of ancient barbarity not only of the Mossi tribesmen but also of ourselves. It was an ironic and enormously instructive experience to encounter the otherwise affable and good-natured farmers turning visceral and raw. The collective savagery of the hunt provided a first-hand

101

glimpse of the brutal tribal instinct that might instantaneously overwhelm the animus of one hundred men and hurl them together in a common cause of violence. The cultivator of the soil turned warrior in an instant. Where did all those spears and hideous looking clubs suddenly come from? And the mothers bringing their children to be blessed so that something that they saw in the savage chase might somehow spill over and conjure a future of significance and renown for their own sons. And perhaps thereby, offer a vicarious escape for them all from a life otherwise of dull peasantry and mere survival.

8. GHANA
South to Prampram

Always striving to stretch our funds, we knew that petrol, among other things, was much cheaper in Ghana and, fuel having been one our biggest expenses in Upper Volta, we decided to buy just enough to bring us as far as the border where we supposed there would be a petrol station on the Ghana side.

We drove along past the landscape south of Ouagadougou that we knew so well and further through fresh countryside until, eventually we reached Pô, the last village before Paga on the Ghanaian side where we expected to buy gas. At the crossing we went through the usual inquisition by the border guards as they attempted to harass us into bribing then. This we never did. We merely went through the various shenanigans and endured threats until they tired of it and stamped our passports and the Carnet de Passage for the vehicle. While it was extremely aggravating we nevertheless had to maintain our tempers. The guards held all the cards and the unsavory process must merely be endured. We eventually settled all the necessary formalities, crossed the border and looked for a garage selling that lovely, cheap petrol.

Crossing the border, a Ghanaian police officer at the road side directed with the club that he was carrying that we must now drive on the left side of the road. We were now entering a former British colony where we would find much that would remind me of the U.K. including school children in uniforms and imported items that I was very familiar with, for sale even in the smallest shops and markets.

Paga itself did not have a garage, so we drove on hopefully to the next town which was only some ten miles away. Then the van began to slow down and the motor coughed and stopped. We rolled to the side of the road, out of fuel. We were about halfway to the town and there were no cars on the road as it was about midday when all things slow down considerably as the temperature rises. Half an hour, two lorries and a motorbike later, a land rover came down the road in our direction. It was a Ghanaian police vehicle and we flagged down the driver to stop. He was a very pleasant fellow and seemed pleased to be able to help. His name was Fred. He took me and the petrol can to the next town of

Navrongo, where we filled up. I told him of our travels and he seemed genuinely interested and was kind enough to drive me back to the van again so that we could continue our conversation. Before he left, he gave us his address and we promised to send him a postcard when we arrived back in Europe.

As we passed through the village of Bolgatanga, the road became worse, almost an earthen track and we weren't sure whether we were still on the right road or not. A farmer was pushing his bicycle along the wayside and we called over to him to ask directions.

"Hello, is this the right road for Tamali?"

"Tamali? Yes, that's right, this is the one."

"Is there another route that we have missed? On our map the road is marked surfaced."

"No, no, the road is just like that until a couple of miles past the town, then it's better!"

"Oh fine, thank you very much."

"There are one or two bridges on the way, so you'll take care won't you!"

Sure enough, we were soon driving along a newly surfaced road and presently we crossed over the first of the two narrow bridges. Now and then a squirrel ran out into the road in front of us or a group of monkeys disappeared away into the tall grass and steadily the sun began to set and it became time to find somewhere to camp.

We found quite a good spot away from the road down a sandy track and I pitched the tent as Karl began to cook "Pesas", little African potatoes that taste like early summer fingerlings, solid textured and delicious.

Our evenings by the campfire were always pleasant occasions. We seldom had visitors at night but during the day there was always a group of kids or a couple of farmers who came by and then often stayed for hours at a time. In this location we had just one visitor who I suspect was the farmer who worked the adjacent fields. He was very courteous and warmly welcomed us to Ghana.

"You know, I find you white people very remarkable," he concluded as he headed back to his village.

The following morning before the sun had hardly risen we were on our way again. With each mile the grass became greener and taller and the trees bigger and more numerous, leafier and sometimes covered with blossoms. We were leaving behind the savanna woodland and entering tropical rain forest.

Before and after every town there was a barrier across the road and a police control post. At the first one the police tried to beg for cigarettes or anything else that they caught sight of in the van, but my British passport seemed like magic and they straightened up, saluting and wishing us both a pleasant journey. Similarly, perhaps those who held French passports in Upper Volta were not so unpleasantly harassed as we were at the border.

Soon we arrived at the ferry station on the edge of the broad Volta River. In the little village of Pwalagu, the Ghanaian women were sitting in rows along the roadside with their baskets, pots and pans, selling everything imaginable from smoked fish to household soap. Sitting beneath a big, leafy tree was a large and jovial lady surrounded by yellow blossoms that had fallen from the canopy above. She was selling bread. We asked her the price of her rolls and she told us sixpence. Ever cautious even when buying a loaf of bread, we went to another stand and compared prices; everywhere it was the same, so we gave the jolly lady the money and bought a tin of milk as well and returned to the van to make some coffee.

As the water was beginning to boil on the paraffin stove, a man came by and told us that it was time to come and buy ferry tickets. I followed him to his little office while Karl continued making the coffee. The price, "one Cedi," half the price we had paid for the Gambia ferry and almost double the distance, a pleasant change.

Somewhere out on the river the ferry blew its whistle and everybody looked up and started to get their things together. I went back to the van and we started our coffee and tasted the excellent bread rolls, but suddenly we were interrupted as the column of cars started to move forward. We drove down the very steep slipway and up the other side onto the ferry, where we then continued our breakfast on deck. Soon the ferry was chugging across the Volta and we smoked the last of our Upper Volta tobacco as it went. On the far bank was yet another police control and, after the usual tedious tomfoolery and initial intimidation, we were

105

again allowed to drive on.

It was almost evening and once again necessary for us to find somewhere to camp. We turned off the main road down a track and beyond the track down a path, where, as was usual, I pitched the tent while Karl gathered wood and started a fire. Lying along the edges of the fields were rows of white roots that had been laid over branches on the ground to dry; neither of us knew what they were.

We finished our meal and, despite the mosquitoes, we stayed out a long time chatting by the camp fire. The sky was vivid in the light of a snow-white full moon and, somewhere, away in the bushes, an army of toads were croaking at each other. We crawled into the tent, killed off the couple of mosquitoes that had somehow gotten inside and slept until our rooster, Max, began to crow in the morning.

We had been given two roosters by a friend in Ouagadougou. There was an Austria school established at the outskirts of the city where European volunteers, skilled in different professions and trades, were offering a practical education in fields that ranged from auto mechanics, electrical installation and carpentry. We had met the director, Kurt Garnel, and the bursa, another Austrian whose name was Rudolf Ebener. Rudolf had treated us to lunch in the cafeteria and offered us the use of the dormitory showers. The cold clean water was unbelievably refreshing and it was great to get thoroughly cleaned up.

Kurt Garnel was in Ouagadougou with his Austrian fiancée. They were to be married within a few days. They invited us to attend the outdoor feast after the ceremony. Among the other guests was a mechanic called Michelé who was also a teacher at the school. He was one of four Mossi men who were Austrian trained auto mechanics as part of an economic development initiative in Vienna.

We became friends with Michelé, another man called Michel Tapsoba and a cousin of Michel's who worked for the city of Ouagadougou. Another relative was a government official. The difference in the spelling and pronunciation of their names was to avoid confusion. It was Michelé who had given us the two roosters.

Karl was up first and let the poultry out for a run before the long journey ahead. I awoke soon after and set about dismantling the tent and packing it away into the van. We finished our breakfast and started to round up the two roosters and their harem. One, two, and three, but the fourth, our young cockerel named Moritz, decided he would rather not go with us that day and would sooner stay here instead. As we chased him up and down, trying to pounce on him or catch him by his feet, an African came down the path pushing his bike. He took off his coat and tried to throw it over Moritz's head but, between the three of us, Moritz only became increasingly agitated and decided to take cover in the bushes. Karl, whose favorite occupation was catching poisonous snakes and biting, hissing lizards, was being out-foxed by a chicken. He climbed onto the roof of the van to see if he could see where the crafty fellow was hiding himself. Then another African arrived while the first one disappeared. The second man spoke excellent English and I told him of Moritz's misbehavior. Just then Karl spotted him moving about in a bush and the three of us encircled the area. Moritz was very cunning and escaped us, running under the van for cover. But that only made him easier still to catch and I grabbed his leg and put him inside the cage with his companions.

I gave our friend some coffee that was still left over from breakfast and asked him what the white roots were called.

"Oh, that's Cassava," he told us and ripped up a little tree out of the ground and showed us the long tuber. He pushed away the outer brown skin and an inner white covering with his thumb nail, revealing the chalk white, fleshy root like those lying on the ground to dry.

"When they are dried in the sun like this, we take them, grind them and then the womans make semolina or soup. That's African food, yes."

He said he had a rice field further down the path and we told him we had heard his frogs during the night. His name was Abdula. We all shook hands and said "goodbye", thanking him for assistance in the capture of the rooster.

The houses we saw as we drove on our way along the main road leading south were no longer round like those in Upper Volta but rectangular and, instead of straw thatch, they had corrugated iron roofs. Now and then we passed a group of huts specially built for curing tobacco and, from all directions, people were arriving with huge bundles of slightly brown tobacco leaves balanced upon their heads.

107

On both sides of the road were also banana plantations and round palm trees with those juicy fruits similar to the ones that we had eaten in Gambia. Sometimes the roads were bordered by high hedges like in the English countryside while behind them we caught glimpses of agricultural training centers, colleges and country schools with African children dressed in school uniforms of English fashion.

Soon we were driving through dense forest with towering trees and thick, tangled undergrowth. Against one stout trunk was a completely wrecked bush taxi with a slogan painted on the front, "Everything by God."

Time passed and we became tired after our long day of driving and drove off the main road to look for somewhere to camp.

We parked in a clearing, away from the sound of the traffic, between tall, impressive, hardwood trees draped with every type of ivy and creeper imaginable. Then, somewhere, the sky began to growl and dense clouds raced across as if they were afraid of arriving too late for the storm and then it thundered louder and louder as the heavens opened up and loosened a torrential downpour. At first a few drops of rain fell and then the whole sky seemed to burst open. It is not called rain forest for nothing.

In the middle of the night, I felt something crawling across my face but squashed it and also one of its brothers with one swipe. But if I had so easily crushed two ants like that together, then there were bound to be more. I groped around in the darkness for the lighter but sent the paraffin lamp flying across the tent before I found it. I was right, there was a whole army of red ants crawling about over the ground sheet. I got rid of half a dozen before I burned my fingers with the lighter. Karl turned over and peered out of his sleeping bag and dreamily asking if I was thrashing corn. I said that we were being invaded by ants. He swore and turned over again. But, by the next morning, we were both covered from head to foot with tiny, irritating bites and scratching did nothing to relieve the incessant itching.

We continued our journey south through Tamale, on to Kumasi and, in due course, we reached Accra and found ourselves in the middle of a large modern city. However, upon the advice of the Austrian Handels-Attaché stationed in Accra who invited us for lunch, we decided

108

to leave the urban areas behind us and to look for a quiet spot somewhere along the coast, away from the bustling city where we could conduct our animal catching activities in peace. It is hard to describe the harassment that we would otherwise have had to endure. We were an easy target for thieves and beggars of every level of devious ingenuity. We did not wish to spend our time constantly have to fend off wheedling swindlers who thought to deceive and ingratiate themselves hoping to relieve us of our property. This is not the Africa that interested us. We found our way out of the maze of roads and started looking for a rural area where we could camp.

As we drove along, another vehicle overtook us and flagged us down. He had recognized our Austrian license plate. The driver was a large stout white man and, as it turned out, he was from the same Austrian village where Karl's grandmother was born. The Austrian was working in Ghana for the German government on a plan to encourage recently urbanized country people to leave the city and return to work on the land. He told us that the place we had intended to camp was the center of all the thieves in Accra. He told us of tourists who had been staying there and had everything stolen, absolutely everything they possessed. We told him we would only be staying in Ghana for a few days and he directed us to a small village along the coast called Pram-Pram.

We drove down the narrow road towards the beach. It was beautiful. The deep blue of the ocean, the pebble beach where brightly painted fishing boats were pulled up and the whole coast-line bordered with coconut palms. We went down onto the shore to see what the fishermen had caught. Some of them were already selling their catch while others were occupied hauling their boats through the surf and up the beach over wooden rollers, with the brawn of half the village men and boys to assist them. The fishing boats were heavily built with space enough for a dozen men. They were constructed of stout timbers with wooden benches spaced at intervals across the gunwales. Some appeared to be built of heavy boards while others were dug-outs from a single trunk.

We asked the cost of the fish but, seeing that we were white men, the price at once increased unashamedly. A woman beside us had just bought a fish for two shillings. They expected us to pay double.

Disgusted, we decided to explore along the beach and see if we could find some ripe coconuts. Two small boys tagged along with us and together we found a tree heavily laden with huge clusters. One of the urchins started climbing up the tree while we stood watching, amazed. He gripped the trunk frog-like between the soles of his feet. Then he reached up and hugged further up with his arms. His feet followed and again he gripped the tree between his soles. Once or twice he rested and was able to remain comfortably for a moment, adjusting his weight so that his legs gripped the rough hide of the palm and held him. Within a couple of minutes he had climbed a thirty foot high tree. One after another, he twisted the coconuts out of the clusters and they fell to our feet with a powerful thud. When several were lying on the ground about us, the boy slid down the tree and they both started breaking them open against the trunk. They hit the ends hard so that the outer shell and mat broke open, revealing inside the inner round nut itself. The tops of these they cracked open and we drank the lovely, refreshing juice inside. Then they broke open the shell completely and we ate the fruit itself until, at last, we couldn't eat any more. We resolved to stay here for a few days.

It was impossible to drive onto the beach itself to camp, so we decided to ask at the police station if we might camp in their yard, as that was immediately adjacent to the water.

The office immediately reminded me of a similar police station in Gambia. There, behind the Sergent's desk, was a gun rack holding half a dozen British military 303 rifles chained securely and padlocked. Above was the self-same portrait of Queen Elizabeth 2 and the Duke of Edinburgh. Both countries had gained independence more than ten years prior but the Queen nostalgically remained in place, no longer Empress but yet beloved as the titular crown of the British Commonwealth. I suspected that she remained in place also for her permanency in a world where African authority might change abruptly and the portrait of a president might have to be replaced on a tediously regular basis.

The policemen were very friendly and welcoming, generously allowing us to park and camp beneath a leafy tree behind their houses. It felt very safe in the police compound and I could scarcely imagine a camping spot more secure. As their guests we were spared the harassment that we had constantly endured at the roadblocks.

110

The sun set peacefully behind the coconut palms, turning the leafy crowns a fleeting, ruby red while the waves ceaselessly dashed in a steady rhythm against the stony shore with a curious rattling and again a chattering as the waves returned to the ocean. A few of the policemen's children came and played happily about our camp, excited at the novelty of having guests and everything was very pleasant and peaceful with the world.

We spent the weekend swimming, fishing and eating coconuts. During the couple of days we were there, we had three offers of marriage from native girls who wanted to get away and live a life of imagined luxury like the Europeans. One father became very perturbed. His daughter had announced that she was leaving to travel with us. She would cook and clean and work for us.

"You must come and talk with me about my Pickaninny. She cannot just leave and go with you. She is my daughter. She is my Pickaninny!"

I was astonished that he used that term to describe his daughter but I realized that he was struggling with pidgin and I, of course, understood what he meant and apologised for the misunderstanding. But strangely he seemed a little disappointed. Perhaps he would have liked his daughter to marry a European but, of course, only properly and in accordance with accepted customs and conventions.

The fishermen were impressive. After a long day of toil out of sight of the shore upon the heaving ocean and having delivered their catch to the market ladies and merchants and having taken a simple meal with the families and friends, they would stand before the sea above the beach of pebbles and smoke their pipes. It was as if they had fought and, while not defeated the expanse, they had arrived at terms of mutual respect. They appeared justifiably content, satisfied with a day's work well done and time well spent. They spoke quietly with one another and occasionally there would be a moderate chuckle as someone quipped an amusing reply. There was never a more profound communion and reverence between man and nature as I witnessed there at eventide, watching the fishermen of the village of Prampram as they calmly contemplated the setting sun slipping behind the waves.

Karl was also intrigued by the skill and impressive, imperturbable nature of the fishermen. Very early the next morning, he approached one who seemed to be the most congenial and asked if he could join them and fish for the day. They discussed it amongst themselves for a moment and then replied, "Yes, of course". Perhaps they were glad of the extra pair of hands to launch the boat or maybe the policemen has spoken well of us or possibly one of them had a marriageable daughter but Karl's request was granted and they manhandled the vessel down the beach and steadily paddled through the surf out over the ocean beyond sight of the shore.

By mid afternoon the first fishing boats began to appear on the horizon and, within an hour or so, the community effort repeated itself while man and child bent his back to push and pull the heavy craft up the steep foreshore and safely beyond reach of the thrashing surf.

Karl shook hands with his new friends and headed up the beach. He had caught a fine fish with only a hook, weight and his line wrapped around a block of wood.

All had gone well but, at one point, he had become considerably alarmed. Amongst the men there was one youth who somehow had displeased his elders. The boy sensed trouble when the men rested their paddles and turned towards him. Karl did not know what was going on but it occured to him that he, too, was miles from land in a fishing boat with perfect strangers and he recognized that they could deal with him also as they liked, if they wished him harm.

The boy became terrified as the men growled threateningly at him and, all at once, he sprang out of the boat and into the ocean shrieking and trying to swim away. The men let him flounder for a while then they hauled him back into the vessel. Thereafter everything was calm and peaceful once more as the men continued with their work.

Karl had no idea what had prompted the sudden meting out of primal justice but he assumed the kid must have somehow crossed an invisible line with his elders. And these were not men to be messed with. But once they had terrified him and successfully addressed the apparently offended convention all was seemingly forgiven and forgotten. I imagine that the boy learned something very significant about manhood, the requirements and standards of admission into the ranks of his seniors and his baptism was hopefully of indelible significance.

A few days later, we found ourselves once again driving through Accra from one traffic jam to another. To drive less than a mile through the town it took us over two hours. We applied for our visas for Togo but were told we had to wait two days and, paying the last of our Ghana money, we realized that we would be living off millet and onions until we arrived in Togo and could change some dollars for CFA francs in Lomé, the capital.

When we eventually found our way out of the town, we headed for the beach at the other side of Accra from Prampram and looked for somewhere good to camp that wasn't too far from the city. Unfortunately, the police station was very small and had no space for us to put up our tent. On the beach, we found a good spot next door to a disused cabana and organized our camp. At first we had too many dubious visitors who looked around too much, too closely and asked too many questions and we had to be constantly vigilant. Fortunately, by evening, they had all disappeared and we were left on our own.

We had steadily developed an attitude of vigilance ever since the early days of our journey in Morocco. Here the watchfulness was entirely justified. We never took chances. Interestingly, we were assisted by the cages of reptiles and, in particular, the snakes including the puff adder and the large python. Without exception, the natives were very apprehensive of snakes and, in some cases, quite evidently terrified. The first thing we did in a new camp was unload the van of the various cages and water the creatures. Seeing this the beggars and thieves kept a more respectful distance.

Karl was absolutely marvelous with animals. His collection of lizards that he had preserved in alcohol for the Senkenberg Museum in Frankfurt was growing all the time. Karl would examine a catch and begin to look for distinguishing characteristics that were not evident in the illustrations of his Klingelhofer volume on reptiles. He would systematically count the scales and conclude whether an animal was well known or if he might have tentatively discovered a subspecies. The first skink that he had caught in the Desert du Ferlo was undoubtedly unusual. He had poisoned it and, after carefully labeling it, injected it with a syringe of alcohol and preserved it for posterity in an huge glass jar that we kept carefully bundled up on the roof of the van.

It seemed a far cry from the Desert du Ferlo where we had enjoyed the villagers who came to visit our camp. There had been unpleasant incidents of overly aggressive begging there, too, and once we had to chase a group of obnoxious women away from our camp with threats. But here on the beach, it seemed a consistent problem. Everyone we met was larcenous.

The beach was, as usual, lined with hundreds of coconut palm trees and we decided to try and climb one ourselves, which proved only moderately successful. We found a tree that conveniently leaned a little but we still paid for the couple of coconuts that we managed to retrieve in grazes and cuts. In comparison the skin on the soles of the feet of the Africans is tough like leather as they are usually bare foot.

These few days passed quickly by and, in all truth, we were both of us much relieved to be leaving Ghana. We had enjoyed the North and Prampram had been an incredible experience but otherwise, during our very short stay, we were constantly pestered by one "Smart Alec" after another and had to be on our constant guard against thieves the whole time.

We collected our visas for Togo and left the city behind us. One after another, we drove through the numerous police barriers before and after every small town and, after one hundred and twenty miles, we finally reached the Ghana-Togo border at midday. By now we were very well acquainted with the formalities, the various forms that had to be filled out and the people we had to see to have our passports stamped. Soon it was all over and we were on Togo soil, once again speaking French.

9. TOGO
From Coastal Range to Mountain Tops

In Lomé, we bought a giant yam. It was a huge root that tasted remotely like potato but with a heavier texture. This one weighed over seven pounds and cost us even less than the price of a hen. The tubers can grow to a length of four and a half feet and, extraordinarily, weigh more than one hundred pounds. The farmers bring them to market on carts because they are so heavy. Sugar had been impossible to buy in Ghana and we had stirred our tea with a length of sugar cane. Here we bought two pounds of crystal sugar, some bread, oranges and tobacco and then we went exploring to see if we could find somewhere good to camp while we waited the week until our mail arrived with our money from Europe.

Initially, when we first arrived in Africa, we had changed currencies at any convenient bank. Gradually we realized that the exchange rate was significantly better on the black market. This is where Karl came into his own. Tourists report of bartering in Africa as if it were a game or a sport. Karl raised it to a fine art. His tenacity was extraordinary and, after experiencing his haggling, the victim was almost reduced to tears. This was particularly disheartening for those who glibly imagined that they could cheat him or who thought that he was merely another white pushover.

Between the two front seats of our van was a hollow space in which we concealed a cash box that held our funds and important documents such as our passports. The box was chained and padlocked to the vehicle and the cavity was concealed from view with an innocuous looking cover made of wood and painted the same green as the van. We carried very little money on our persons unless we intended to shop for provisions and consequently we successfully avoided being robbed.

But one of the most irritating experiences was not the attempt of direct robbery but the almost constant hassle that we endured whenever we visited a city or large town. In Togo and Dahomey (renamed Benin in 1975) the cry of "Yovo, Cadeau! Yovo, Cadeau!" was constant wherever we walked. It was mildly interesting that this was the consistent chorus whereby Europeans were tormented. It means *White-man! Handout!* Did they really imagine that someone was going to reply, "Oh, yes of course. Here you are." But strangely I have seen whites, particularly those newly arrived, give them money in response.

Karl once said to an Austrian teacher who had just flown in from Europe and was getting to know his way about, "Do not give them money. They will steal your wallet and your watch before you know it. And you only encourage the hassle and badgering". To which the young Austrian replied, "You know I am here on a different mission than you!" But later he discovered the malice of some of these people when a group of surly, city youths threw rocks at him.

We motored along the coast away from Lomé in the glorious sunshine and past some very modern buildings that lined the shore. We reached the harbor and continued on until we reached a junction where another road followed the palm trees down to the beach itself. The road ended very abruptly right by the shore where part of it was washed away. It had obviously once been the main coast road but the ocean had worn it away. Along the shore were a few cabanas and most of them were empty. We imagined that the huts had once belonged to fishermen and had been left because the waves had denuded the beach and made it too steep for them to land their boats. And perhaps also because, sooner or later, all of the structures were doomed to be washed away.

We drove a little ways along the grassy shore-line until we found a hut that suited us and we moved in. It was completely made out of coconut palms. A frame of wood from the split trunk was covered over with palm branches with the leaves platted. Everything was tied firmly together with palm fibers. Our house had one inner room, which sheltered us from the strong sea wind and a second that was open on two sides where we put up our tent.

Once settled, we feasted like kings on the tasty yam and devoured at least a third of it. It was enormous. After the meal, we smoked the local tobacco, which was rolled together in bundles like cigars. Three such bundles had cost us just a few francs. Finally, we finished off the day drinking sweet, milky coffee outside in the moonlight in front of our fine house.

The Lomé market was an open building of several stories but the vendors spilled out around the surrounding streets and alleyways. As usual the shop-women were huge. A well-fed wife, as elsewhere in West Africa, was a status symbol and her girth granted the husband a certain financial prestige. But the ladies were good humored and enjoyed a lively banter with one another and their customers. And, remarkably, their prices were fair and appeared consistent for both us and the native consumers. As we left the market we realized why this was. There was a European style super-market a short distance away. The market vendors had not tried to cheat us because whites frequented the other market and seldom used the open air one. This was easy to understand. Amongst the tobacco stalls and those selling grain and produce were tables piled high with the dried up limbs and the organs and skulls of every conceivable creature. These were grisgris used to make amulets and charms as well as medicinal concoctions. The mix of odors was almost unbearable but fortunately the sea breeze wafted some of it away.

The derisive saying in West Africa, originally attributed to Albert Schweitzer regarding religious affiliation, "50% Muslim, 50% Christian and 100% animist," is absolutely authentic but it is not only idiosyncratic of that continent but typical wherever there is extreme ignorance and poverty. The education of people dependent on the soil and susceptible to the inconsistencies of climate and season arises through their closeness with nature.

The next day the sea was very rough; the waves were pounding against the shore angrily but the sun was shining brightly, quite indifferent to all the commotion going on below. It was very hot and dozens of fishing boats were bobbing about among the waves way out to sea.

We decided to try our hand at fishing from the beach. An African woman had spread a huge basket of little fish out to dry in the sun along what was left of the road and she gave us a few for bait. We had to cast far out over the breakers to where the water wasn't so foamy and to where the sea was deeper. Time and again we threaded new bait, waited and wound in again. Midday passed and then the afternoon, but we caught absolutely nothing. It was late, we had to give up. We would try again the next day somewhere else.

Our hut was right in the middle of a belt of coconut trees that followed the coast out of sight. Because the fishermen had left the area, the coconuts had been left as well, some of the trees were topped with as many as sixty or even seventy fruits, most of them a green-brown color: ripe! We could climb the easier trees, but it was very strenuous and often painful. The bark was as rough as sandpaper but the climbing had to be done barefoot because wearing shoes made it impossible to grip the trunk. The ascent was so arduous that by the time any significant height was attained the climber was too exhausted to do anything but slide back down. The coconuts usually remained untouched. I wanted to try to discover an easier way. In the van, we had two canvas straps about three feet long which we had brought with us to lash our blankets in neat rolls inside the van. Since then, though, we had built a partition out of wood into which we could squeeze the blankets and camping bags and so we had no particular use for the belts.

I fastened the two straps loosely around the trunk and stepped into them and then started to walk up the tree. With strings attached to the lower strap, I could raise it without having to bend down to pull. Slowly and steadily, with remarkably little effort, I climbed higher and higher until I reached the top where I still had enough reserve strength to cut down the fruits. The descent was simply the reverse and just as relaxed as the upward climb. I took twenty, some of which we gave to an old Togolese lady who lived in a hut a short distance behind ours. Upon reflection I wondered if the coconut trees really belonged to her in the first place and were not there simply for the taking but her own property.

The next morning Karl was up very early and I could hear him preparing breakfast. He had been fishing during the night by high tide and had caught two medium-sized fish and an eel. Later in the afternoon, he disappeared again and didn't arrive back until evening. Two good things occurred in succession. Firstly, Karl had been looking for shell fish by the harbor and had come across an oyster bed. He brought back thirteen, huge rainbow colored shiny shells. Thirteen must have been our lucky number because as the oysters were sizzling in the frying pan, a native girl came past our hut carrying a dead baby goat by its hind legs down towards the shore. We asked her in sign language if it had been dead long. It did not smell putrid. But she didn't understand and climbed down onto the beach and threw it out to sea.

As soon as she was gone, I ran quickly down the beach and waded out among the waves to retrieve the carcass. Just then Karl called

118

and I left the goat on the sand and went back to see what was up. The old Togolese lady was talking to Karl. It was her daughter who had thrown the animal away into the sea. She said that they don't eat the meat of animals that die naturally, but that it was quite fresh and we could fetch it if we wanted to.

I returned to the beach again to fetch our dinner but the waves had meanwhile carried it out to sea and I had to swim after it.

Back at the hut, we skinned it and boiled it thoroughly to make sure that it was safe to eat and then sat down to a meal of oysters as a first course followed by goat meat with yams. What a feast!

On the following Monday, we retrieved our mail from the Togo Post Office and then we packed all of our things back into the van and set off for Lake Togo. When we left the coast road, we headed inland along a washboard track that shook the van to pieces. Our own dust cloud pursued us as we drove while the sun beat down and cooked us inside the van. We were glad when we at least caught a glimpse of the beautiful lake reflecting the sun's rays, shining like silver and surrounded on all sides by coconut palms. We wanted to camp on the edge of the lake if possible and we tried one track after another, driving through several villages, but we found nowhere peaceful that suited us. We were exhausted from driving and it was getting later and later, so we made our camp about a mile away from the lakeside beneath a mango tree.

Our first visitors were the women folk who had been collecting firewood that evening and stopped by to see what on earth a van and a tent were suddenly doing there in the middle of one of their fields. None of them spoke French and we didn't speak Ewe except the words for water, fish, and good morning, but, as usual, we managed to chat a little in the language of hands and feet. The ladies left, bundles of firewood balanced upon their heads while nursing babies, securely bundled in a shawl-sling on their backs, peered at us wonderingly out of the folds. The women waved as they departed, calling out greetings and laughing at the fun of it all. *Two white-men having arrived from nowhere were now living in the bush just as they did. Did you ever hear of such a funny thing!*

Before long, a little man turned up. He was dressed in a burlap tunic and was obviously a farmer. He began an excited conversation with us in his own language and seemed to be very annoyed and agitated.

119

After a short while he realized that we did not understand a word that he was saying and he strode off in a huff.

A little later, as we were securing our camp and preparing for the night, he turned up again, but this time with a hoard of yelling school children. They came down the path as a mob, calling and shouting, all very excited about something. Marching into our camp without greeting or the usual respectful deference that was the convention of their culture, their yelling continued. It was a few minutes before the old man caught up and could make the children stay quiet long enough for him to speak. Finally, the noise diminished and we found ourselves surrounded by a hoard of impudent brats waiting expectantly to see how the game would advance.

We had never experienced anything like this before but similar incidents involving gangs of kids occurred in Togo three times during our stay there. During the last such incident, the men were mortified with embarrassment and came down from their village and whipped the kids soundly.

But now the old farmer in his burlap kirtle pushed his son forward and indicated that the boy would act as his interpreter.

"My father say, what is?" the child announced rudely in French. His father nodded vigorously in agreement with his arm clutching the boy's shoulder as if he were a ventriloquist's dummy.

"What exactly is it your father wants to know?" Karl asked.

"My father say, what is?" he repeated impertinently.

Karl looked across at me with an amused expression and we remained calm.

""Speak French!" yelled the boy abruptly.

Karl explained that we were tourists spending just one night here and that we would probably be gone tomorrow.

"What does your father want?" he asked the boy again.

"My father live over there," said the boy, pointing towards the lake.

Now we began to think that maybe this piece of grass on which we were parked belonged to the old man and Karl asked if this was so.

"I speak French," announced the boy becoming ruder and louder.

No reply.

"Good, give a hen!" ordered the boy.

"Go!" shouted Karl loudly at the group and, at the same moment, I also stood up with the intention of shaking the old man out of his sack cloth for his disrespect. But the sudden reaction of us both had been too much for the group, half of whom had been standing on one leg ready to run anyway in any case. Panic spread and, after three seconds, there was no old man, no children, just dust and a small piece of moon shining in the sky surrounded by lots of stars, and us, quietly laughing.

The next morning we had intended to leave early but the battery was too flat to start the motor, so we had to wait until we saw a bush-taxi speeding down the path. We hailed the driver to stop and asked him if we could get a jump. Unfortunately his battery was flat as well, but he agreed to give us a tow so that we could jump start our vehicle. Soon we were driving away under our own steam, leaving Togo Lake behind us and heading back towards Lomé to buy acid for the battery and to prepare for a feast for the next day, the eighth of November, my birthday. We always celebrated our birthdays.

In the town, we bought the acid and distilled water and I waited in the van while Karl disappeared on his own. Later, he came back carrying a large wooden whiskey case that made rather a pleasant sound, a sort of "clink, clink..."

This time we chose a different spot to camp on the beach where we were lucky enough to find yet another empty cabana to live in.

Karl was up at the crack of dawn and busied himself making a fire and preparing breakfast. When all was ready, he came to the tent with a saucepan and a lump of wood and gonged me to the breakfast table. The previous day, he had bought beer, bread, biscuits, jam and margarine, things that we hadn't eaten since we had left Europe. That was a feast fit for a king, a very fine birthday breakfast indeed!

* * *

As soon as we had recovered from our festivities and became once again accustomed to our usual mono-diet, this time of yams, we decided to head north towards the mountains and explore the region near

121

Atakpamé.

We started off at about midmorning and drove away from Lomé, along a very fine road in the direction of Palimé. (Since renamed Kpalimé) We did not enter the town itself but, as soon as we saw the mountains, we decided we'd like to drive up one of them and make our camp at the summit.

The track leading up was very rough indeed and there were signs that bulldozers had been at work. We engaged the first gear and slowly crawled on up. Karl started to yodel. It was the mountain air.

The way became worse and worse, rougher and rougher, but fortunately Karl's singing improved. Then, as we crept around a long bend, the van springing about wildly, we met the cause of the trouble. Bulldozers, not one or two, but half a dozen churning up the earth at one place and flattening it down at another. We drove on past and the road became better but much steeper. The whole mountain was covered with very dense jungle vegetation and a low cloud was hanging in the treetops and, as we stopped by a stream to collect water, we noticed how motionless the air was and how our voices echoed from the canopy and the mountain wall.

Finally, we reached a spot that wasn't quite the summit but nevertheless suited us very well. It was about three quarters of the way up. We parked as far away from the road as we could on the top of a freshly bulldozed hill of earth. I began to raise the tent and Karl went to collect wood for the fire.

Evidently, someone had already spotted us and came driving down from the summit with a tractor and trailer full of rock. There were three men riding on the tractor and they all started grinning and waving as they drove up to us. We called "Hello" and, as the workmen were all very friendly, we shook hands several times as was their convention with strangers. Eventually, the driver came to the point and told us that they would be blasting with dynamite further up the mountain very shortly and he suggested we drive down and come back again later.

The tent was already standing, we had already let the hens out and Karl had his fire going. In addition, it had been a very rough ride up the mountain and we didn't really want to go down again unless the blasting would be really dangerous. Nobody knew if there was, in fact, a risk, so I climbed on the tractor with the men and we returned up the mountain path to ask the man in charge if we were in significant danger or if we might remain where we were. Along the road were scores of men at work and they all laid down their tools as we passed and called out friendly greetings. Eventually, we reached the foreman's hut and found him there, stuffing a whole lot of papers and plans hastily into a briefcase. He was a middle-aged man from Dahomey and was very amiable. He told me that they were building a television mast on top of the mountain, the first in Togo, and he was working with two other engineers, a Frenchman and an Italian. The next day was Sunday and no one would be working, of course, but that evening there would be one or two very minor explosions which shouldn't bother us. We could stay until Monday morning.

Back at camp one of the workmen advised us to stay inside the van until the detonations were over and suggested we cover the windscreen with a blanket just in case any stones should fly in our direction. This was very sage advice and very much appreciated. We were well aware of the African tendency to always offer good news or to tell someone what they wanted to hear and thereby avoid disappointment or displeasure. This seemed an appropriate and valuable instance when that custom was wisely neglected.

We sat inside the van; it was very hot. We had laid the blanket over the windows and waited for the explosions.

There were eight in all. The first few were in the distance and the last brought a rain of small stones showering down on the van like a hail storm.

Somebody drove up from below and called to us that it was all over and we climbed out, looking around apprehensively. We put our pots and pans on Karl's fire and set about preparing our evening meal. It was a strange scene because our camping spot was so bleak. We were essentially camped upon a mound of loose rock and earth from the blasting and road-making. The forest itself was a hundred yards away. It was like a moonscape with two strange white wizards on top of the mountain, sending out clouds of dense but savory smelling smoke which mingled with the clouds shrouding the treetops and the mountain peak.

We had a few young visitors who gaped at us uneasily from a

distance. They were fascinated with everything that we did until Karl became weary of being stared at and gave them a wildlife magazine to look at instead. That was an excellent idea; they forgot completely the strangeness of the situation and sat together in a tight circle, whispering loudly with one another and releasing occasional cries of astonishment.

We practically forgot our little group until they came to return the magazine and to gave us a gift of a dozen ripe oranges still attached to a branch.

Darkness settled early because of the dense foliage and towering peak that obscured the setting sun. It quickly became darker and darker. The workmen had already descended the mountain truck after truck and everything was quiet except for the night animals who made a thousand different whistles and grunts that echoed continuously among the trees and rocks.

The next day we were eating our breakfast while the hens were hunting insects in the undergrowth. As yet nobody had arrived to spoil the peace and quiet. Suddenly there was a rapid rustling in the grass a couple of feet away from our fire pit. We both kept very quiet and watched in hypnotized astonishment as a long green head appeared out of the grass. Neither of us breathed and the snake stayed watching us for what seemed an eternity, turning its head from one to the other. We didn't startle it which must have seemed very unusual to the snake. The natives will typically club or stone to death every wild thing that can walk or crawl. But it suddenly decided it was time to leave and hurried off in a flash and a rustle out of sight. Karl said that he thought it had been a Boomslang or tree snake, (*Dispholidus typus*). It is a large green snake with enormous bulging eyes. It is venomous but it must bite deeply as its poisonous fangs are located rearward in the jaw. We realized that what had happened had been unique and it might never occur again.

The day passed and we rather enjoyed our stay on the mountain but, towards evening, the village boys, who had been around the camp most of the day, decided not to go home and became rather a nuisance. One of them, running about, turned over a saucepan on the fire and I nearly twisted his ear off his head. We told the children we were going to eat and that they should now go off home for their own suppers. But they became annoying and troublesome so that finally we had to drive

124

them away. Some of them retreated to a safe distance and called out insults. A group of village women laden with firewood and carrying bowls of spring water on their heads were wending their way up the track to a village some distance beyond our camp. They became concerned at the behavior of the boys and called out but the kids ignored them and continued taunting us. The women continued on until out of sight.

Suddenly a company of half a dozen big, strong Africans came down the mountain path, each armed with a long cane. One after the other, they rounded up the mischievous boys and marched them off up the mountain to the village. In due course, some of the men came back and, of all things, came over to us to apologize, mortified at their children's behavior. They clasped their hands before them and to their chests in abject distress. The women had seen what the boys had been up to and had gone to tell the men in the village. The men told us that all the boys had to go to the village headman where each received a sound whacking. We were almost speechless and we shook hands with the men and told them what wonderful people they were. They stayed with us, chatting a long time before, finally, darkness fell and they retreated back up to their village.

The next day was Monday and the tractor driver came up to see us to say goodbye and to wish us a good time in Togo. Another brought us some palm wine to take with us and, finally, we left feeling very pleased and much encouraged and headed back towards Lomé to apply for an extension to our visas.

* * *

A few days later we decided to drive up north again, this time we wanted to visit a waterfall, "Cascade de Kpime," which was about seven or eight miles away from the mountain where we had stayed a week or so before.

We filled up the tank with petrol and the canisters with water and were soon on our way again, leaving the beach and the beautiful palm trees behind us, heading towards wilder countryside where we hoped to catch some more animals for export.

On the way, a battered old French car with an African driver came swerving across the road towards us and only at the last moment did he manage to bring his vehicle under control. We stared back after him, outraged, as he sped out of sight but then we saw the cause of the trouble. A big, fat snake was wriggling its way across the road. We skidded to a halt and raced back to the spot, armed with a towel and a blanket. Karl was naturally the first to arrive. I was becoming an increasingly reluctant snake enthusiast and was quite willing to leave them to their own devices and catch harmless lizards and turtles instead. Fortunately, the snake had already vanished somewhere out of sight and retreated deep into the undergrowth.

About mid-afternoon we reached the waterfall. Although the water fell from a great height, there wasn't a great deal of it. Most of it ran down a pipeline to a generating station in the valley. There was a watchman at the gate of the station and he told us that there was a dam right at the top of the mountain. We asked him the way up. He ran inside to fetch a key and soon came back to open up the gate that barred the entrance to the mountain road. We told him that we would probably stay a few days at the top and he replied that there was a house by the lake with accommodations. We thanked him and drove on up the winding, rough, but remarkably beautiful road. Through the tunnels made by the branches of overhanging trees platted together with creepers, we passed banana groves, cocoa plantations and papaya trees heavily laden with fruit, as we continued up to the summit.

We found the house at the edge of the lake and saw the huge, curved wall of the dam. As we drove up, a small man dressed in an African pajama suit of baggy trousers and a loose shirt came to meet us. He was a very friendly and pleasant man and led us along a path to the dam wall, where we looked down into the lake and saw thousands of little fish swimming about close to the surface.

We discovered that the little man's name was Felix. We told him that we found the area very beautiful and would like to stay a few days. We asked if we could pitch our tent behind the house. He said that that was alright by him, but first he would have to telephone the man in charge to get permission and he went into the house to his office. We wandered about a bit by the water's edge, watching the birds diving into the water to catch fish and a fisherman laying his basket traps carefully in special places

126

where the fish were known to congregate. There were a couple of chairs on the veranda and we seated ourselves as we watched the sun slowly sinking down behind the mountains. It was like paradise.

The watchman came back evidently distressed and told us that unfortunately it was not allowed for us to stay on the mountain after night. "Je suis vraiment désolé. Très désolé!" *I am so very sorry. Very sorry!*

I asked him if I could speak to his manager myself and explain our situation as naturalists. But our friend told us that the man in charge was in Palimé and that it was the watchman at the bottom of the mountain who he had in fact telephoned and who had then contacted their superior.

I convinced him to asked him to get his friend to ring up again because it was getting late and we didn't want to drive down the mountain in the darkness. He rang the man below again and I spoke with him and told him what we wanted and why we didn't want to drive down that night. But the man below said that it wasn't allowed and that we would have to come down. I told him we would come down tomorrow and abruptly hung up.

We found quite a pleasant spot to camp a little way in the forest among the cocoa trees and there we pitched our tent and cooked our meal and slept very well indeed.

The next day, in the morning, the watchman came to see us and brought us a large bunch of ripe bananas, which was very kind of him. He told us that the boss wouldn't know we had spent the night there and we could go and wash at his house if we wanted to.

We spent a little while sitting with Felix on the veranda by the lake and then we took some photographs before finally wending our way back down the mountain path. Before we left, Felix gave us four ripe papaya fruits and his address and we promised to send him a Christmas card.

Further down the mountain we crossed over a narrow bridge. The water looked so cool and inviting that we stopped and washed in it and then continued on towards the main gate. The man was upset by my phone call with him the previous evening and he offered his profuse apologies that we could not stay longer. We told him that we would ask permission in Palimé and he gave us directions to the manager's office.

We drove to Palimé and called on the manager in his office to see if we could return to the mountain. He proved to be a very helpful gentleman and, although he could not give us permission to go back to the mountain, he did show us the road leading to another area that also had a waterfall and where hardly any people lived, so that we could camp there and pursue our animal catching quite undisturbed.

The road that he indicated led a little way west of the town and then started to wind up and up another mountain side. We passed a breath-taking waterfall where the water splashed down the rocks like a million droplets of silver and where the air was damp and the vegetation a deep lush green. Finally, passing a few buildings that seemed deserted and which we found out later was an old hospital, we drove into the forest itself along a grass track, through the trees to a clearing where we found an ideal camping spot.

We hadn't been there ten minutes but we had already raised the tent and begun to make ourselves at home. We were very efficient. Suddenly a wizened little man appeared before us as if by enchantment. He welcomed us warmly and shook hands vigorously, offering to help us arrange our things. He could greet in both French and English and knew some simple phrases but we relied mostly on sign language to communicate. He had cut his leg with his machete and had bound the wound with leaves and palm fibers. It looked very professional and effective. After a while, he just as suddenly disappeared and we didn't see another soul for the rest of the day.

The hens were glad to be out of the cage again and ran about the place, scratching up the earth and chasing grasshoppers. Then we noticed that the white hen had wandered off somewhere on her own. We assumed she had gone to find a good hiding place to lay her egg. I was concerned and went to look for her roughly in the direction where I thought she had gone. I struggled through the brambles and knotted undergrowth, through veil after veil of spider webs when, suddenly, I heard something moving about a little distance from me in the trees. It was the old man and, in his hand, he was carrying something white, which looked like our hen.

I waited until he had put it down and walked away, so that he wouldn't have time to hide it if he heard my approach and then I came out of my hiding place and went to have a look. The white thing wasn't our hen but a round bottle of palm wine. The old man was making palm wine! He shook hands once more with the same enthusiasm he had shown at camp earlier in the day. The old man poured out some wine for me to taste. It was still foaming and was immensely refreshing. In fact, because of its freshness, it was the best palm wine that I had ever tried. Then he preceded to explain to me how he made it. He had chopped down a palm tree and cut a deep groove near the branches at the top. In the groove was a hole bored all the way through the trunk to a funnel which, in turn, conducted the sap drop by drop into a bottle. One half of the groove had a palm wedge in it which stopped the juice coming from the branches. It was the sap from the trunk that he wanted. At the roots, he had set a modest fire. He plunged a torch of dry palm leaves into a lower cavity in the trunk and it burst into flame as he blew it to a red heat through a blow pipe. Then he cut away the burned wood with his knife and covered over the hole so that it stayed hot inside. The heat from the root fire and the hole in the trunk forced the sap to flow up the trunk and through the funnel that he had set at the top end. It was a remarkable procedure. But I could not help thinking that, while extracting maple syrup or the latex of a rubber plant did not kill the tree, this process of making palm wine did. He let me taste the sap. Before it fermented, the juice was rather sweet and sickly.

After the demonstration, my new friend led me through the forest to his house, which was built entirely of bamboo and palm. The hut was surrounded by cassava plants, coffee bushes and cocoa trees and the purple heads of ripening pineapples. The old man lived there most of the time on his own, although he had another house in a nearby village where his family lived. I told him that we would come and take his photograph the next day and I returned to back to camp.

The white hen and I arrived back at the same time. Somewhere or other she had hidden her egg away in the forest. I decided to follow her the next day when she left but I never did discover her hiding place.

We actively explored the surrounding countryside always eager to discover places where we could trap lizards or amphibians but while the forest was lush and pleasantly cool, the creatures we wanted were more

129

readily to be found in rocky and marshy areas.

As we were eating our evening meal, my forest friend appeared again, this time with a whole bottle of palm wine, which we poured out and the three of us drank together. We offered him some food, but he had already eaten so we gave him a cigarette instead. That made him very pleased but before long, after many warm salutations, he departed and, just a few steps from our camp, disappeared completely into the dense forest.

* * *

As time passed and people got to know us, we developed a small circle of very good friends. The old man in the forest visited regularly. We learned that the hospital had been converted into a hotel and was called *Le Campement*. We came to know the gardener who kept the grounds and also grew vegetables. Kofi, the hotel cook, became an amusing friend with his dry sense of humor and Edwin, who also worked in the hotel, was very pleasant as was the owner himself, who was a Lebanese.

Kofi suggested that we make a feast in the forest and he said that he would bring the meat and do the cooking. We had some potatoes and could make some fries and we would also kill a chicken. The houseman in the hotel brought three bottles of beer and Edwin one more and a bottle of *sorabi* moonshine which was distilled palm wine. The old man had left us a bottle of palm wine that morning but didn't arrive for the party until it was nearly over. We bought another five bottles of beer just to liven things up a bit and after the houseman had spoken to the spirits of the dead people who lived in the forest and told them that, although we were white, we were not so bad and had poured water, beer and sorabi on the earth for them to drink, the party began. Kofi had prepared a dozen skewers of meat and roasted our chicken with potatoes. We ate and drank like lords around the campfire.

Some days later, we were driving back to our camp in the forest of Klouto, after having visited the monastery of Dzogbegan on a high plateau, when a long, sinuous snake writhed out across the road followed by two muscular Africans armed with clubs and huge stones. It seemed

130

they had already wounded the snake. We drew up and got out. Karl put his foot on the snake's head and caught it behind the neck but, although it struggled at first, it soon became limp. The men had stoned it so brutally that at least ten inches of skin from its back was torn away. We took the dead animal with us and later Karl skinned it properly. It was an olive-green, grass snake and almost golden in color underneath.

We had been told of a nearby Benedictine monastery and it was suggested that it might be a place of interest that we should visit. Some of the monks were French while others were Togolese. They ran a farm and an orchard. A very pleasant French monk was intrigued by our interest in reptiles and our export enterprise. He persuaded us to stay overnight because he would help us catch Agama lizards after dark. We were delighted and could hardly wait until sunset. Before long our friend returned and led us among the buildings of the monastery. He carried a large metal bucket and a flashlight. Karl and I also did most of our catching at night. A chameleon on a bush, for example, was easy to spot in the beam of a flashlight but virtually invisible amongst the foliage during the day. As we climbed a flight of concrete stairs, the monk shone his torch. One after another the beam betrayed colorful agama that were easy to pluck off the wall and drop in the bucket. The bucket was perfect because the agama could not climb the metal with its sharp claws. Very soon we had gathered a fabulous number of healthy and colorful lizards and we vowed to keep this new technique in mind for another occasion.

As we journeyed back to Klouto, we recognized an African who lived in a village a short distance away from our camp in the forest and we gave him a lift home. He told us that he had been in Lomé a few weeks before with dancers and musicians from his village and that they had danced and played a welcome to President Pompidou of France upon his state visit to Togo. He invited us back to his village to visit his brother, the chief. The name of the village was Adekbega and it was situated within the proximity of the borders of Togo and Ghana in a valley just a mountain away from our Klouto camp.

Eventually, we arrived at the chief's house which was made of bricks but built solidly, something like a rectangular prison, including bars on the windows. The chief welcomed us as if we were Pompidou himself, or at least two of his chief ministers, and even the little children followed us along the way between the houses, chanting "Pom-pom-Pompidou." The chief gave us each a beer and we sat down in front of his house as all the important villagers were presented to us. The next day would be Sunday and the chief invited us to visit him again and they would perform the "Tam-tam" dance, the same way as they had in Lomé for the President.

Sunday came but, at midday, we had four interesting visits. First of all Marcel, a dentist who had lived in Dahomey for fifteen years but was originally from the West Indies. He was staying in the hotel, convalescing after a liver operation. We had met him once or twice previously. He came with his African assistant, a young fellow from Dahomey called Raymond and they brought with them drinks, ice and fruit.

Raymond was the son of a significant Dahomean business man. Marcel remarked out of earshot that, in all the years that Raymond had worked for him, the young man had never stolen. This was a considerable compliment and a reputation of which Raymond was enormously proud. He once told me discreetly, "I am very honest and I never steal!"

A little later a woman arrived from the nearby village with some food called "Yeki-Yeki," which is a cassava porridge served with a hot paprika meat stew, which Marcel had organized. Then came Kofi and Edwin from the hotel and, still later, the hotel proprietor himself with armfuls of beer bottles. With him he brought a Togolese friend and three prostitutes from Palimé.

The girls were very unpleasant and tried to steal things constantly. They even stole some book matches that we had out on our table. After they had eaten an enormous meal, they left and we were glad to see the back of them. It was truly a situation of anything not nailed down would be stolen.

But our friends remained and soon it became a real party, the likes of which the forest of Klouto had probably never known. As the evening wore on and our companions scattered back to their homes and to the hotel, the man to whom we had given a lift on our return from the Dzogbegan monastery came from the village to tell us the chief was waiting. We drove Marcel back to the hotel in the van and, remembering our promise to revisit the chief of Adekbega, set off for his village.

132

In the village masses of people all gaily dressed were gathered, crowding the central meeting area and all the paths around. We were led around about until we arrived at the chief's house, where we took his photograph. He gave us palm wine, which was almost as good as the stuff the old man had made in the forest. We drank, poured a little on the ground for the dead people as was the custom, drank from each others' bowls to check that it wasn't poisoned and then we were led off once again to the village center. As we approached the drumming started and the women began dancing. We were shown to a small table beneath a shady tree, which was covered by a plastic table cloth and had two chairs —places of honor! We shook hands with scores of people and all the time the drums were beating and the women were dancing. Somebody gave us some palm wine and somebody else suggested we get up and dance which we did for over half an hour until we were drenched with sweat and had to rest. Eventually, it became dark and we decided to leave and said goodbye to all the wonderful people.

* * *

Shortly after this event, Kofi invited us to his village. We wondered if this other area might be better for catching reptiles and we agreed to join him. He told us that there was a house there and that we should spend the night. We accepted his suggestion and took him along with us in the van. We drove to his little hamlet on a hillside that was surrounded by fields of coffee bushes.

We met the village chief, a young and seemingly well educated man who spoke fluent French. He showed us around the village and placed the guest house at our disposal. The view from up there was impressive: mountain slopes and hillsides covered with dense forest.

The following day we took the chief to visit some relatives of his who lived some miles along the main artery north. We stopped at a roadside eating house and treated the chief to a delicious stew of cane rat. The cane rat is call Agouti in West Africa although it is misnamed. Agouti is a South American rodent. The correct name for the Togolese creature is the Greater Cane or grass-cutter rat (*Thryonomys swinderianus*). It is a big meaty nocturnal rodent that can grow up two feet long. It has a short

133

tail.

The stew was hot and peppery and made with palm nut oil and it tasted somewhat like a goulash. Karl found the head of the cane rat in his bowl and kept it. Later, he cleaned it up and retained it for a souvenir, along with the baboon skull from Upper Volta.

We returned to the chief's home and were preparing to leave for Klouto when we became aware that a pair of the older men of the village were having a heated discourse with the young chief. Our friend was becoming embarrassed by the conversation but finally was able to escape and rejoin us. It transpired that the older men had wanted the chief to charge us for the nights' stay in their village. The younger man had explained that we were his guests and that we had bought him lunch. This was the first time we had observed a mercenary attitude towards hospitality anywhere in West Africa but shortly it would reoccur.

A few days later, after a brief trip to Lome where we dispatched another shipment of reptiles, we decided that it would be a nice gesture to buy a gift for the chief of the village of Adekbega for his kindness and for sharing a little of the excitement of the Tam-tam dancing and celebrations. We bought a large fish at the market but Karl pointed out that Africans give gifts in threes. So we added a bottle of sorabi and a couple of bottles of beer.

On our return to Klouto we drove into Adekbega and found the village chief seated before his house with some other tribal elders. We were greeted warmly and then we offered him our gifts. To our utter surprise he treated them with contempt. One of the men was Ghanaian and spoke good English. He translated the chief's words.

"You have been here how many times? Two, three. This is not enough payment". The translator was himself becoming embarrassed.

We recognized that perhaps our gift was slight and that we may have offended a convention but the chief seemed out-of-line by any measure. We assured him that we would mail him a nice photograph of him when the pictures were developed.

"Some white men tells the truth while others are liars..." The Ghanaian translated the chief's reply.

"This man is going too far". I heatedly retorted. "We were

134

unaware that here in Togo the African sells courtesy and hospitality where traditionally a stranger was always welcomed!"

When this was translated, the chief became ingratiating but we had no further patience with him and we left abruptly.

Back at our camp, we went to see the Lebanese hotel patron and told him our strange tale. He merely shrugged and offered us some of his dinner.

It later occurred to me that the Pompidou visit had undoubtedly introduced the concept of easy and abundant money in return for an exhibition of the traditional ceremonies and dances. And the largess had provoked a deviation from their usual spirit and custom of goodwill towards strangers. Africa was changing rapidly even before our eyes.

That night we slept very well for at least for part of the night. But soon it became evident that something was bothering the hens. They were clucking and screeching in the cage, very perturbed about something. I opened the tent flap and looked out with the torch, but I couldn't see what it was that was upsetting them. I tried to get to sleep again, but they continued to make a din. Suddenly, I felt something crawling over my body and something else was in my hair. I found the torch again and looked around to see what it was. The tent was full of ants, thousands and thousands of them all over the ground sheet and climbing up the walls. I woke up Karl and we decided to evacuate to the van. But when we were outside we got the shock of our lives. The entire area was covered with millions of ants and we were standing there in our naked feet. Suddenly, we felt their bite and we started to yell and hop about. We ran for the van and clambered up onto the roof. The hens' cage was absolutely full of the little devils—no wonder the poor animals had made such a fuss. Karl climbed down the side of the van and opened the door without touching the ground. He put on his boots and started splashing kerosene around the place. It seemed to work. He poured half a gallon into the cage and the hens began to settle down a little after a while but remained disconcerted. Then he poured some more all around the tent and then inside as well. Finally, I clambered down from the roof and ran, still without shoes, into the tent. We slept the few hours left until daybreak and then got up, glad that the miserable night was behind us. Meanwhile, the ants had established a narrow road and were still streaming through our camp, millions strong. They were nomadic driver ants on their seasonal march whereby anything in their path risked being devoured. The huge soldiers with their helmets and formidable pincers formed a protective bridge over the river of workers streaming below. Disconcerted by the kerosene bath, they had reformed and, by the million, now continued their devastating march through the hill-top countryside, consuming any unlucky animal life that they came across.

Camping in West Africa was a significant challenge but at night there was seldom any real danger. However, we always had flashlights and our machetes at the ready and would be instantly alert and up at the least disturbance. The driver ants, however, were a wholly unexpected hazard.

Fortunately, that was our last day in the forest and we collected our things together and packed everything into the van and set off to spend our second African Christmas in Dahomey.

10. DAHOMEY
Fantôme and Voodoo of all kinds

On the 23rd of December, after buying ample provisions including beer, wine, and tobacco, we said goodbye to Togo and left to celebrate Christmas in the adjacent country of Dahomey, since renamed Benin.

As we journeyed along the main coast road, we passed the wreck of a new Volkswagen car that was completely crushed against some low trees at the side of the road. The surface of the road was scarred with skid marks and the bushes along the side were torn up and lay scattered all about. The car had obviously rolled several times because nearly all the windows were broken. Inside, the upholstery was covered everywhere with brown, dried blood. On the dashboard was a small plastic plaque with the name and address of the owner, a lady doctor from Cotonou. We never found out what had happened nor discovered any further information concerning the victim of the crash. It seemed a very ominous beginning to our stay in Dahomey.

Soon we had to leave the surfaced coast road and head inland in the direction of Tori-Cada along another of those dusty washboard tracks. In Ouagadougou, we had heard from teachers at the Austrian school of an agricultural cooperative established by the Germans to encourage rural development and offering instruction in the trades.

Before the First World War, the protectorate of German Togoland which had encompassed parts of Ghana, Togo and Benin was a self supporting colony administered with predictable imperial brutality.

I wondered if we might meet a native in some isolated village who still retained some German words from sixty years before.

As usual, it was very hot indeed and when other vehicles drove by we had to close the windows to keep out the choking dust, which made the van like an oven.

We noticed that other motorists placed the palms of their hands flat on the windshield when we drove by and we realized that they did this so that a flying rock would be less likely to shatter the glass.

Along the way we passed a chain of little school children holding hands as they marched along. They shouted after us as we drove past and

137

we remembered the words of Marcel, the dentist, who had been convalescing in Klouto. He had once told us that those Africans living near the coast in Dahomey are the most terrible beggars, even the smallest children. "If they see you, they shout *Hey! White-man, give me a handout!*"

We bypassed the ancient Portuguese slaving community of Ouidah but promised ourselves a visit upon our return. We drove through a little village by a railway station where the road was so rough that each time we drove over a bump the hens in the back of the van started clucking in consternation.

The village was called Tori-Gare and we knew that we couldn't be far away from our destination. We stopped by a market adjacent to a rail crossing and asked a massive, market woman, selling onions and red peppers, if we were nearly there. She assured us that we were and waved her chubby arm in the general direction.

We traveled the one or two hills from Tori-Gare until we came to a crossroads where, on one side, there was a clinic closed for Christmas and in the middle stood two wooden figures, one of a colonial soldier with a helmet and rifle and, by his side, the other of a woman with huge, protruding breasts. Both of them were life-size and painted gray and white and were set upon a hillock surrounded by a low earthen wall.

We had entered the land that was the birthplace of Vodun or Voodoo.

At Tori-Cada the Germans had established a Project in order to encourage the farmers to cultivate their land more intensively. They offered interest-free loans so that the natives could buy seed and they had formed a cooperative in order to sell the harvest more effectively in the city.

The German cooperative was just a short distance further and we drove up and parked in the shade of one of their numerous garages. As we got out, someone called over to us from the far corner of one of the sheds that was piled high with sacks of maize and coffee. We climbed up the wooden steps leading to the office and were greeted by the Dahomean watchman, Etienne, and two of his friends. We asked them where we could find an Austrian called Johann, who was working with the Germans, instructing the Africans in building houses of bricks and one of them offered to lead us the way on his moped. Off we went, back along the same road, past the crossroads and those strange figures, until we reached a house a little ways from the road about a mile from the Project.

Johann wasn't at home, but Elly, an African, Johann's houseboy, was feeding the rabbits. He hardly spoke a word of French but managed to explain to us that his master was in Cotonou that day but would be returning shortly.

While we were waiting we looked around the compound, which was really like a small farm. In a tree, a kennel was secured and inside lived a beautifully colored Patas monkey. Although it was chained it seemed quite tame. In front of the house was a vegetable plot enclosed by a bamboo fence, next to which Johann had built a straw-thatched canopy where he had set up a ping-pong table. All around the garden were dozens and dozens of pineapple plants, some with nearly ripe fruit. It was all impressively organized.

Suddenly we heard the sound of a motorbike and a middle-aged man came speeding around the corner in a cloud of dust and parked beside our van. He sprang from his machine and approached us with an outstretched hand. This was Johann.

We told him of our mutual friend in Ouagadougou, with whom he had trained in Austria for development work. Johann was delighted to have news of his colleague and of the success of the educational Project in Ouagadougou. His friend, Gerhard, had told us to pay a visit if we should come to Dahomey. Johann seemed very pleased to see us and, straight away, he opened up three bottles of refreshing beer, and we drank to one another's health. The clinking bottles reminded me of a joke. There is a saying in West Africa among the white people. During the first year of your stay you go into a bar and ask for a beer. There is a fly in the beer and you send the drink back. The second year there is a fly in your beer and you remove it with your finger and drink the beer. But after three years if you receive a beer without a fly in it, you ask for one!

We had an amusing afternoon telling stories of our adventures while Johann filled us in with information about the surrounding countryside and culture. He added that he had an African mistress who lived in a nearby village. But, as there is no romance between men and women in West Africa, it was pretty evident that she was a prostitute and not a girlfriend as we conventionally understand the term.

139

The strange figures that we had seen at the crossroads, Johann told us, were supposed to represent the fantômes which were spirits that guard the Africans against thieves. There were much better ones further along the road from the house which looked even more menacing.

We put our provisions in Johann's fridge, which ran on kerosene, and then the three of us sat down on deck chairs in the garden beneath the shade of the thatched canopy.

Before long another Volkswagen van like ours drew up and two men got out and came over to greet us. Both of them were from Germany, the younger, Hartmut, was a draftsman who planned and designed everything to be built by the Project, while his older associate, a man of about forty-five, Mr. Hanke, was in charge of the commercial side and served as the bursar. They both invited us to their various Christmas festivities and we promised each of them one of our roosters as a Christmas contribution.

The first celebration was to be with Hartmut the following day at lunchtime at the home of a nurse named Dorothy who ran a clinic in one of the nearby villages. It was several miles to the house, along the dusty roads past enormous, towering trees, little villages of red adobe huts and more of those sinister fantôme figures that seemed to be placed in front of every village and at every crossroads. When we arrived, Mr. Hanke and Hartmut were already there and they introduced us to Dorothy.

It was obviously a welcome respite to have European guests and the talk was ceaseless. They were intrigued by our animal catching enterprise and offered some interesting suggestions where we might find abundant reptiles to catch. We learned a great deal about the region and places of interest to explore in the surrounding countryside. They also offered us interesting insights into the temperament and character of the native Dahomeans, as well as the flora and fauna. Yet, while it was very refreshing to be within this oasis of European expertise, we knew that we would only really become properly familiar with the region, its inhabitants and culture through direct association with the indigenous population in the bush.

The following evening we left Johann's compound where we had temporarily pitched our tent and this time drove to celebrate Christmas night at Mr. Hanke's house. His home was very European and stood all on its own some distance from a swamp known as the Marigot which is the French for backwater or creek. There we met the rest of the German team, including the director of the Project, Mr. Dietz.

It was a splendid evening seated around a large dining table and feasting upon good food and enjoying pleasant company. While at dinner we learned that the Project was going to be relinquished to an African administrator named Mr. Fassassi early the following year and that most of the company would return to Europe or relocate to other West African countries. Mr. Hanke was going to work in Togo.

The Christmas festivities over we set to work exploring the countryside around the Project to determine the best places to catch reptiles.

It was an extraordinary experience just to walk the tracks and roads around a village or from field to field across the African countryside. The bush was unlike anything I had experienced. While the dusty road might change color depending on the geology of the region and the trees and bushes differ from rain forest to savanna or the coastal areas, wherever we found ourselves it was always unique and exotically fascinating. But if one did forget for a single moment that this was Africa then suddenly something incongruous would occur as a reminder. It was not that something exciting and extraordinary was always happening. Sometimes the days passed by in very ordinary ways. Rather, it was the recognition of actually being there, in Africa, a most thoroughly foreign and fascinating place.

As we hiked from our camp to some remote stream or to explore a rocky outcrop that might conceal geckos or agamas, there may be a rustling by the wayside, a creature such as we had never met in Europe might spring out and dart across before us. Or, up in the foliage, a troop of monkeys might shriek an excited warning of our coming. A farmer or fisherman could appear in the distance and already be peering ahead at the unfamiliar sight of two white-men up ahead with buckets of frogs or perhaps carrying a net or catching pole. These were extraordinary things for the native to observe just as their own appearance and culture were equally curious to us.

An overladen bush taxi would sometimes hurtle by in a cloud of dust and confusion and you could hear the excited chattering through the

141

open windows of people off to market. Or perhaps a trussed-up goat would bleat piteously, complaining of its miserable condition among the hodge-podge of bundles on the roof. Or a cage of bewildered chickens would be clucking while a baffled rooster senselessly crowed merely because that is what it is supposed to do even if dangling awkwardly, almost upside down, parched and bedraggled from the roof.

Perhaps the most delightful experience far away in the solitude of the bush is an encounter with a group of native women with babies bundled on their backs and toddlers in tow as they make their way home, laden with firewood or huge bowls of water balanced on their heads. Even the little girls are already sharing the burden, each with a more modest bowl but equally and just as skillfully held aloft while their eyes dart about with interest at the two unfamiliar men who greet them in their own language. Somehow the white men sound strange and, after the first enthusiastic words, the conversation falls flat and as they pass by and you wonder who they were.

The Christmas parties at Tori-Cada seemed to have come to an end and, while we had had a very enjoyable time and we were very grateful to the Germans for their hospitality, we longed to return to the mystery and enchantment of the African world.

Additionally, friction had arisen between Karl and Johann that developed into a quarrel that could not be patched up. Johann was a strange man, at one moment extremely friendly but easily aroused and aggressive. He enjoyed tormenting his African neighbors with his pet monkey. Some evenings he would visit them in their compound and we joined them one evening around the fire. Johann would suddenly release the monkey's leash so that it would run at his neighbor's wife and terrify her. Africans have no concept of keeping an animal for a pet. For them, they were a source of food or transport. If possible they swiftly dispatch every wild creature they encounter as if the supply was inexhaustible. Indeed we noted a dearth of larger animals in the Tori-Cada region. Johann repeated his tiresome game, so distressing to the African woman, over and over again so that when he came to visit his neighbors knew that they were in for yet another ordeal. I found this very crass and it only revealed his lurking contempt for the African.

Before we could explore further we needed to return to Cotonou to see if we had any letters and we decided to take a look at the city itself. We left at about midday, expecting to arrive in the early afternoon. But then, only about ten miles away, the engine started to slow down as if we had run out of petrol, although the tank was still more than half full. We drew up at the side of the road on a grass verge beneath a group of swaying palm trees, which offered us a little respite from the brutal sun. Opening up the motor cover to look inside we were horrified to see clouds of smoke pouring out from everywhere. There was no oil in the engine! There had been a leaking gasket somewhere and the green oil pressure warning light had malfunctioned.

We waited a couple of hours for the machine to cool down and then gingerly poured in some fresh oil. Karl tried to start it, but it wouldn't turn over. Everything was seized up! We had no choice but to sit tight and hope that someone we knew might pass by and maybe tow us back to Tori-Cada.

Sometime later, Hartmut came down the road in the direction of Cotonou, driving one of the Project's vans. He stopped and we showed him what had happened. He agreed to tow us back to Tori-Cada, where he suggested we could work on the engine in the Project garage.

Soon we were once again in Tori-Cada and very relieved not to be stranded somewhere in the bush with such a serious problem to address.

Unfortunately, we had a reconditioned engine which meant that all the internal bearings were a little larger than standard, a size that just wasn't available in either Cotonou or Lomé. We had to send away to Europe for new big end bearings to replace those that had seized up, which meant we had a few weeks to wait.

Mr. Hanke was very gracious and suggested that they might have a spare crankshaft in storage but there was none to be found. Some considerable time later we discovered where it was. Pierre, one of the African mechanics, had been pilfering over a considerable time. He now had everything necessary to build an entire engine that he intended to then sell in the city.

After the Christmas holiday, work started again at the Project for the carpenters, the mechanics, the builders, drivers, and laborers. A Dahomean was sawing poles lengthwise. These would be used in

143

construction. At first I thought it strange that, unlike a European, he held the handsaw with the teeth pointing away from him. But, upon reflection, I realized that he was working just as the pit sawyers would have done years ago in Europe, long before the work was performed by machines.

Other men were loading and unloading bags of maize that the farmers brought in from the fields. These would be trucked to Cotonou for sale at the market.

In another location, there were a score of rabbit cages where the Germans were introducing rabbit husbandry to the rural farmers as a possible and easy source of protein. A young African man named Germain was in charge of this enterprise. He had attended school in Germany under an African development plan. "They know that I don't like to work", he explained, "We understand each other just fine." And sure enough he never seemed to be very busy. He just puttered around with his rabbits at his leisure. But he was an extremely nice man and we enjoyed talking with him. He knew all about the Marigot swamp. A crocodile had been killed there during the previous year and was given to Mr. Hanke for a gift. Germain, also a taxidermist, had preserved and stuffed it for him.

One evening, just as work was over, the store manager, Alphonse, came over to invite us to his house at a village called Zoungoudou. He told us that he would send his little brother to fetch us at about seven that evening.

Eventually, a young schoolboy arrived and told us that Alphonse was ready for us to come. The boy led the way down a narrow path away from the Project buildings and about a mile and a half along the dusty road until we reached the village of Zoungoudou, just as darkness fell. We made our way through the maze of thatched red adobe huts where goats and sheep were still wandering about, not sure whether it was night time yet or still day because of the glow of the log fires. The African women were preparing the evening meal for their families already seated together on the sandy ground in front of their homes. Those who noticed us greeted us as we passed by in the shadows.

We were shown Alphonse's house and found our host waiting for us, listening to his transistor radio. He jumped up and welcomed us several times, shaking hands almost constantly. Before we had hardly sat

144

down, his wife appeared and offered us water to quench our thirst. Then our host disappeared and then returned with a bottle of sorabi, which he said was to kill the *les microbes*. It had not occurred to me that sorabi was considered medicinal. But I had heard that same excuse in Europe from those who were also too fond of spirits.

Maize is the main part of the Dahomean diet and it is prepared mainly in two ways, either finely ground and cooked so that it sets solid and is scooped up with the first three fingers and dipped into the sauce (abassa or à bassa), or coarsely ground, it absorbs less water and is fuller (pâté). Alphonse's wife had prepared pâté with a sauce of red palm nut oil, hot peppers, the leaves of a plant that grows in the Marigot, and a little dried fish.

The meal was excellent and very filling. We knew the protocol of eating with the hand. We washed both hands but only the left hand was used to eat. It is enormously offensive to eat with the right because the right hand is the one used for cleaning oneself. Afterwards, Alphonse drove us in turns on his moped to visit a friend of his who lived nearby. It was Germain. It was he who had studied agriculture in Germany and was the same man that we already knew who bred and looked after the rabbits. At Germain's house, we were offered still more sorabi and finally returned the short distance back to the Project where we had pitched our tent, a little unsure on our feet.

On our way we heard a weird howling and moaning coming from the crossroads a mile or two away where we had noticed the two fantôme statues upon our arrival. The watchman, Etienne, warned us that they were keeping watch for thieves. We asked who *they* were. And he replied ominously, "Les fantômes!" *The spirits!*

The next day was Saturday and a rest day at the Project. All was empty and quiet. Karl had been doing his washing most of the morning and had left some things in a bucket to soak by the faucet in the yard.

About midday, a group of youths came down the path and into the yard in a cart pulled by oxen. They stopped by our tent and begged for cigarettes, alcohol, or anything we might have to give them. I told them to go to hell and they went away laughing and one of them promptly emptied Karl's bucket of washing out onto the ground and used the bucket to water the oxen. Karl went over and cursed him, which attracted the attention of Etienne, who came and told the boys to buzz off. But they seemed to be just looking for trouble and one of them started badmouthing Etienne and finally hurled a piece of broken brick at him. It narrowly missed, but then a real fight started and the boy hit the watchman several times with a plank and a last time across the face, which sent the man to the ground. Karl caught the boy in a half-nelson and held him like that until some friends of Etienne's arrived and led him off to the village chief and, later, to the police station in a small town close by.

That blow across the face kept Etienne away from work for three weeks, but he very proudly told us that the police had thoroughly beaten the boy in a like manner at the station and that now he walked with a limp and had one eye permanently closed. It seemed the *fantômes* were not the only ones capable of swiftly meting out appropriate justice. The youth also had to pay Etienne damages, but, having neither work nor money, Etienne didn't know when he was likely to see any of it.

* * *

Gabriel was one of the drivers at the Project and his best friend was one of the mechanics called Pierre. One Friday evening they told us that they would come and fetch us the next day to take us to Tori-Gare to spend the day with them.

Sure enough, the next day they turned up two hours later than arranged in a battered old Citroen deux-chevaux van that had, at some time or other, fallen apart in the middle and then been welded back together again.

We were not disconcerted by the lateness of their arrival being long since accustomed to the flexibility of time in Africa. There were no clocks and only a few men wore watches. The time of day was an approximate thing determined by the sequence of activities such as waking, eating or labor and by the position of the sun.

We reached Tori-Gare and drove on to Gabriel's house and compound a few hundred yards from the station. Beneath a shady tree in front of the house, they had already prepared mats, a table, deck chairs, and a record player with a separate and enormous loud speaker.

At about midday, Pierre left to go and eat at his own house and

146

we followed Gabriel into a room where mats were laid out on the floor and a meal of pâté and roast chicken was waiting for us. The absence of cutlery told us that we would be eating with our fingers in the same manner that we had at Alphonse's house.

After the meal, we relaxed a while as everything was loaded into the back of the Citroen, deck chairs, table, and even the enormous loud speaker. There was a ceremony in a village a few miles away and that was where we would be going.

Before we drove off, a huge crowd of people came dancing and singing down the road, waving bottles of sorabi. One young girl was carrying something wrapped in a gaily colored cloth, swinging it here and there and dancing madly with it. She was obviously the center of the parade.

As one of the dancers poured out a glass of sorabi for each of us from his precious bottle, we asked what it was the girl had in the cloth.

"The head!" he shouted to us above the noise, banging himself on the top of his own head with the hand that carried the sorabi and spilling some of the contents. We looked at each other, startled for a couple of moments while, in the meantime the dancer slipped away to join the rest of the company, wildly dancing off down the road. We wanted to ask Gabriel if it was true, but he had already started the car and inside there was so much noise from the engine and groaning suspension that no one could understand what was said.

On the way, we went to pick up a friend of Gabriel's, Ciprian, who had a small tailor's shop in Tori-Gare. Now the tiny vehicle was thoroughly overloaded. But Gabriel was both a skillful and nonchalantly confident driver and we were not concerned.

Gabriel had started driving trucks when he was still young. He hauled grain and produce from the Northern regions down to the coast. The first time when he passed through his own village, he had stopped to visit his family and everyone had gathered around him cheering and clapping because he was still just a small boy while the truck was enormous by comparison.

It was beginning to get dark as we arrived at the village and the celebrations were already underway. In fact, they had already been "under way" a day and a half. There were two sets of musicians with bells, differently styled drums and a few other simple percussion instruments. They were forcefully pounding a frenzied rhythm and the dancers were wildly hopping and spinning with fantastic energy.

Gabriel led us through the village to a house on the hillside where a relative of his lived, a farmer called Barnaby. Barnaby was an extremely strong man with a very serious face, not angry, just solemn. Another man who was Gabriel's immediate neighbor had also impressed us by his giant physique. There were some herculean men around here. Barnaby produced a bottle of sorabi and we all drank before going back down into the village together to join the amusements. Sorabi, distilled from palm wine, was evidently ubiquitous and I imagined that moonshine must be a formidable local industry.

There was a special shelter thatched with palm leaves already prepared for us and a table with two bottles of sorabi, several bottles of beer, and two packets of cigarettes. Gabriel organized his record player and almost everyone left the conventional tam-tam and started dancing to his modern music.

The evening wore on yet nobody wearied of dancing. We had experienced these events before and they always seemed interminable to me. I supposed that they eventually would wind down and break up through sheer exhaustion. I decided to question Barnaby, who was looking very serious sitting next to me, about the dancers we had seen that day in the road carrying the skull.

Barnaby spoke excellent French and didn't have to be asked twice to explain in great detail.

"The day after somebody dies, the first ceremony begins and usually carries on for several days. It depends how important the dead person was, but usually the relatives kill an ox or a couple of sheep and chickens and give food and drink to all those taking part in the festivities. Some time later, the person is dug up and his head is put in an earthenware jar and wrapped in a cloth to be carried about the roads and other places that the dead person had known. A young virgin is paid to do it. After the second ceremony, the skull is buried in the family grave that could be a cave or an underground room. These ceremonies cost a great deal of money and make life very difficult for poorer people.

"Sometimes people steal the heads and sell them to witch

doctors who make grisgris with them that produce money! They could be sold in Ghana or somewhere for a fortune. But that doesn't happen very much anymore."

I told Barnaby that we were intending to visit Abomey before leaving Dahomey, to see the renowned museum there.

"That will be very interesting, some of the kings of Abomey were quite famous. In fact, the name Dahomey comes from the last king who was called 'Dah' and the name Abomey together making 'Dah-Abomey,' which is Dahomey!"

He told me how important the dead were to the Ayizo people and how the relatives would put all the dead man's personal belongings in a basket and destroy them. These days they simply leave them in the road so that the cars drive over them, killing the possessions so that they go with the dead man. I told him that we had often seen baskets of old clothes and rotten fruit lying in the road, but had thought it to be just rubbish.

The celebration continued all night long and, even when the sky slowly began to brighten as the dawn approached, it still showed no sign of coming to an end. We were told that it would probably continue for one or two days more.

Everything packed into the Citroen, we said, "Au revoir" to Barnaby and drove off back to Gabriel's house, exhausted.

Towards midday, we heard a great commotion going on in the lane outside. A huge and high-spirited crowd was coming along the path, escorting three vigorously whirling figures dressed in heavy grass costumes. Their entire bodies including their faces were completely concealed and their feet were barely visible beneath their gyrating forms. Gabriel said that they were fantômes who were on their way to perform at a feast not far from there. The leader of the group came over to us and boomed something or other in his native language. Gabriel translated that the fantômes had asked if we had anything to give him, money, cigarettes. . . . Unimpressed, we said nothing and went back inside the house as the fantômes three continued on their way. It seemed that the word *fantôme* described something both supernatural and something else very human.

During the next week we were invited to observe yet another

African celebration. This time it had nothing to do with the dead; it was a *fetish* feast.

These observances were wild occasions stimulated by an excess of moonshine. In fact, it occurred to me that Dahomey had a national alcohol addiction. Perhaps that was part of the reason why the police and government officials who we were obliged to deal with were so impatient and testy. The festivities and animistic observances that we witnessed bordered upon hysteria and seemed to induce a collective frenzied agitation in the onlookers. It was this that we recognized after our initial interest in the masks and the costumes had subsided. The music itself was unbelievably monotonous and almost unbearable because of its incessant repetition. But it worked its magic and threw the villagers into transports of euphoria.

Jean was another African who had spent a couple of years learning about agriculture in Germany and, after he had finished work at the German Station one evening, he asked us if we wanted to go and watch the fun. We left, Karl on the back of Jean's moped and I on the rack of Michel's bicycle. Michel was another mechanic working at the Project.

Fortunately Michel was strong. The fetish village was a long way away and we didn't arrive until sunset. However, the music and dancing would carry on all through the night. The several score of villagers had formed a ring around the drummers and the men dancing and they were all chanting to the music. The dancers were dressed in very gaily patched dresses and wore colorful headdresses, bracelets, and bands. They were dancing wildly and women similarly dressed were singing to the pounding of the drums and the ringing bells. Every now and then the men did somersaults. Indeed, they were very skillful gymnasts and we were quite impressed with their tumbling. We watched for a few minutes and then Jean led us through the village and among the round huts, until we arrived at one where the mother of a friend of his lived. The old woman was in front of the hut, cooking pâté and ran to meet Jean as she saw him coming. She welcomed us, practically throwing herself at our feet and, in quick succession, we were presented with water, sorabi, cola fruits, and cigarettes. Then Jean disappeared with the old woman into the hut and reappeared alone half an hour later. Apparently, it being the time of the

150

fetish ceremony, she had been expecting her son who worked in Cotonou to visit her, but he hadn't arrived and that greatly upset her.

It had become late and the four of us were eager to return home. We left the fetish village, the dancers and singers, and made our way back to the Project, Karl on the back of Jean's moped and I again with Michel but also accompanied by Vincent, Jean's brother, who had also attended the ceremony. He ran along beside us.

When we were within a few hundred yards of the crossroads by the clinic at Tori-gar, we heard the hollow crying of the fantôme and Michel stopped to listen. He seemed apprehensive. We got off the bicycle, he switched off his lamp and we approached slowly and in silence. When we were quite close, Michel rang his bell to warn the fantôme that we were coming. Suddenly, the fantôme started to boom and scream and we stayed where we were, frozen. It seemed to be interrogating Michel from somewhere in the darkness and, now and then, he called back a reply. Finally, it appeared that the fantôme had given us permission to continue and we carried on slowly towards the crossroads as it resumed its howling. At the crossroads it started booming at us again and Vincent handed over two or three cigarettes to a figure who appeared out of the darkness.

After we had passed by, Michel told me that the fantôme had just asked who we were, from where we had come, what we were doing on the road at night, and if we didn't have something to give him.

Some days later the sentinels of the night proved themselves to be of some other purpose than just intimidation and graft. They caught a thief with three small tables that he had stolen from a house not far from the project. Unfortunately, the man had managed to get away but the fantômes had recognized him.

In his stead, they took his wife and children to the police station, where they were imprisoned and the woman was beaten to encourage her husband to turn up as quickly as possible. Several days passed by and still there was no sign of him. Perhaps he did not know what was happening. But beatings by the police seemed to be the typical procedure. He must have guessed that his family was being mistreated.

* * *

151

Finally, the bearings for the engine arrived from Europe. Karl's father had mailed them promptly as soon as he received our letter and included some lengths of emery cloth to facilitate the repair job. I had already stripped down the engine and cleaned all the parts in kerosene. But the crankshaft was badly damaged. Some of the steel from the bearings was welded onto it. With the emery cloth I spent hours and even days smoothing the hard steel. When I had to stop Karl took over until gradually the job was completed and the engine could be finally reassembled.

Karl had gone to Cotonou to check for mail and to buy provisions and while there he was hailed by someone who at first called him by my name. Then the young man got Karl's name right and Karl turned to find himself face to face with Marcel's young Dahomean assistant, Raymond, who we had met while staying in the forest of Klouto. Raymond welcomed Karl enthusiastically and took him to his family home for a meal.

* * *

While writing the notes for this chapter, we were camped about ten miles from Cotonou at a place called Powou, which is a beautiful location beside a lake. I was interrupted by a visit from the police who, after much harassment, finally left, taking Karl, my notes and our passports with them.

But before I go on to explain what happened in greater detail, I must tell of a chain of preceding events which deal with the same subject.

Once, in Lomé, we had managed to sell a royal python to the captain of a German cargo ship. We had met some of the crew while fishing from the harbor wall and had told them about our journey and mentioned during the conversation that we had a python at that moment in the van. They asked to see and we showed it to them. Somehow word got to the captain, who was very interested and asked us to come on board and bring the snake with us. He paid us generously for it and we were very pleased with our good fortune.

Our customers in Europe, to whom we had sent many consignments of reptiles, offered us two-thirds less for royal pythons so

152

our retail profit was considerable. On another visit to Cotonou, we decided to try our luck again in the harbor where we saw an East German cargo vessel.

It was early afternoon and, with the snake in the sack, we went to see what we could do. The harbors always have uniformed guards at the gate but they usually let whites go through unhindered, thinking that they belong on one of the ships. We called to one of the ship's crew in German and he invited us on board. The man took us to the officer's mess and we introduced ourselves. One man was very enthusiastic about the snake but, unfortunately, the officer didn't have a currency that we could exchange and he offered to pay us in kind. He gave us two khaki jackets, a pair of shoes, some bread and butter, and a dozen bottles of beer.

It was already dark when we left the ship. It must have been about nine o'clock and we thought we would avoid the main entrance because we expected to be hassled by the guards who would be curious about the sack and pester us for a bribe. There was an area of fence to one side of the harbor that was close to the water and easy to swing around. We decided to leave that way instead of through the main gate. That was a very bad idea. Some distance from the harbor two men approached us, one uniformed and on a moped. They asked us to show them what was in the sack and we told them to first to tell us who they were. The man without the uniform tried to pull the sack from Karl's shoulder, but Karl didn't release it. A crowd of people gathered round and a few of them tried to help the two of them take the sack away, but fortunately a policeman turned up and we agreed to show him and the other uniformed man what we were carrying. The policeman said that there was nothing to declare, but the other wanted to make trouble and went to telephone one of his colleagues, who arrived also on a moped about ten minutes later. We were escorted to a shabby little office not far from the harbor, where they started to interrogate us. Their intent was to get a bribe. They spoke *Fon* amongst themselves and shouted us down each time we tried to reply to their questions. I made the second big mistake of shouting back at them which only infuriated them further. They refused to allow us to telephone the English or German consulate which we demanded they do upon arrival.

One of the men sat on the window sill swinging his feet in the air, finding the whole business highly amusing while another sat with his naked feet on his desk and the third strolled around the room with one hand in his trousers and carrying a pole with which he threatened to beat us.

Had we been thinking we should have cracked open some of the bottles of beer with them and just made a party of it. They would almost certainly would have let us go.

They gave us a form to fill out, said that our writing was illegible and whipped it away again before we had written more than our names. We realized that it was quite impossible to talk to them, as there wasn't one among them who was interested in whether we had done anything or not. They were all just amusing themselves at our expense and didn't care if it was legal or not.

After several more attempts to get them to telephone the consulate and, after being threatened with a beating, we said no more, not a word. We just waited to see what would happen next.

At about ten o'clock, a young Dahomean prostitute and her pimp were brought in. She had been working on a ship and the interrogators learned that she had earned one thousand francs that evening. One of the men amused himself, searching her body and clothing for the money and the others looked on with round eyes and watering mouths. They suggested having sex with her.

The pimp was distraught and tried to reason with them but they treated him in much the same way as they had dealt with Karl and I.

At midnight, a riot van arrived and one of the policemen spoke very quietly to the pimp who relayed to us in English that they wanted to see an end to the matter and we just had to go and fetch our passports from the van and then we could leave.

We started off on foot, but then were called back and told that we had to go in their van and we climbed in, suspecting nothing and glad that the game was almost over.

But instead of driving to where we had parked our vehicle, they turned off and drove away from the harbor. I told the driver that our van was in the other direction, but he ignored me and we realized that we had been tricked.

After a ten minute journey, we arrived at the prison and were led through the office to a cell that was full, packed with naked and half-naked Africans. But it wasn't the Africans that repulsed us, it was the smell, a horrible, overpowering stink, and the heat was unbearable. We refused to go inside and insisted on seeing the officer in charge. We were led off again to the commissioner, who was sleeping on a grass mat in the yard. A policeman woke him and, because he was half asleep, he listened to what we had to say and told us that we could sleep in the bicycle shed where there was a bench and an officer on guard.

Back at the office, we pestered the men so much that at last they allowed us to telephone. We had to ring for directory inquiries because the men claimed that they didn't have a telephone book. We were told that there wasn't a number for the British Consulate and when we telephoned the German one there was no answer. We realized that it was already after midnight. Finally, one of the men slammed down the receiver and shouted at us that it wasn't a public telephone and we were led off to the bicycle shed.

Perhaps half an hour later we heard a terrific argument between one of the policemen and the commissioner. The man shouted that the prison was there for everyone, even the *Yovos* (whites), and we thought that we would soon be finding ourselves in that stinking cage. But fortunately we were left where we were and the quarrel quietened down and soon we only heard the buzzing of mosquitoes and the murmur of a couple of men talking quietly somewhere in the darkness.

In the morning, we thought things must become better and that we would be able to telephone and get away from those depraved African policemen, but, on the contrary, things became quickly much worse.

The chief on day duty was drunk. He swore and threatened us and had us literally thrown into the cell. The other prisoners warned us not to say anything or we would certainly be led off to the little room where they beat people up. We took their advice and watched horrified as the chief snarled at us through the bars and played around with his pistol. Suddenly, he accidentally fired a shot, narrowly missing a small boy sitting with his mother on a bench. There were several women in the room apparently waiting for their husbands to be released.

In the cell itself was one man who had been arrested on the

street nine days before and still hadn't been told what it was he was charged with. There was also a little boy of eight or nine and God knows what he was doing there.

Suddenly the chief roared, "The prisoners can go and wash two by two, except for those two white imbeciles!"

Then he came to the cage, gripped the bars, and told us to our faces that we were, in fact, imbeciles and we thought how small he would look without his uniform and pistol and how nice it would be to beat his brains out, but, as he was obviously looking for an opportunity to do the same thing to us, we kept quiet and calm.

Most of the men left the cell to wash in spite of the fact that they were supposed to go two by two and fortunately they took with them the bucket that had made the room smell so bad.

About mid-morning we were loaded into a van with about a dozen other prisoners and driven back to the office where we had been the previous evening. On arrival, all the others were handcuffed and we wondered if we would be too, as yet another humiliation, but fortunately we were led straight to the commissioner's office. The commissioner seemed to be remarkably reasonable. Perhaps he had realized that his men had gone too far. He questioned us as we stood in front of his table, our hands at our sides, like two naughty children being reprimanded by the school principal.

He read to us the charges that the men had dreamed up the previous night and we became furious as he told us that we were supposed to have assaulted a policeman in the harbor, to have insulted the men in the office and that we had refused to fill out the forms they had given us.

We replied angrily that none of this was true and that the men had assaulted us in the harbor and that we had been insulted, ridiculed and threatened. Then we mentioned the behavior of the chief in the prison who had fired a shot and that, at nine o'clock the previous evening, we had first asked to telephone the consulate and had been ignored and threatened with violence.

The chief glanced at us and looked quickly away and we knew that we had managed to get him worried. He then telephoned both the British and German ambassadors and explained to them on the phone

156

briefly with what we were charged. He told us to sit down in the meantime as he dealt with some other matter.

Very soon the German ambassador arrived and we explained to him what had happened and he replied, "Now you see how they make an elephant from a fly."

It was quite clear that the commissioner felt very uneasy having three white men to argue with at once and, although he rudely tried to interrupt the ambassador several times, he was no longer in control of the situation and the very intelligent German succeeded in destroying one charge after another as ludicrous. When there was nothing left to charge us with, the commissioner started to threaten us anew and gave no peace until the ambassador, with our approval, offered him the bottles of beer as a bribe, which he readily accepted.

The whole affair had been quite delicate as it was very clear that the police themselves were the law. They did as they wanted and were so corrupt that probably, if we had given even a small bribe at the gate the previous evening, we would have saved ourselves a lot of trouble. They could lock anyone away whenever they wished, for as long as they wanted. They kept a law and order of their own by intimidation, lining their pockets at the same time.

The German left and a secretary from the British embassy arrived who was a Dahomean, but, as everything was already settled, we thanked him for coming as we also left.

The first thing we did was to go and thank the German ambassador for getting us out. He had not yet returned to the Consulate but another official warned us sternly, "You must obey the laws of a foreign country just as you would at home!"

And we realized that the Africa of his experience was completely different from that of our own. He really imagined that the country ran on a basis of law and order.

The second thing we did, free once more, was to go to an African outdoor café where we drank hot, sweet coffee and devoured the German bread and butter that we had received in exchange for the python. It was remarkable that no one had stolen our stuff while we were in jail.

Dahomey was a Marxist state from 1972. Mathieu Kérékou was

the most recent president during the time that Karl and I were there. The Marxist practice of radio propaganda and the use of socio-political aphorisms had an unsettling effect on the minds of the uneducated Dahomeans out in the bush. Transistor radios were becoming fairly common. A least one or two could be found in the southernmost villages. Hostility towards whites was an unpleasant aspect of that propaganda that we experienced first-hand.

Gabriel had to haul a load of maize from the German Project into Cotonou. He asked if we would like to join him and told us that he would introduce us to his second wife who lived in a village between Tori-Cada and Cotonou. We readily agreed, recognizing an opportunity to visit both an isolated village and to check our mail in Cotonou, accompanied by a native companion and guide.

We climbed aboard and set off down the dusty trail towards Cotonou, enjoying a lively conversation as we drove.

Gabriel told us of his special fetish that he applied to his face every day and which assured that people would always like him. It was a paste that contained all the things that are considered desirable including certain foods and outlandishly, the pubic hair of a virgin girl.

Soon we arrived at the compound where Gabriel's wife lived. A young woman with a small child in her arms came running up to greet him and to welcome us to the village. Gabriel held his son with great affection as the child chuckled while the mother smiled with obvious delight. Suddenly an elderly man of the village rushed at us in a blind fury and tried to attack us. He spewed his wrath and venom towards us in Fon and the few words of French that he knew. It became hard for Gabriel and some of the other men to intervene as he became increasingly incensed. However, we did not come directly to blows but we were considerably astonished and quickly headed back to the truck while Gabriel fired up the engine and we made a hasty retreat.

A week later there was a great unrest in the town. Apparently, a Frenchman and a handful of Dahomeans, among them army officers, had tried to assassinate President Kérékou. Their attempt had failed, but the President retaliated by making things very hot for any other Europeans in the town, in particular the French. We were told by a friend of ours living in the town that militia mobs were organized under the direction of the police to roam the streets, breaking up people's cars, smashing windows, and beating up any white people they saw. The soldiers with machine guns harassed whites and held them for questioning. We knew exactly what that was like.

Finally things got a little out of hand and shops were broken into and looted. A house was burned down and even a priest was beaten and very badly injured. White people arriving by air were told that they weren't allowed to stay and those trying to cross the frontier were interrogated and questioned by specially appointed officers before being allowed to pass. In Cotonou a nine o'clock curfew was established and, for a few days, the roads were closed.

One night, about a week after all this, we were woken up by the sound of several shrill blasts of a police whistle. We called out of the tent, asking what the devil it was they wanted in the middle of the night and they answered back that we had to get up, they had some questions to ask us.

We came out of the tent but couldn't see a thing because the men were dazzling us with their torches. Finally they shone them to the ground and began to aggressively interrogate us concerning our "mission" there, who we were and just about anything that suddenly occurred to them. Only one of them was a policeman; the others were the village chief and his interpreter, as the chief couldn't speak French. After telling them as calmly as possible the things they were curious to know, they asked us if we didn't have something to give them so that we could remain friends. We told them that we would visit the chief in his village before we left the area and this seemed to be enough for them and they left. Relieved, we returned to the tent to wait until morning.

An afternoon some days later, two policemen drove into our camp in their little van and snooped around the place and similarly asked a string of strangely irrelevant questions that had nothing to do with our being there. This was very obviously the prelude to the usual racket of extracting a bribe. Before they left, they asked if we had anything for them to drink and, when we said that we hadn't, they threatened us that if we should cause any trouble then they would have us beaten.

The significant business of the Dahomean police force seemed to consist of intimidation and extortion, anyone, black or white who they considered sufficiently vulnerable to this sort of shakedown was fair game. Had we remained at the German Project, they would never have dared to offend us.

Only half an hour later, they returned obviously disappointed with the failure of the earlier visit. This time they took my notes from the table and asked for our passports and insisted that we go with them to the police station. At that time, Karl was fishing on the lake in our inflatable canoe and I was ordered to go and fetch him. Fortunately, just at that moment, two African friends of ours drove up. The one, Mr. Fassassi was to take charge of the German project when the German director was due to leave in April while his companion was to assume Mr. Hanke's job when he left. Mr. Fassassi was educated in Germany. I asked him in German to keep an eye on our belongings while I went to fetch Karl, as I didn't trust the two policemen at all. He agreed and I went to the edge of the lake and shouted myself hoarse until, at last, the wind carried my voice and Karl heard what amounted to a whisper. Soon he paddled up the shore where the police glowered, insisting that we both go with them. We explained that we had all our things around the place, including the tent, and that it was unwise to leave them unattended. After a lot of persuasion, they said that I was to stay and Karl was to go with them, together with the two from Tori-Cada who had to vouch for us that we were, in fact, tourists and not "up to anything."

Before they left they noticed that I'd also written some letters and not yet put them in envelopes and, only, after a great deal of trouble, did we manage to persuade them that they were simply letters to the family and nothing important, which was just as well because I'd written to some friends telling them of all our troubles in Dahomey. It would have been unfortunate if someone at the police station had been able to read English.

Karl arrived back well over an hour later in the car belonging to our two friends and explained what had happened. Karl knew some curious folk rhymes and chants that the native men who we had come to know used disrespectfully amongst themselves. One of them runs: *Everything is going wrong. What shall we do? Let's make a fetish.* This at first seemed enormously flippant in a country that was the traditional birthplace of voodoo. But the irreverence of it revealed a tell-tale sign

160

that voodoo was also the object of a mild ridicule and no longer intimidated the younger men in the way that cultism had once gripped entire communities. Animism had been reduced in the twentieth century to an abstract of superstitious practices and rituals. And it was also a smoke screen, concealing what amounted to a thuggish system of graft and extortion.

Karl had learned several such sayings in the Fon language which he now used with great skill to win over the two officers by making them laugh. Karl had an enormous and contagious sense of humor. He realized that the police were drunk anyway and it was not hard to get them laughing. By the time they arrived at the police station, they were all the best of friends. If it had not been for the commissioner they would have gone for a beer and all would have been well. But the commissioner turned out to be just as rapacious as his officers. He aggressively interrogated the two African men with Karl, more than he did Karl himself. Telling them to translate my notes, Mr. Fassassi replied, "I do not speak English but the notes appear to be a few pages of a travelogue." It was remarkable that the commissioner showed such little respect for Mr. Fassassi because he was of a prestigious, professional family in Dahomey. But these were flagrantly lawless times exacerbated by political unrest and an extravagant dissemination of Marxist propaganda that caused considerable unrest.

The commissioner turned to Karl. "So you are a natural scientist. What is this called?" He reached behind him and plucked a leaf from a bush beyond his office window.

"I do not know," Karl replied. "I know about reptiles, amphibians and fish which is of course a huge subject."

Finally the commissioner merely ordered a sack of maize from the cooperative at Tori-Cada and let everybody go. Our two friends said that had we given the two policemen some money in the first place, then we would have saved ourselves all that trouble. They would have gone away again and left us in peace. It was the same lesson all over again and we began to wonder if we should practice a refinement of the graft by offering small tips. Later, we elaborated this further by inviting difficult officers and the sometimes belligerent airport agents that we dealt with when we shipped our animals simply to join us for a beer. And it worked

161

miracles.

We decided to stay in Dahomey just long enough to explore northward and then to send off another consignment of reptiles before leaving for Nigeria and Cameroon.

We needed to extend our visas and approached the appropriate agency with that in mind. "A visa extension! Why do you want to stay here any longer? Another three months! What are you up to?" The usual refrain.

The visa officer was a large man who had the demeanor of low blood sugar that we had often detected in a country adept in brewing and distilling, with hidden moonshine stills concealed throughout the bush.

"We wish to visit Abomey." I replied. "We are going to see Mr. Fèliho."

"You know Mr. Fèliho?" He looked impressed.

"We are friends with his son."

Our passports were duly stamped and we were once more on our way out of Cotonou.

Raymond Fèliho, who was Marcel's assistant, had once invited us to visit his home in Abomey. His father was very wealthy. Mr. Fèliho had purchased twelve trucks from Germany in order to expand his haulage company and Mercedes had given him a thirteenth truck for free. When Karl had met Raymond again in Cotonou the invitation was reiterated. Raymond himself had been harassed by the Cotonou police and he had hit one of the officers. But when they discovered who he was he was immediately released. The mere mention of the name Fèliho worked magic more effectively than any grisgris.

11. ABOMEY
The Bloody Kings and the Throne of Skulls

So far most of the time spent in Dahomey had been tied up with repairing the van and we were more or less stuck in one place so that we had been unable to visit the historically very interesting town of Abomey. We intended to export a second consignment of reptiles before we left Dahomey and we thought we might be able to purchase some animals at the markets. We decided to combine the two and visit Abomey to increase our stock of animals.

It was interesting that living, wild creatures were also for sale in the markets. Usually they arrived ready for the table. But, in a country of pervasive grisgris and magical fetishes, every animal had some kind animistic value, not only for its skin or its bones and teeth but also its blood.

We had often seen fantôme statues and wayside shrines that showed signs of recent blood sacrifice. A fantôme representation constructed of hardened clay might be smeared with chicken blood and feathers or the shattered jaw and teeth of some hapless creature would be seen embedded in the form.

Some miles before we reached Abomey was a less historically significant town, although of the same size, called Bohicon. We immediately saw from the basket balancing African women, who were heading towards the town on both sides of the road, that today must be market day. The nearer we approached, the denser became the crowds of people on their way, heavily laden with wares to sell. We parked our van right opposite the market beneath a leafy, blossom covered tree and strolled across to look around. Along the journey we bought enough *akassa* to last us for several days. Akassa is a thick maize pâté wrapped in a packet of banana leaves. It was very cheap and filling and became one of our principle foods. Three akassa packets were enough for a good meal for one person. In addition, we bought a supply of "gumbo" or okra with which we made a tasty sauce. We were now subsisting almost exclusively upon the same regional diet as the Africans. And this necessary eccentricity opened all kinds of doors to us. As whites we remained curiosities but also somehow more accessible simply because we ate the

163

same food and, for the most part, lived in the bush just as they did.

But at this market we were not looking to buy food. We hoped to discover some live reptiles for sale.

A thorough search revealed nothing of interest but just as we were about to leave the market to continue on our journey, we came across a group of stalls huddled together in one corner and laid out with all sorts of strange and astonishing items. As the salesmen saw us coming, they came to meet us, loaded up with armfuls of carved wooden figures, skins and hides, and one of them had a live but wounded chameleon. We followed them back to their tables and they presented us with the heads of birds, the skulls of monkeys, the skins of snakes, in fact, everything necessary to make the finest grisgris. Then, one man, who had only one hand, led us quietly to one side and produced a mysterious medicine bottle from the folds of his robe. The bottle was full of bits of bone, dried grass and grain. Half covering the bottle with his stumped arm, he whispered to us that it was a good luck grisgris that should be tasted and smeared on the face every day. I wondered if it was the same ointment that Gabriel used.

Like a conspirator to a confidant, he whispered his price and we whispered back that we would think about it. From one of the other stalls, we bought the hide of an antelope for very little and a live tortoise that we would export with the other animals we hoped to soon catch or buy.

At this time, we exclusively caught animals at night. It was colder and the reptiles were slower and sometimes they would scarcely move at all to avoid us. Using flashlights, we would scan the bushes and quickly spot a chameleon or a small snake reclining in the branches. Chameleons glow green like a Christmas tree light in the glare of a torch and they are easy to lift from their roost like picking a fruit.

We left Bohicon and continued on our way to visit the museum of the past kings of Abomey. It seemed that we were the only visitors that day and had the vast forecourt to ourselves to park in. We bought our tickets and followed the young African guide through the outer courtyard to the main door leading to the palace itself. The compound was a group of oblong huts covered with corrugated iron roofing and surrounded by a high wall. Set in the palace walls were painted terracotta

164

models of the emblems of some of the kings.

In the first hut, called the throne room, there were carved wooden throne-stools of the various kings and around the walls hung a linen "tapestry" depicting the history of Dahomey. Colored figures similarly cut from dyed linen were sewn onto the tapestry. The guide explained what everything was supposed to mean and then hastily led us off to a second hut which housed the totems of the various kings. They were made of bronze and seemed too recent to be historical. But there was one figure made of wood that looked most authentic. It was very old and was the figure of a woman about three feet high, carrying in one hand a moon and supposed to be carrying in the other a sun. Our guide told us that it had been made over two hundred years before and had been a war goddess who could change day to night or night to day, depending on whether the warriors were winning the battle or losing it. The arms of the statue were movable and in battle it was supposed to come to life and move to regulate day and night, depending on which condition was most advantageous for the soldiers.

In the yard outside there was a row of old, black canons that had been traded from the Portuguese for fourteen slaves each. The Dahomeans sold enemy captives to European slavers for three hundred years. Presumably their enemies practiced a similar commerce of their own. In another yard, there was a round hut that contained two more round huts inside. The clay walls had been built with the aid of the blood of forty-one captives from another tribe.

Along the wall of yet another building were the bones of hundreds and hundreds of animals that had been sacrificed at various rituals in bygone days.

The last hut contained relics from the time of the coming of the first white men. A collection of flintlocks, swords, pots and jars, an umbrella, things that had been presented to the kings throughout the ages by the slave traders and other merchants.

Some of the carved figures were impressive both for their sculpture and the earth-tone coloring. Animals motifs were consistent throughout though we did not know their specific significance.

The king's throne rested upon human skulls but was otherwise unimpressive. I wondered how significant you had to be to support the king's throne with your skull. Surely not just any old skull would do.

We left the museum and crossed an area where there was a small market place. A couple of young women called to us and I thought it was the usual harassment and demand for *cadeau*. But it was not. Karl had met these young women before on his visit to Raymond's house in Cotonou. They were daughters of Mr. Fèliho who, at first, I just ignored and tried to avoid. I recognized my mistake and we greeted and chatted with them for a while. They seemed both pleasant and well educated, speaking fluent French. It seemed that Raymond was still in Cotonou.

At about midday, we left Abomey and took the road in the direction of Cové which was very rough and dusty. We wanted to visit the river there to see if we could spot some crocodiles or perhaps find a native who might have trapped them in his nets and have some small ones to sell.

After passing through Cové, we arrived at a crossroads that was guarded by a huge crucifix with a copper verdigris figure of Christ. It seemed to me that this was the Christian answer to Voodoo, similarly situated at a road junction just as the Dahomean fantôme or the fetish shrine elsewhere. We were not sure which of the tracks led to the river, but there was a sign pointing the way to a monastery where we decided to go to ask for directions.

Within a few minutes we arrived and, driving through a huge archway, we parked in the shade of the monastery wall.

Before we even got out of the van, a monk appeared, a tall, bearded, European man in a faded yellow habit. He welcomed us graciously.

We explained that we had just stopped by to find out which of the roads led to the river, but the amiable man was so interested in our journey and adventures that we talked and talked, suddenly realizing that it was almost sunset and hardly prudent to drive out searching for a camping spot in the darkness of the bush.

The abbot remarked that it had indeed become late and invited us to stay in one of the newly built guest rooms beneath a water tower just a few yards from the main part of the monastery.

We were very glad to accept, being quite weary after our long journey in the heat along the terrible, dusty washboard roads. The abbot fetched the key and led us to the water tower, where he showed us two rooms on the first floor with bunk beds, mosquito nets, and showers. We made ourselves at home in the first room and prepared our evening meal in the monastery kitchen.

There were two Africans and seven other French Benedictine monks there, some of whom had been in Dahomey continuously during the nine years since the monastery had first started. They had built up enormous plantations of oil palms, coffee, fruit, and vegetables and had constructed the very beautiful monastery and the numerous out buildings. A clinic and dispensary was established to care for the local population and treat them for simple injuries as well as tropical diseases.

We washed away the sweat and dirt that had accumulated on our bodies during the day and slept on the straw mattresses of the bunk beds to the sound of the monks chanting at evening prayer.

It was an extraordinary contrast. We had glimpsed a little of the savage brutality of the slave kingdom of old Dahomey. We had seen the walls mixed with human blood and the skull-supported throne from where ruled the ancient line of predatory despots who thought nothing of human life. And now, through the myriad bush noises of the night, wafted the angelic, beautiful harmonies of the Benedictines at their prayers.

The next morning we got up at first light and saw that the monks were already about their various duties. We were eager to take a look at the river and, after a hasty breakfast, we said goodbye to everyone. After being made to promise to revisit them before leaving the area, they wished us good luck and we drove off to see what we could see.

We arrived back at the monastery sooner than we expected. We had arrived at the Zou Ouémé river, but had found so many Africans fishing and farming along the banks that our hopes of seeing crocodiles rapidly disappeared and there was obviously no possibility of camping there in peace.

Returning to the monastery, the abbot produced a map of the area and showed us a spot less disturbed, along the river half a dozen miles away where we might camp in peace. We thanked him and drove off once more to the new place, which was indeed much quieter but nevertheless, after two days, we found nothing of interest. It was denuded of wildlife.

On the Sunday, we returned to Abomey intending to visit the market to see if we could buy some more tortoises or chameleons, but we had been misinformed and were told that the market wasn't until the next day.

We decided to visit another monastery to see if we could camp in their grounds for the one night. It was increasingly difficult to camp without being harassed by natives crying, *Yovo cadeau!* and thrusting their open hands in our faces.

Just a couple of miles from the town, we turned off the road and followed a sign pointing to the monastery of St. Paul.

It was roughly midday as we drew up in the courtyard, parked beneath the shade of two mango trees growing tightly together and were welcomed by an African monk. We told him that we were waiting for market day and looking for a peaceful spot where we could pitch our tent.

But the very kind novitiate insisted we take one of the rooms reserved for visitors and, in the same breath, invited us to have dinner with them that evening. He then looked at his watch and, smiling, hurried off out of sight, leaving us to arrange ourselves in our new quarters.

As we were moving in and getting ourselves organized another monk appeared and welcomed us. He was a Frenchman who had been in Africa for the last half a dozen years and taught general science in the monastery school. We showed him the few animals we had already collected for our consignment, including the three different snakes, which interested him immensely as he had a small collection, himself, preserved in alcohol. He led us off to his laboratory and showed us not only the snakes but also animal skeletons, which he had prepared himself, his insect collection and some small animals that he had set in plastic resin. He told us of another school in Bohicon that was run by Spanish monks where the science master, Brother Alloy, had a very much larger collection of preserved snakes. Brother Alloy was gathering samples for a colleague, Dr. Roman, who, ironically, we knew personally. We had met him in Upper Volta, where we had visited him to view his reptile collection in order to learn of the species of the region.

We decided to drive over and visit Brother Alloy that very afternoon, hoping to view the animals he had managed to collect.

Brother Alloy was very friendly and knowledgeable. He was delighted with our connection to his colleague, Dr. Roman. We enjoyed a cup of coffee and then he showed us around the school and afterwards led us to his classroom where, in a glass cabinet, he kept his collection of snakes. He had found at least thirty different types from the green mamba and the puff adder to the tiny, harmless burrowing python. Karl was able to converse with the scientist through their mutual knowledge of the Latin names. I was able to take up the shortfall with my French.

That evening, after an excellent meal at the monastery of St. Paul and armed with nets and torches, we combed one building after another, catching geckos and sleeping agama, the science master having showed us all the best hiding places. We caught enough to make a reasonable consignment and decided to head speedily back to Tori-Cada the next day. We knew we could gather a considerable number of frogs at night and then to head to the airport at Cotonou.

We arrived at the market very early the next morning and bought five more tortoises and two large chameleons, asking everywhere where we could buy small crocodiles. Before we left, we met the one-handed man again and happened to mention that we were looking for crocodiles. To our surprise, he told us that he knew where there were two for sale near his village and he agreed to go with us to show us the place. We left the market and drove once more in the direction of Cové and then along a very rough and remote track and finally a winding path through the bush. The van lurched and bumped along until we eventually reached the village.

The villagers were apprehensive and uncertain about us as no one could speak French except for our one-handed salesman. He explained what it was we were looking for and one of the younger men ran off to fetch two small crocodiles, both under a foot long and very beautifully colored. Then our guide began to translate what the men had to say. He told us that crocodiles were grisgris for them and if we were to buy them and keep them in our "lorry" we could be sure that we would never have a breakdown and, for the two together, they wanted what amounted to a sack of maize.

We thanked them for the valuable information and told them that we wouldn't pay more than a quarter of that price but finally agreed to pay one third. Everyone was content and we set off in haste to reach Tori-Cada by evening.

Now all we needed was a few frogs from the Marigot and a box to pack them all in. We left soon after we had driven the one-handed man back to the market and by evening, reached the German Project and found our African friend, Germain, who invited us to pitch our tent behind his house, which we readily accepted.

We shared the evening meal of maize pâté with the family and then Germain took us to one side and spoke very quietly. That evening there would be a meeting of the "fantômes" at the crossroads and he would try to persuade them to let us attend. He told us that normally, when people go for a first time, they must pay a great deal of money and buy refreshments for all those taking part.

"But I'll tell the others that you are in a fantôme circle in Togo and have only come to visit them to compare the music and see how things are done in Dahomey."

This seemed to be a ridiculous ruse but we decided that Germain knew best.

After the meal was over, the family slowly started to prepare for sleep and we left with Germain to visit a friend of his in a neighboring village. After the usual lengthy greetings and the traditional glass of sorabi, we all went off into the woods behind the house where the farmer had his moonshine still.

Private distilling of sorabi was illegal in Dahomey, but Germain told us that practically everyone did it, everyone who had the palm trees to make the palm wine first. This still consisted of a huge oil drum full with fermented palm sap that murmured over a log fire. A tube led from the drum to a tank of water which was another oil drum cut in half. There it cooled and the spirit condensed dripping, steadily into a bottle.

We bought the half liter necessary as a gift to the fantômes and, at about ten o'clock, made our way to the crossroads, armed with tape recorder and camera with flashbulbs.

We could already hear the wailing in the distance and Germain told us that the leaders of the group were calling the others together by their secret names.

The stars were well hidden behind a dense rain cloud and we

170

didn't know if there was a moon or not that night; it was very dark!

When we were only about fifty yards away, Germain left us alone, taking the bottle of sorabi and telling us to wait quietly while he explained to the fantômes why he had brought two whites along. Ten minutes later, he returned and softly called to us to come, warning us again that, if we were asked, we were to say that we were already in a fantôme circle in Togo.

We stumbled down the road in the darkness and, as we came nearer, the wailing became a hollow howling until we arrived and were bluntly greeted by the fantôme leaders and told to conceal ourselves somewhere out of the way and to keep silent.

The howling and screaming was produced by yelling through a huge ox horn. We had heard this sound several times when we had been out catching reptiles at night. Once we had imitated it and called back. Suddenly a complete silence had descended. I wonder who they must have thought we were. Authentic fantôme spirits perhaps?

The roll-call continued until about a dozen members of the group had arrived and the circle was complete. One of the men was completely naked. They started a fire and began to make a different music, striking hollow sounding bells and cymbals in accompaniment with the steer horns. Suddenly everything was interrupted as someone noticed the headlights of an approaching car. They darted off like rabbits into the bushes, dragging us behind them particularly concerned that our white skins would be revealed in the headlights. When the danger of being recognized was over, we all resumed our positions again and the fantômes began their ritual singing to the fetish fantôme, which was supposed to give them information whether thieves were out or not. They sang to it three times, one of them wearing a dried grass costume and dancing wildly, representing its dis-incarnated spirit.

As time passed, Germain crept over to us and whispered that we could now tape the singing if we wanted to and take a photograph, but we may never show it to any woman and we must give it to them when it is developed. We agreed and, during the course of the night, Karl took three photographs while I discreetly recorded the entire event.

All at once everyone jumped to their feet and we were told that they were going to pay a visit to someone who lived down by the swamp.

171

Howling, wailing, screeching, and shouting, the sinister group made its way hastily down a side path towards the Marigot, with us drawn along in their midst. A couple of times Karl fell back to ask Germain various things about the fantômes and this annoyed the others very much and he was told to keep silent and to stay in the group. Once down by the Marigot, we got into trouble again. The moon had at last escaped from behind the rain cloud and our white skins reflected the light and they howled at us to keep in the shadows.

By the house, the men bellowed threateningly until, at last, a very frightened and timid voice answered. Later Germain told us that the fantômes had asked for refreshment and the farmer had promised them ample the next day but that he had nothing to offer in the house at that moment. They terrorized the poor man for half an hour before finally heading off in a frenzied knot of mayhem, back to the original place at the crossroads.

When we had first arrived in Tori-Cada three months earlier, we had asked the Africans about the fantômes and were told that it was their prevention against theft. But, after what we had seen that night, we realized that there was, in fact, far more to it than that. The fantômes were the controlling force in the community. They kept respect for themselves by scaring the wits out of the Dahomean people just as the police did more overtly. The man who lived by the marshes was obviously intimidated by the nocturnal gang and its claim of supernatural authority. They merely wanted more drink. They kept the identity of the members and details about their rituals top secret. No woman was allowed to know anything about the circle because, we were told, "they would talk too much!"

Discipline within the circle was very strict, as we saw for ourselves. That night one of the group fell asleep by the fire and the others pounced upon him and beat him with sticks so that he should realize the seriousness of it all and never do such a thing a second time.

Returning to Tori-Cada, we still had our frogs to catch which we did easily being very familiar with the region around the Project from previous excursions.

The next morning we left for Cotonou very early as we had a great deal to do. The previous week we had written to the airport to make

172

a Telex reservation for the animals, but as yet we hadn't even a box to pack them in. We met the freight representative in Cotonou but he told us that he had only received our letter the previous evening. Clearly nothing was arranged. We would have to wait several days. That was too long. We were very annoyed but this was Africa. Who said anything was easy? But if we had to wait those few days then a lot of the animals might perish because they had to be fed regularly and that was not always easy to manage. The frogs, for example needed living flies. The flight to Europe was quick and they could last a day or two without difficulty but not an additional four or five. We assumed that our letter had been intercepted and consequently delayed as had been the case with one that had arrived from Europe, already opened!

There was still one chance; we decided to leave immediately for Togo, where the service to Europe was much more frequent and we would send the animals from there.

Karl was a master at packing the creatures, making sure that they had sufficient moisture while he gave the chameleons a leafy branch to cling to. Other creatures were housed in individual cloth bags, each within a separate cell within the box so that they would not unnerve each other. The TelEx communication was essential to ensure that the airport in Paris would know to keep the animals warm before they were shipped on, in this case, to Holland.

The next day was a Sunday and, at eight-thirty in the morning, our box, full of live reptiles, left for Holland from Togo Airport. Another successful consignment from West Africa.

12. AGADJI
An Oasis in the Bush

We were relieved that our shipment of animals was on its way but, rather than continue with our travels, we were obliged to remain in the coastal region of Togo for a while longer. Once again, we were having mechanical problems with our van. Fortunately, I had become adept at stripping the engine down and systematically rebuilding it once more with replacement parts. But Karl and I began to have serious doubts about the wisdom of using air-cooled vehicle in the tropics. It was different with the commonplace little Citroen deux-chevaux. Somehow the simplicity and unsophisticated nature of its construction made it ideal in most circumstances and it was easy to cobble a simple repair if it broke down, even though it, too, had an air-cooled engine. The Project at Tori-Cada had numerous Volkswagens and they, also, kept breaking down, usually from overheating because the engine was concealed in the back where there was very little airflow. Fortunately, they had a complete workshop and mechanics who kept the vehicles in running order.

We needed a garage space of some sort. A complete engine overhaul was hardly practical while camped on the beach. It had to be somewhere out of the wind and away from the sand.

We discussed this problem and decided to simply ask a European with an empty shed or garage if we could work there for a few days and perform the necessary repairs.

We limped into Lomé and drove a few blocks around the European quarter. We were in luck. A French lady was walking towards her house and we drew up and explained our situation.

She was very eager to help and assured us that we could effect the repairs and even stay in a small out-building to the rear of her property while we did the work.

Soon we were gratefully settled in and already preparing to strip the motor down when the French lady's husband arrived. He was a Corsican businessman named Robert and a marvelous character. He was extremely forthright and candid and that nature was revealed in his powerful appearance. His hair was cut severely short and seemed to be composed, brush-like, of thick strands of wire. His head was pear-shaped

175

with a broad and powerful chin. The rest of his body was similarly tapered towards his powerful legs while his skin was a shade or two darker than that of his Parisian wife. He seemed to fill the space wherever he happened to be. I wondered how he would handle the corrupt authorities with their nasty shenanigans. Nobody would mess with this guy. He and his family had lived in Bangui, the Central African Republic but, during Bokassa's reign of terror, he had finally had to flee, escaping with others down the Ubangi river to safety. He also told me that many Frenchmen who had escaped and returned to France still owed him money. He had a little book with all their names and he was going debt collecting when they eventually return to Europe. In the meantime, he and his wife, who was a splendid cook, were planning to establish a fine French restaurant in Lomé.

His wife was high-spirited and somehow also coquettish in the way of a blond French woman. They were both great fun to be around.

While Robert was intrigued by our animal capturing enterprise he was particularly impressed when he heard the tapping of my typewriter. I explained that I was writing about our various adventures and exploits as they occurred. I believe that he hoped that he might also receive a mention. The typing seemed to put people on their most agreeable behavior. I found the same thing in Ouagadougou at the Austrian School where the director himself clearly hoped to be included with a favorable acknowledgment.

In terms of snake catching, Robert described how, in Bangui, he was in the bush and while seated on a log a snake had wriggled up the leg of his trousers. He had slammed the ball of his hand against his own thigh, dispatching the reptile but giving himself an almighty bruise.

In the evenings, they would often sit outside on their front porch and sometimes we would join them. "It is very pleasant in the evenings", mused Robert. "Sometimes I also like to read. There is nothing like a munching on a juicy apple while engrossed in a good book."

Next door to our friends was a young English woman who worked for Oxfam. "You must go and visit her", said Robert. "She is from England like you".

The following afternoon I decided to introduce myself to the neighbor. Jane Harrison was very sweet and intrigued to meet us both so

176

that we could relate some of our adventures. We invited her to join us on her neighbor's porch. Robert and his wife were away for the afternoon.

Jane worked as a secretary in Lomé. Oxfam was endeavoring to encourage small business growth as well as to assist with famine relief in the Sahel. The drought lasted from 1970 and continued for fifteen years. Over a million people perished from Senegal to Ethiopia, along the region between the Sahara desert and the more verdant savanna to the South. Their pastoral livelihood was destroyed through the decimation of their livestock.

Jane was a quiet and gentle girl with a warm sense of humor. While we were in Lomé she had two house guests, both teachers from England, who worked near Niamey, in Niger. One of the young women was suffering from a terrible cold while her friend was chronically adverse to mosquitoes and being bitten almost brought her to tears. Her plight was a very unfortunate one. There was no escaping the little demons. In fact I had sometimes imagined myself being bitten when there were none. There was a slight tickle on my arm and I imagined a mosquito piercing into the flesh but there was nothing except perhaps one hair merely brushing against another. The poor young teacher feared the mosquitoes dreadfully and it was if they sought her out.

Jane's house had a large area of concrete that was a sort of a carport and she allowed me to work on the Volkswagen engine there where the task could be performed much easier than next door because there was more space to work and it was shaded.

Meanwhile Karl went fishing from the Lomé pier where he became friendly with the Togolese fishermen who were also working there. Sometimes a man would catch a large fish and his partner would jump into the ocean to retrieve it, concerned that it might writhe off the hook somewhere between the water and the pier twenty feet above. One man proudly showed Karl the scars on his leg from the bite of a barracuda.

Another manner of fishing for those without a boat was to swim with a long line of baited hooks far out beyond the breakers. The coastal Togolese were superb swimmers. Their livelihood depended on it. We watched the men, line in hand, swim steadily out to sea, avoiding the power of the surf that would otherwise have thrown them back onto the beach by swimming under the waves as they approached. Then far beyond, almost completely out of sight, a tiny head would be seen turning about and the fisherman would steadily work his way shoreward until the surf carried him the final distance to the beach. The line would remain in the water in this way while the men set others and then waited for that optimum time when experience had taught them to retrieve their lines and the deserved catch.

Karl caught a huge orange colored fish from the pier. He did not jump in the water but retrieved his prize by winding the line steadily around the board of wood that he used as a reel. Promptly, after showing off his fabulous catch, he took the ocean-fresh fish and sold it at a nearby hotel.

While in Lomé we heard of a Frenchman who was also in the animal exporting business but on a much larger scale. We drove to visit him as soon as the van was repaired. It was just a few miles from Jane's house. Unfortunately, the Frenchman was not at home but some of his Togolese helpers were glad to show us the animals that he had in tanks and cages. There were over one hundred Royal pythons (*Python regius*) in one enclosure. The royal python is considered, along with the chameleon, a sacred creature in Dahomey. Apparently, the Togolese had no such scruples. Many of these creatures must have been brought in by the natives. There were far too many for one man to have caught. Additionally, there were at least fifty crocodiles, several hundred parrots and a cage full of monkeys.

I could see the wheels of Karl's mind turning as he recognized that if we, too, established a permanent base and stayed in one location we could greatly profit from a systematic approach towards animal catching that would be far more efficient. We were both weary of the long delays we had to endure while waiting for our funds to arrive by mail from Europe but if we started to think on a larger scale we could then manage this thing far more efficiently.

We discussed the idea at length. For some time I had considered our plan of continuing on to Nigeria and Cameroon in much the same manner as we had traveled everywhere else, with a certain dread. Nigeria was the notorious pariah of West Africa. If we imagined the ever-present graft, harassment and theft of Ghana and Dahomey to be bad, from

178

travelers through Nigeria we had only heard grimmer stories. There seemed to be no reason to go there. I expressed my concern and pointed out that Upper Volta (Burkina Faso) had been very good for us. We knew exactly where to go to find hundreds of geckos, turtles and frogs and it was a benign country where we had a number of friends and contacts. We also knew the airport and the somewhat crusty employees quite well which would expedite our enterprise. Karl was in whole-hearted agreement and, from that time on, he further elaborated the idea and conceived of an approach that seemed very workable.

We spent roughly three months in Togo after we left Dahomey, most of that time in Lomé due to the renewed trouble with the van and then a later disaster of a blown up engine. We were very grateful for the kindness and hospitality of the English girl, Jane Harrison. When Robert and his wife moved away to another house, Jane had us stay with her. Sadly, soon after we left Togo that August, Jane's Oxfam contract expired and she set off for home, unfortunately, only reaching Amsterdam where she was taken very ill, went into a coma and never awoke. That was the 12th of August, 1973. Nobody seemed to know for certain what she died of but an Oxfam volunteer who we later met in Ouagadougou said that he thought she had died of malaria. I suspect that also a broken heart had much to do with it. Jane and Karl had grown very fond of each other and I am convinced that she had thoroughly fallen in love with him. Their parting must have been devastating to her.

When we were finally mobile again, we were also almost out of money and had to get to work straight away catching animals.

We headed north to a town called Atakpamé, which lies among the forest covered hills about seventy miles away from Lomé. Unfortunately, our tent, after a year and a half of use in tropical Africa, had been soaked by torrential rains so often during the rainy season and then dried out crisp afterwards by the terrific heat of the sun on the dry days between storms that it had become utterly threadbare. Even the fly canvas was no longer waterproof. We could camp in the van but sometimes if we found ourselves near a mission, of which there were hundreds if not thousands in West Africa, we would ask for shelter and sleep upon the floor of one of their buildings in our sleeping bags. It was also increasingly expedient to do so after our several alarming encounters with both official and unauthorized thieves, particularly in Dahomey. Often a mission might be found in the most unexpected places in the middle of the bush. There they would be running schools, clinics, agricultural centers, and cooperatives. If we were near one of these we would stop by and ask if we could put up for the night. Often they were very pleased to have European visitors and we were always made very welcome and comfortable. Sometimes we found that the missionaries lived off the land, building up small-holdings or even farms and selling the produce. This was the case in the village of Agadji which must be the only village in Togo with street lighting.

Incongruities, such as street lighting in the bush, were a source of considerable astonishment to me. I never ceased to be amazed at the oddness, when indigenous rural culture, bound to the land in every respect, was suddenly overlapped, in stark contrast, by European culture.

Once we had been driving in the bush along an isolated track when we had suddenly come across a small storefront structure built of adobe and capped with a tin roof. Standing by the entrance was a stocky Frenchman with a rounded belly. With a Gaulois cigarette hanging from his lips, he was the epitome of Parisian *boulanger* grafted here haphazardly upon the African landscape.

In Togo and Ghana we had seen dug-out fishing boats fashioned from a single tree, just as they had been made since time immemorial, but equipped with out-board motors. Or, sometimes we saw a native woman in the bush wearing a bra, while all her companions gathering firewood or hauling water, remained topless because, traditionally, a woman's breasts were not considered sexually provocative.

Agadji was rife with such contradictions whereby European culture and the ancient customs and traditions of the indigenous people coexisted in eccentric correspondence.

There were two missions in Agadji, one run by Catholic nuns and the other by two Catholic priests. All of them came from the Alsace-Lorraine district of France and they were bilingual in French and German, in fact trilingual, because they also spoke the local native dialect. There are thirty-nine indigenous languages in Togo. We ourselves used French or, if necessary, the sign language of hands and feet.

Between them and, with the assistance of half a dozen African girls who were being trained to take over the mission when the Europeans would eventually leave, they ran a school for African women, teaching them improved nutrition, hygiene, and handiwork.

A few miles from Agadji our engine actually exploded. Something had stressed inside and broken through the housing, spreading hot black oil all over the place. This time there would be no simple repairs using recycled parts. We would have to find a whole new engine. We walked to the mission and one of the kind monks made arrangements to get us towed to the convent where the nuns offered to let us stay and make repairs. Karl set off hitching to Lomé where he hoped he could procure a motor and conveniently visit his girl friend, Jane Harrison.

When we arrived at the mission it was recess time, which lasts until after the harvest. The women were needed to work in the fields. Consequently, the classrooms were all empty and, as there were no guest rooms, the nuns allowed us to move into one of them for shelter.

Only a couple of weeks previously a huge old Afrormosia tree (*Pericopsis elata*) behind the school had been struck by lightning during a violent storm and had fallen and smashed the shower rooms adjoining the newly completed school house. Consequently, there were now crowds of Togolese workmen about the place, rebuilding the structure. There appeared to be an apprenticeship system whereby the young men were indentured to learn the trade. This was an entirely European concept. Typically, in a village, the entire community was involved in the construction of its own dwellings and even small children would participate, carrying bundles of straw back to the village for thatching. Apparently, those who actually did the work at the mission were the apprentices who were not only unpaid but had to pay the master themselves before they could begin their training and again, upon its completion, after the three or four years. In theory, they could then in turn employ apprentices of their own to do their donkey work for them.

The former communal practice of sharing everything produced other consequences. It was extremely difficult for the African entrepreneur to establish a viable business. This was because they could never accrue sufficient capital. There was always a relative or a neighbor who needed something and the savings of a small-businessman were constantly depleted. Thus, in this sense, the communal system obstructed commerce and business. No one could open a garage or a store without a crowd of relatives hanging about and bleeding it dry. Businesses run by Africans always appeared run down and shabby. Those run by Arabs or Asians, however, thrived and profits were plowed back to increase the yield through continuing improvements.

Agadji was rather like an oasis in the middle of a forest, surrounded by mountains. It proved to be a paradise for snakes. The generator at the monastery provided electricity not only for the street lighting but also for the convent. The outside lights were kept on until about ten each evening and attracted thousands and thousands of flying insects. The insects, in turn, attracted fat toads who sat beneath the lights in groups and gorged themselves almost to bursting so that they could hardly waddle away to take cover when the lights went out. And, of course, the snakes liked toad for dinner and I was there to catch the snakes, as was Karl when he returned some two weeks later, but with much greater enthusiasm and success than I.

During our stay we caught rhombic night adders, harmless black house snakes, a burrowing snake, an interesting nonpoisonous colored snake that Karl could not identify and two cobras. One of the cobras I caught with the help of an African apprentice. He was enjoying his siesta after lunch, lying on the balcony in front of one of the classrooms when he noticed something gliding slowly along by the wall at the far end of the terrace. He jumped to his feet and howled in horror, attracting the attention of one of his colleagues and myself. We ran over to see what the matter was and saw the cobra, shiny black with a white zig-zag of spots down its back, thin but very long, with a yellow head and beady eyes. It was curled up trying not to be noticed, as shocked as the apprentice by the sudden commotion. All at once one of the apprentices started spitting wildly at the snake, so that the saliva ran down his chin. I was a little bewildered and quietly amused; this was the first time I had seen an African tackle a snake. I had heard once before that if they managed to get in the first spit before the cobra was able to, then the snake would become so scared or shocked that it would not spit back. Evidently that wasn't entirely true because the cobra had now raised itself and was looking towards us, very annoyed and dangerous.

Some distance behind me stood the second apprentice, holding an empty paper cement sack against his body in case the snake should suddenly make a mad rush at him and try to bite his legs. I borrowed his paper sack, ignoring his squeals of horror as he darted off to take cover behind a pile of bricks. I threw the sack over the snake's head. The first apprentice continued spitting, although God knows where all the saliva came from and the snake used the concealment of the sack as an opportunity to glide off to the safety of the flower bed. The second apprentice, covering his legs with another cement sack which he had found behind the pile of bricks, threw the first sack roughly in the direction of the snake, crushing some of the beautiful flowers. I trapped the snake between the earth and the cement sack with my foot and, following the writhing tail forward until I found the head, secured it and carried the snake off into captivity. The first apprentice was convinced that his spitting had confused the animal so much that it had been unable to spit back, but Karl later revealed that the creature was not a spitting cobra at all. Nevertheless, I secretly wished that Karl would do the snake catching part from now onwards. I did not relish the excitement.

While Karl was away I bought some simple foods from the local native market. The people was very nice in Agadji perhaps because of the kindnesses of the monks and nuns working there and improving their well-being. Or perhaps it was the prestige of street lighting. But nevertheless there was no harassment or begging nor the perpetual cry of *Yovo cadeau, Yovo cadeau* that was so annoying in the cities. A group of ladies was walking down the hillside, carrying baskets of bananas upon their heads. These were the largest bananas I had ever seen anywhere in West Africa or anywhere since, even in an European supermarket. Once again, the people of Agadji revealed a transition to modernity by charging me the correct price straight away without the customary haggling. The bananas were sweet and delicious. One was sufficient for a whole meal.

The nun in charge of the convent school was a lovely lady. She showed me her vegetable garden and expressed her joy at living off the land. They even grew and harvested their own grains, rice, in particular. As we walked down the rows of vegetables, I began to share in her delight. The setting was a magnificent and beautifully maintained clearing surrounded by a dense forest of giant trees. Togolese carpenters had even made the school house furniture from timber from a fallen forest tree.

183

The plain tables and chairs were simply and beautifully fashioned of exotic hardwood. Smiling, the nun reached down and picked a ripe eggplant that she offered me for my dinner. And, at that moment, I recognized a kindred spirit. I, too, loved to garden.

The forest around Agadji was very extensive and quite dense in parts and although, when Karl returned, we found enough reptiles to bring together a small consignment, there was otherwise surprisingly little other wildlife. Then one afternoon I went for a long walk as it was a cloudy day and quite cool. I had been walking for about two hours and hadn't seen a soul all that time, when I almost fell over an African as I followed the track around a corner, never expecting to find anyone crouching on all fours in my way.

"Shhh . . ." he whispered, grinning and signaling to me to crouch down beside him.

"Il ya beaucoup des monkeys là bas!"

His mixture of French and English was typical for Togo, especially here not far from the Ghanaian border. We had visited a native market nearby before our engine died and had seen currencies from both countries in use as well as products that were distinctly both English and French.

I crouched down beside the hunter and peered with him through the undergrowth in the direction he was pointing with his shotgun. I couldn't see anything, but I whispered an encouraging noise and wished him "Bon Hunting" and crept on my way, being careful not to frighten off his game.

I followed the path down into a valley where there was a stream with refreshingly cool water and there I rested on a mammoth weather-worn boulder. About me where enormous, towering trees covering the majestic mountains in every direction. Overwhelmed by the grandeur, I hoped that someone would not one day realize their commercial value as timber and destroy this incredible vista for temporary profit.

Feather white clouds were partly covering the sun which dappled through the canopy. I sat listening contentedly to the bubbling water, the cries of the birds, and the screeching of the monkeys—the monkeys!? Just a little way up the side of the mountain that I had just descended, a whole tribe of green monkeys were on their way, springing about through

184

the branches and flying recklessly from tree to tree. Every moment I expected to hear the shot from the hunter's gun echo across the valley, but none came and the monkeys continued their aerial journey, some stopping and nibbling at the fruits and leaves that they found irresistible along the way. I counted about thirty in all, but there must have been more, all the trees on the mountainside seemed to be swaying from the weight of them swinging from the branches. Finally, the last of the group was out of sight and I sighed, then decided to go as well, starting off slowly back up the mountain track the way I had come.

About half an hour or so had passed when I was met by the hunter, this time not on all fours but still grinning. I asked him if he had been lucky, but he didn't understand what I was saying and merely grinned all the more, wishing me "Good evening" as we passed one another by.

When Karl returned with another engine I ran to meet him, eager to get to work on the van. He had managed to get a lift from a European civil engineer who worked on the new Togolese highway project that lead north from Lomé. The engineer had brought Karl and his engine all the way to the Mission even though it was miles out of his way. It was unusual that he drove himself as most Europeans employed a chauffeur which helped the local economy. But he said he felt safer with his own driving.

Karl had one or two small adventures in Lomé, somehow managing to break Jane's kerosene refrigerator, piercing the coils with a knife while trying to extract a frozen fish. He and Jane had also dined at Robert's new restaurant where Robert's wife, convinced that they were in love, kept at them purring, *Mariage! Mariage!*

The engine was used of course but very serviceable and I had it quickly installed while Karl went to explore. He arrived back later and had in his possession some very large frogs that he had captured in a nearby pond. He preceded to skin them and fry them up. He offered me some but this time I refrained and preferred instead a modest bowl of rice. Karl said that the frogs tasted really good. I think I was beginning to feel unwell again with some intestinal problem and I simply couldn't face fried frog's legs.

One thing I had been able to do was prepare some tobacco from the market. I had constructed a small box exactly the size of the base of our van jack. Into the box I laid the leaves, lacing them with a splash of sorabi. I placed the box with the jack in it under the van and raised the back of the vehicle into the air. I left it this way for three days by which time the leaves had compressed into a solid brick of tobacco that could then be sliced for pipe tobacco. But it was very strong. Hopefully, the thick smoke would help keep the mosquitoes away from biting our necks and faces.

There was a tennis court at the Mission and Karl and I hit a ball around for a bit but neither of us were any good at the game. We decided instead to press on and, thanking our kind hosts, we set off on our return journey to Lomé.

Once more near the water it struck me what a beautiful country Togo was. The great rollers sweeping the Gulf of Guinea ponded the sandy shore. Giant coconut palms lined the strand where fishermen worked upon their boats, mended their nets and prepared their lines. Colorful fishing boats dotted the ocean or crashed through the surf returning with their catch.

It was now that we put into practice our idea of inviting port officers to join us for a beer. It worked and thereafter we had no difficulty entering the harbor. Karl was eager to try filming under water. He secured his 8mm movie camera inside an aquarium which he then sealed entirely with silicone, allowing a small hole for the remote cable that ran the camera. Binding the camera, he lowered it into the swell and waited for some sea creatures to swim by. Before long we caught a glimpse of a large turtle as it swam into view and click, Karl started the film rolling.

There were many turtles in these waters. One such creature had been captured alive by fishermen and we had seen the animal secured with rocks upside down on the beach, desperately trying to right itself.

On another visit to the harbor, we met some Germans from a cargo ship who invited us to have dinner with them. We ate and drank like kings. One of the officer's wives was intrigued by our adventures and asked if we had a scorpion. I had several dead ones preserved in plastic resin and I returned to the van on the quay and found a small black one that I had captured in Mali. It may have been a juvenile Emperor scorpion (*Pandinus imperator*), the largest scorpion in the world that can grow to a length of nine inches. In the African tradition where one good

186

gift deserves another, she gave me a bottle of German schnapps.

Finally we were about to leave. The chef suggested that he could give us some provisions for our trip north, particularly as the ship was being decommissioned upon its return from African. He filled a sack with tined foods of all kinds and even included a sack of potatoes. We had enough food to last us three months! Further, our friendliness at the harbor gate allowed us an easy retreat without any of the usual difficulties.

In Lomé, Karl said his goodbyes to Jane and we set off once more for Ghana.

13. OUAGADOUGOU
Much Better Hunting

We had to apply for our Upper Volta visas in Accra which we did without delay so that we could head north, away from that congested city and its odious tricksters and thieves.

The rainy season was approaching but it was still very hot and, becoming increasingly cautious, we stopped and rested frequently to allow the engine to cool down. On one of these occasions we noticed an oil leak and realized that we needed a new drive-shaft gasket. The severe West African climate, together with the punishing off-road and wash-board beating that the vehicle had endured during the last couple of years, demonstrated how the Volkswagen, wonderful on European roads and ideal in a moderate climate, was severely inept in the tropics. This was four-wheel drive Land Rover country. Had we traveled with such a vehicle, I think we would have fared much better. As it was, I had stripped the VW engine down several times already and was intimately familiar with every nut and bolt. But it would be pleasant not to be so constantly hobbled, dreading the next break-down.

We met an Englishman who stopped while we were examining the engine, trying to decide what to do, and he asked if we needed help. He was traveling north with his Ghanaian wife and their two daughters to visit his son who worked as a teacher up-county.

This was a remarkable family. The father, when he had first arrived in Ghana, had exported raw unprocessed lumber from the bush and exported the trees to England. He would drive into the bush and approach the chief of a remote village and negotiate for the giant hardwood trees. The chief would be delighted to have the money and sold his birthright cheaply, even sending men to assist in the felling. The logs were dragged out and trucked down to Accra for shipping to Europe.

"I see now that it was exploitation," our new friend said. "But I did not know Ghana and the Ghanaians then as I do now."

Eventually, the market declined and he sold a cargo of lumber for a loss and that abruptly ended that particulate enterprise. Now he ran a factory in Accra that made VanHeusen shirts.

It was yet another incongruity. This was a typical middle class

189

family as English as any at home. They were entirely oblivious to the underbelly of West Africa that we had experienced through living as strangers in the bush or as easy prey to the villains in the cities. They did not regard the police as corrupt.

"I like the flexibility of the Ghanaian character," our friend explained. "You can talk to an official and work a problem out. They do not merely follow the rules".

His wife was a lovely woman but his daughters were gorgeous. Their skin was an exotic bronze and their eyes were as black as coals. Their father kept them on a short leash.

We followed the Englishman to the small town where his son worked. We had to take a bush taxi to another location to buy the part we needed but soon the repair was complete and we suggested to the family that we take their teenage daughters out for a drink. The Englishman thought that was a great idea and invited his wife and himself along as well. It was a pleasant evening but not exactly as we had expected or hoped.

Early the next morning we headed north once more, taking advantage of the coolness of the early morning. After a couple of hours, we pulled over to check the engine temperature and to make sure that the oil leak was successfully mended. A car and its attendant dust cloud appeared in the distance. It was our English friend and his family. He pulled up to see what wrong.

"I hope you are not broken down already", he asked sympathetically.

"No, we are merely checking and everything seems just fine." I replied.

We thanked him for his kindness and they continued on their journey, the pretty daughters looking back wistfully.

Karl was feeling feverish and was sweating alarmingly. He clearly was suffering from a severe attack of malaria and needed time to rest and recuperate. We always took our anti-malarial tablets religiously and used mosquito coils to deter the little devils when we camped. The coils were sold cheaply everywhere. Once lighted, they filled the tent or the van with a smoky stench which may or may not have deterred the mosquitoes but it had the effect of allowing us a respite, imagining that they were indeed working. Before the tent had finally disintegrated beyond repair, we had fired up the coils and left them inside. But even so, those most wretched of insects could be heard buzzing in the darkness and, by the light of the flashlight, we would squash them dead against the walls realizing that the red smears on the canvas were of our own blood that they had already drawn. When we thought they were all vanquished once again, in the darkness, we would be tormented by their unnerving buzzing as they sought a patch of vulnerable skin to sting and suck.

Wading in the swamps, catching frogs and turtles produced inevitable bites. The mosquito could pierce heavy cloth and, if loose clothing afforded some protection for our bodies, our faces remained fair game. The Anopheles mosquito was a constant enemy.

We knew that if Karl could sweat it out he would be on his feet again within a few days. As we motored north we came across a road sign indicating a mission or project and I motored down the trail towards the cluster of modern buildings. Karl was feeling wretched and the monk who came out to greet us, sympathetically, ordered Karl to lie down in one of the guest rooms. He took his temperature and insisted that Karl stay until the sweats relieved the symptoms. Karl fell into a fitful sleep.

Within a day or two Karl was significantly recovered and we continued once more along our northerly route. The bout of malaria Karl had endured was merely one of the miserable maladies that we had to contend with. I, myself, at that time, was tormented by prickly heat which is a heat rash where the skin breaks out in red itchy bumps. Its real name is Miliaria and I endured it for months until, in Ouagadougou, we managed to find an appropriate treatment.

Navrongo is a small town in northeastern Ghana just a few miles below the border with Upper Volta and there, in a church hall, we sheltered from a terrific thunderstorm that erupted in the night, announcing the beginning of the rainy season.

The whole night long the storm raged, the howling wind driving the torrential rain and flailing the tin roof of the hall so that talking was impossible. Outside the hot, dry, dusty sand had greedily sucked up the first few drops of rain and turned into mud, then later disappeared altogether under the flooding rain that had turned the yard into a lake and the ditches along the fields into rivers. The bushes and trees that had waited thirstily for the beginning of the rainy season were now bent with branches sagging and leaves drooping under the weight of the rain and the pressure of the furious wind. We wondered how many African huts would lose their thatched roofs that night and how many clay walls would be washed away but, nevertheless, we eventually slept, exhausted by our long journey and relieved at least to be dry and beyond the reach of the raging storm.

With the dawn the rain continued but with less intensity until midmorning by which time we had already crossed the border and were steadily motoring on our way along the newly completed road towards Ouagadougou.

A few miles past the frontier we were flagged down by a very wet African on a moped who, in spite of being soaked, was smiling, showing his full set of strong, white teeth. We drew up, leaned out of the window and asked him what was up.

"The bridge about a mile down the road has been washed away, it is impossible to go further. It collapsed just before I was about to cross," he announced in French.

We said that we would drive down and take a look and, once again, he assured us that it would be impossible to pass.

A little way further down the road a group of farmers gestured and shouted frantically, hopping in the air, waving their short digging-hoes, trying to get us to pull over.

But we knew what it was they wanted to tell us and we assured them that we were going to look at the situation for ourselves. We drove slowly on towards the bridge but there was a massive hole where the structure had once been. The foundations had been completely washed away and the concrete had simply sunk four feet down into the river bed. On both sides the road had disappeared entirely, leaving a gap sixty feet long that was uncrossable. As the African on the moped had said, "Impossible to pass!"

There were two other ways to reach Ouagadougou apart from the main road. One was a track leading off to the east at Pô and the other ran westerly towards a town called Leo. The way on the right was no longer in use and impractical as it was virtually cross-country, but the

192

route to Leo is "quite good," a passing Gendarme heading south assured us.

We started off once again, this time along a very rough track pitted and muddy and crossed by streams. It was supposed to lead to Leo from where Ouagadougou was not so very far away along a better road. But before long the streams became rivers, the road could scarcely be differentiated from the surrounding bush and the mud so deep that we finally decided to wait a while, at least until the water had gone down and the mud had started to dry rather than become impossibly stuck in the slurry.

We made our camp right in the middle of the way, certain that no one else would be using it and needing to pass. About mid-afternoon the sun decided to show itself and steadily the water rushing past on both sides of us began to slow down and then soon ceased altogether. The river that had barred our way had already sunk to half its depth since we had been there and we decided that we would soon try to cross. But then an African came wading through, pushing his bicycle with half a dozen screeching guinea fowl hanging upside down from the handlebars and a huge sack of millet roped on the rack behind the saddle.

He looked like a simple rural farmer who wouldn't be able to speak a word of French but, to our surprise, he came up to us just as we had finished our meal of boiled dried beans and fish and said, "Bonjour, you're not going to try to carry on along this road are you? After this river there is a second where the water is waist high!"

We looked blankly at one another at the thought of waist high water and an African farmer who spoke French more fluently than we did and lived out here in the middle of nowhere. He held his short handled digging-hoe to his stomach to indicate the level of the water, repeatedly emphasizing the impossibility of continuing any further. And then, with an overemphasized shrug that was typically French, he abandoned us to our fate and cycled away through the bush.

We finished off our early dinner of beans, packed our things together and drove back up the muddy track again towards Pô. The fierce sunlight had scattered the clouds and was rapidly drying the swamped fields all around. The road was already completely dry as if scarcely a drop of rain had fallen. And, at the collapsed bridge, the water had already gone down markedly.

The road was crowded with half a dozen bush taxis, private cars and a lorry piled high with firewood. There was a gang of Africans splashing about in the middle of the river, pushing this way and that, and even against each other, trying to get a Renault across which had gotten stuck in the middle. The driver was accelerating like mad, churning up the muddy water and the Africans were chanting as they heaved. They didn't seem to be making much progress, in fact the car seemed to be sinking deeper all the time. But then reinforcements arrived to help and, yelling furiously, pushing and dragging, they managed to get the car rolling and soon reached the far bank.

After watching similar maneuvers with about four other cars and helping to push as well, we decided to try our luck. We prepared a sort of yoke so that some of the men could pull while others could push from the back. We also fixed snow chains to the rear wheels to get us through the mud that had accumulated along the bank. Gingerly, we drove down the steep slope from the road and across the marshy area a little further away from where the other cars had been and where the mud hadn't yet been churned up and was still fairly firm. About twenty yards from the bank, we got the Africans organized, some to pull with the yoke while the others helped at the back and along the sides of the vehicle. We were confident with this arrangement; there were more than twenty men to push and the chains would grip the turf along the bank so that we could take a really fast run at the river and would probably get halfway before the wheels started skidding. The farmers would then pull and push and we should easily reach the far bank. The difficulty was that it was getting late and soon the sun would abruptly set as it always did in the tropics and there was no managing this maneuver in the darkness. Nevertheless, we decided to go ahead, convinced that we would achieve our goal first time round.

The Africans at the front pulled and the crowd at the back started to push as Karl drove off in second gear. A few times the van started to skid but, by chanting with the farmers at the back, we all pushed together and the van went racing off towards the river. Karl had already switched on the headlights as it had started to drizzle and it was becoming hard to see ahead of him. Suddenly, there was a loud crack and the van

194

stopped dead and skidded a little to one side. Karl was leaning from the window, swearing and cursing with a group of Africans when I came round from behind and saw what had happened. The group that had been towing at the front had run straight for a three-foot high tree stump, jumped over it and carried on, pulling the van into it!!! Now we were sitting in the mud a few feet from the river bank in the increasing drizzle and approaching darkness. Fortunately, we had a winch and sheets of iron track which we could put under the wheels and, although intended for sand, they would also prove workable in muddy conditions. The winch was strong enough to pull 1,500 pounds and with it we managed to get the van a little way away further from the riverbank where we secured it to a tree as it was now raining heavily again and the water was rising uncannily fast.

So there we were. We spent the night with the van stuck up to the axles in mud with water creeping all around us. But we were not alone. The truck laden with firewood was abandoned, stuck right in the middle of the river! It had become dark and the farmers had faded into the shadows and to the shelter of their villages. Additionally, there were now two Peugeot sedans on the opposite bank that had attempted the crossing even later than we had and quickly became mired and remained in the mud until late the following morning when, at long last, they managed to get themselves across with the help of the returning farmers. It was fortunate for all that rain stopped once more before the river rose much higher and particularly fortunate for the truck in the middle of the river and ourselves poised precariously upon the edge of the river bank.

We ate some sardines and bread that we had bought in Ghana and made ourselves as comfortable as possible for the night, Karl in the back of the van and I, in the front, alert in case the water should rise once more which might make our situation dire.

The next morning we woke up very early as crowds of farmers from the surrounding villages arrived and were at work, amidst much chanting and yelling, trying to get the lorry out of the middle of the river. The water level seemed to have gone down a little during the night and the sun was beating down, drying out the mud which cracked into jagged patterns as the water evaporated. Nevertheless, we decided to wait until afternoon before giving it another try when we hoped the mud would have hardened and the water gone down even more.

During the course of the morning,the lorry at last managed to get across with the assistance of maybe forty Africans. Two other cars crossed as well and soon, after midday, we started to get ourselves ready for our second attempt. We jacked up the van and laid iron boards under each of the wheels. Inch by inch, we crept along, replacing the boards all the time. When we got to the water's edge, we attached the winch to a tree on the other side and then, with a long doubled rope, secured it to the chassis of the van. Unfortunately, the rope tended to stretch, so, although it was some help, the winch didn't show its worth until the distance was less and we could triple the rope. We carried on replacing the boards beneath the wheels under water and, although the engine was no help because the wheels just spun, we managed to move very slowly and steadily with the aid of the winch alone. There were huge pot holes everywhere in the river where other people had crossed and become stuck, spinning their wheels. We had to be careful that the van did not lurch sideways off the boards into one of them and sink, flooding the engine. But we persisted, inch by inch, and gradually crept onward.

Much later in the afternoon we were about three-quarters of the way across when the winch seized up. So there we were now, out in the river itself, in an even worse position than the previous evening. I set about dismantling the winch, sitting on the fallen tree trunk to which we had attached it on the far bank, when a group of young Africans came over. They were students from Ouagadougou on their way to Ghana. They saw that we looked as if we were in the middle of the river to stay and asked why we didn't get the farmers to push us across that last bit. I replied that unfortunately the farmers had been pushing cars across for two days and had earned far more money than they had ever seen. They had become greedy and wanted to charge us an extortionate amount for their help.

It was true, the sensation of so much money had had an unhappy effect on the simple farmers and, on several occasions, we saw them arguing bitterly with one another. A Frenchman had given them a bundle of notes equivalent to a week's work for a laborer in Ouagadougou. And there was a steady profit to be made as car after car attempted the crossing and had to be helped.

One of the group of the students waded across and spoke with the farmers where they were waiting, watching us, curious to see how we would manage with the winch broken. We don't know what he said to them, but suddenly the whole group surged across the river, gripped the van wherever they could and pushed harder than they had for anyone else during the whole two days. The air was filled with their rhythmic cadence as they surged forward in unison. In no time at all we were on the far bank, up the steep embankment and onto the asphalt road once more, grinning like fools and shaking hands with every one of them. The farmers were as delighted as we were at their magnificent achievement. We said goodbye to the students and started off at last for Ouagadougou.

Soon we were on the outskirts of the town. The round clay houses, thatched, standing in circles, were replaced by oblong ones with tin roofs and again superseded by the very modern houses with walled-in gardens where the Europeans and wealthier Africans lived. We drove through the town center, recognizing landmarks from the previous year and, finally, we arrived at our destination, the Austrian Technical School where our good friends, Mr. and Mrs. Rudolf Parizs both worked as volunteer teachers.

Rudolf was a Hungarian who, as a small child in 1956, had, with his family, escaped Hungary ahead of the Soviet invasion. Over 200,000 refugees fled their homeland. Rudolf's family settled in Vienna. Louise, his wife, was an Austrian native and they had been married just a short time.

We found Rudolf, using some of his spare time from teaching, repairing a Puch Haflinger which is an Austrian vehicle something like a miniature jeep. It is remarkable in that it has an extremely low climbing gear. It could creep up a very steep incline under four-wheel drive. When it was handled in that manner the steering locked and the Haflinger could only be driven straight ahead. In trials and competitions this little vehicle had out maneuvered far more powerful German military trucks. It was virtually unstoppable and could climb an astoundingly steep grade. Both Karl and I would have several times willingly traded the VW for one of these. This one had been abandoned in disrepair by the school and Rudolf decided to see if he could rebuild it. I agreed to help him and, after six days, we had completely overhauled the whole thing and were eager to try it out.

There was another week until the Austrian school was due to open after the recess, so we decided to drive down to Pô on the Ghanaian border to see how the Haflinger would cross the flooded river and then we would continue towards the Volta Rouge, another and more significant river that meandered its way south into Ghana. This was an area called Kaboré Tambi National Park and it abounded with wildlife. In particular, we were eager to see elephants before we left Africa because, during more than two years, we hadn't seen as much as a shadow.

At about midday we set off and soon had Ouagadougou behind us, motoring along the boiling hot tarmac in the direction of Pô. The rainy season had already made its mark on the otherwise dry, rocky landscape; everywhere tufts of grass had shot up, making the earth look like a threadbare carpet. Here and there, curiously, a telephone pole sprouted a cluster of leaves. Everywhere, the landscape was greening and the grass was growing frantically. Before long it would be tall enough to hide an elephant.

Soon we arrived at the collapsed bridge, but the water had already sunk right down and the Haflinger purred across without difficulty. So far it had been a very disappointing rainy season that year. Not only later than usual in starting, but also much less rain than was hoped. This ominous and foreboding situation was prompting frantic relief operations for the inhabitants of the Sahel zone. The alarm had already been sounded and daily we saw cargo planes flying overhead, bearing grain and powdered milk from Abidjan, Ivory Coast, to be distributed to the people of the North who were in imminent danger of starvation. Because of the slight rainfall there was much less greenery for the cattle and other livestock to feed on and incredible numbers of domestic animals had perished. The Sahel dwellers were nomadic tribes who raised cattle. Without forage, they were devastated from the lack of rain.

At Pô, Karl bought a very tame and brightly colored parrot to keep company with our pet Gray Hornbill (*Tockus nasutus*), which we had bought in Ouagadougou for small change. The Hornbill was a fledgling with ragged feathers and tufts of down yet already it had an enormous beak. Consequently, it was justifiably named Ugly. Thus, we had Beauty and the Beast to keep each other company. We also bought a young billy goat and a few other provisions.

On one occasion Rudolf had seen elephants along the main road itself, but this time we saw nothing but their dung and one or two enormous footprints leading off into the forest. We also saw a small group of baboons bolt for cover but, apart from that, there was nothing more to see that day.

At Pô, there was a Catholic mission with a small hospital and, as Karl was complaining of a pain in the area of his kidneys, we went to the clinic for help. The lady doctor who was in charge was an American who had been in Africa for eleven years and seemed to prefer to stay there rather than ever return home. She said that Karl should leave a urine sample at the hospital for analysis and that we should return the next day to hear the result. Karl announced that he felt much better again and we decided to continue our journey to the Volta Rouge and collect the results of his test upon our return.

We set off on the road that led almost directly north and at once noticed a complete change of style in the houses. The Mossi people, who are in the majority in Upper Volta, build houses of clay, round conical huts in a circle connected by a wall enclosing an inner yard. Each structure is thatched and nowadays some people plaster the walls outside with cement so that they won't be damaged by the sudden heavy deluge in the rainy season. Now suddenly we saw completely different houses. There was always one main building, square with a flat roof (sometimes we saw them with an extra story) surrounded by a few lower huts, round but also with flat roofs and each connected to the others by a wall, often very attractively painted with colored geometric patterns or with writhing serpents. The smoothly rounded walls and richly flowing organic architecture was quite enchanting. These were the houses of the Gurunsi people.

The Gurunsi have developed a considerable sophistication of culture and organization that was evidenced by their gorgeous architectural expression, the elaboration of their murals and the order that operated within their communities.

That night, we slaughtered the billy goat and roasted the meat over a huge log fire. As Rudolf and I were hacking away at a stout dry branch from a Karité tree for firewood, it suddenly whined strangely and

199

split in half and we saw that it was hollow. At the exact place where it had broken and where we were chopping, there wriggled out a very long and very beautiful, shiny green snake. We gave chase as it tried to get away to the cover of some longer grass and Rudolf trapped it against the ground with the flat of his machete. I took it by the head and we left our firewood and returned to camp with the snake instead.

The next morning we paid a hasty visit to the chief at Kampala and he indicated which direction we should drive to reach the Volta Rouge. There was a track that wasn't too bad, although in places it had been washed away by rain. We thanked the chief and continued towards the river. The potholes did not prove much of a problem for the Haflinger, which was as well because I, in particular, didn't feel much like pushing the vehicle if it became stuck in the mud after a miserable previous night's sleep. The goat, before we had eaten it, had been in the back of the Haflinger and had urinated on the tent. The tent was already very dilapidated and discolored by the elements but, when we raised it, we found that it stank foully. Rudolf and his wife were comfortably sleeping in the Haflinger so, of course, we had no choice but to try to forget the smell and make the best of it. In the night there was a terrific storm and the old, battered tent just didn't stand up to it. My side became waterlogged, soaking my bedding. As soon as the rain stopped, I got up and vigorously chopped wood to keep warm. At dawn, the others got up as well and we cooked our breakfast and I dried out my bedding as best I could before we finally set off. This part of the trip with our Austrian friends was proving more reckless than necessary and I wondered at Karl and myself for embarking upon it so badly prepared. I think being around other Europeans we had forgotten our usual caution. Rudolf showed a certain nonchalance and bravado towards the bush and failed to respect it in the same way that Karl and I had learned through experience.

We wanted to try to reach the Volta that day but, soon after we had set off, it started to drizzle and the road became muddier and steadily began to flood. Twice we sank down so deeply that the chassis was no longer visible and even the four wheel drive couldn't help us. In one case we had to lever the whole thing out of the mud with an enormous branch and onto a track we had prepared with rocks and branches. It took us four hours to progress only five miles and then we found that our way was completely barred by a deep pit half full of water and several feet deep. All around the grassland was swamped. Our way forward was blocked and we had no choice but to retreat. Fortunately, during our return journey, the rain stopped and the sky seemed to clear. We decided to head across land to a rocky hill about half a mile away from the road, where we could make a fire and cook something warm to eat.

Driving across was very tricky as the whole area was intensively burrowed by aardvark and we only narrowly missed driving into their holes. They were hard to detect because of the grass which in some places was as tall as a person.

At the foot of the hill, we managed to get a fire going by splashing the wood with petrol and we cooked our meal of rice with tomatoes. Afterwards, Karl complained that he felt unwell again but, nevertheless, by foolhardy consensus, we all started climbing the hill. Around about were the fresh tracks and manure of buffalo. This was enormously dangerous because the tall grass hid everything from view and we had no way of knowing if the buffalo were in the immediate vicinity. We could have been standing three feet from an elephant and would scarcely have seen it. Fortunately, the noise that the vehicle had made as we drove up must have frightened practically everything away for miles around or, at least, I quietly hoped so.

Once on top of the hill, we found fresh baboon droppings but that was all. Looking about upon the magnificent panorama of lush green vegetation, even through binoculars, we failed to spot any large wildlife. The grass was simply too high everywhere. The sun decided to shine as we stood on the hill looking around. It floodlit the panorama, setting the rich canopy alive with every imaginable and splendidly vivid nuance of green. The soaked trees and bushes of the savanna seemed to shine like silver, each little droplet of water on every leaf reflecting back the sunlight mixed with every shade imaginable from black green to almost yellow. Nowhere was there the slightest sign of civilization to be seen, not even the smallest dwelling or the wisp of smoke from a fire. We were entirely alone, a score of miles from the nearest village.

Soon we were on our way back to Kampala, this time only getting stuck once on the way. We paid our respects to the chief as we passed his castle-like house and then we returned to our previous camp.

Karl wanted to try and catch a crocodile he had spotted in a swamp half a mile away from camp and he and Rudolf went off together while Louise and I went to petition the village school master to let us all sleep in the classroom instead of having to use the tent again. We had already spoken to him once on our arrival the previous evening and he was a very amiable man indeed, very glad to give us the shelter of the otherwise unused classroom.

But then, as we were getting our things organized, Karl came back, bent double and said that he had a terrific pain in his kidneys. It was so bad, in fact, that he could do nothing but lie down, curled up on the ground, moaning.

Karl urgently needed a doctor.

The first thing we did was give him an aspirin to relieve the pain and then we went to fetch the village "doctor," whom the school master had highly recommended. He was obviously a very sincere and knowledgeable herbal practitioner. This good man advised making an infusion of a certain plant and drinking it several times a day. But this was impractical given the circumstances. We decided to head back to civilization immediately. Rudolf soon returned from the crocodile hunt. Somehow he and Karl had become separated in the descending darkness. We threw our things into the vehicle and returned as fast as we could to Pô.

Rudolf drove at top speed but that was the trouble with the Puch Haflinger; it was excruciatingly slow. The road was extremely rough and I had the same feeling of dread that I had known on other occasions that something must sooner or later snap, fall off, or come apart, but luckily we arrived at the town with everything still intact. In fact, the journey even seemed to have done Karl's kidneys some good and he was no longer in pain.

We didn't waste any time but drove straight to the mission to try to find the American doctor to see if she had the results of the test and to see what she had to say about Karl's attack. At the gate, she rushed out to meet us and straight away advised us to go back to Ouagadougou and see that Karl had a thorough medical check-up. She said that the results of the test had shown that Karl was badly infested with schistosoma which are blood-flukes that live in a parasitic cycle from snails in still-water to

202

man who comes into contact with the water and then later passes the eggs back into the lake or pond through his urine. The way the water is decontaminated is by killing the snails and thereby interrupting the cycle. We decided that, although Karl was no longer in pain, it would be better to take the doctor's advice and straight away we headed back to the city.

For our friends, this was a weekend jaunt. For us, it was foolhardy. At the beginning of our adventures we had quickly learned that the West African bush is underestimated at our peril. At first, we had been reckless too. But our friends had flown in from Europe and arrived abruptly in Ouagadougou to teach at a school where everything was provided for them and where their well-being was assured. They had a comfortable house, money, food and medical attention if it was needed. They knew nothing of the real Africa and Karl and I should have known better than to set off with them in the rainy season to a region occupied by significantly dangerous wild-life without adequate preparation.

It later transpired that Karl also suffered from kidney stones as we suspected. The French doctor in Ouagadougou gave him enormous quantities of medicine to destroy the schistosoma, together with tablets that apparently were necessary to keep his heart going. It took Karl a week to recover. During that time he was barely conscious.

We frequently retreated to the bush where, not to be outdone, I came down with dysentery. It was particularly severe and although Karl was solicitous, preparing special rice soups that his Austrian cookbook indicated as beneficial, I lost weight alarmingly fast.

I began to hallucinate and my dreams took on a profound and existential quality. I was in the sky, peering down at the Earth below and, one by one, I pulled heavy metal hatches shut, obscuring my view. A kindly voice said, "There are some good things in life, too, you know."

And then I heard the bedlam of my own mind. A thousand voices were chattering and arguing. The noise was excruciating. All at once I found that I had control over the noise and I made it stop. There was a delicious quiet.

Sitting under a tree as I began to feel stronger, I had the tape-recorder running. I stopped the machine and listened to the tape. Suddenly, I was aware that I was surrounded by the most beautiful melodies of hundreds of exotic birds. I had not realized that I was in a

203

virtual paradise of exotic avians until I had replayed the recording. It was enormously delightful and refreshing. I was amazed that I had not noticed the splendid chorus. I felt myself growing stronger.

Karl had left for Ouagadougou where he had managed to procure some effective medicine. Before long I was on my feet again. But I had lost a great deal of weight and the belt around my waist seemed of a sudden to have grown remarkably long.

Rudolf and Louise generously offered Karl and I the use of a spare room at their house. This was enormously welcome as we both needed to become well and strong again in order to reinvigorate our business with Karl's new ideas and to eventually prepare for our return trip to Europe across the Sahara desert.

There was a large stone quarry near the Austrian school that had probably provided rock for road building. In all seasons the quarry was flooded, providing a significant habit for all kinds of small creatures. While in Austria, Karl and I had fabricated a trap for fish that consisted of a large cylinder of flexible clear plastic with a funnel at both ends. The funnels faced inward so that the fish could enter easily, attracted by the bait, but they would be unable to find their way out. We set the trap in the quarry with some scraps of meat to lure whatever creatures might be interested.

The following day we went to retrieve the trap and found it overloaded with turtles and, to our delight, two Nile monitors. This was a splendid catch which we repeated with great success.

Another location that was also conveniently close was a flooded rice field. We had heard frogs there and were determined to return at night with flashlights and see what species they were. The water was very shallow but occasionally there was a deep hole. Twice I slipped in. It was disconcerting because they were difficult to detect in the dark. I think they were shallow wells.

The rice was only a couple of feet high and it was easy to make our way between the rows. The frog sounds were delightful and very specific. Karl suggested that they made the sound of a blacksmith hammering upon an anvil but, of course, in miniature and henceforth we called them *Blacksmith* frogs. It was mating season and this was a lusty frog paradise. Hundreds of tiny golden bush frogs clung to the rice stalks with their throats puffed out, oblivious to our intrusion and determined to find a mate. In the midst of the *ting ting ting* one or two other croakers could be recognized but these little jewels were a delight.

Catching them was easy. The flashlight beam picked them out in the darkness and then it was simply a matter of picking them like golden berries from a bush and filling our sacks. We easily gathered a hundred of them.

Ouagadougou seemed to be a great deal easier location than out in the bush where we did not know the terrain. I went on my own after dark. There was a swampy area beside a stream that was surrounded by low trees and bushes but not dense enough to be impenetrable, just enough to offer cover to turtles. I walked around for a couple of hours, just picking them up one after the other as they wandered about in the mud. I even found a particularly unusual turtle alike to the others but with the addition of a hinged shell.

After a while the mosquitoes became overwhelming and I made my retreat with a heavy sack full of klinking and clunking Testudines thrown over my shoulder. Along the lane I came across a little coffee shop. It was little more than a long table set up in front of a modest store. There were a couple of benches and on the table was a solitary kerosene lamp. Arriving out of the darkness, the young man had not noticed that I was white until I ordered a coffee. Then he was quite surprised. This was a first. "Yovo!" He blurted in astonishment. But he did not mean any offense. I had learned the Mossi word *Moro* which means Blackman and I sometimes used it as a retort. But the surprise was quickly replaced by a friendly smile and he prepared my coffee. The typical drink was instant Nescafé sweetened with syrupy cream. Both canned products were safe and, with the addition of boiling water, it made a pleasant drink, free from germs. I quietly enjoyed my coffee in the lamplight, listening to the million insect sounds, the chirping and scratching, the sudden call of a night bird or the nervous scamper of a rodent, scurrying to safety somewhere in the darkness.

I paid my friend and set off back to the house.

Karl discovered a clever way to catch skinks. There was a small shed built of hollow red blocks that housed some garden tools. The cells of the blocks proved to be an ideal home for colorful *Chalcides*. Karl discovered them living there and caught many by placing a bag containing a short stick over the entrance. Securing the bag so there was no escape, he tickled the hollow chamber of the brick until the skink became alarmed and fled into the sack. He successfully trapped numerous beautifully colored creatures using this simple method.

Upon our arrival in Ouagadougou, we had shipped a consignment to Holland that did not survive. There was either a union strike or a fire at one of the airports in Europe, we never discovered which, and the boxes had not been keep warm on a hot-pad as had been arranged from Ouagadougou through Telex. The poor creatures perished from cold and our customer sent us a photograph of the animals in a heap, everyone of them dead.

However, now we had a wonderful consignment and quickly dispatched it to Europe. It included some chameleons for whom Karl carefully provided a leafy branch, each in its own separate cell.

Karl bought a young female Patas monkey and several yellow-billed hornbills from the Ouagadougou native market. Together with some multicolored parrots, we soon had sufficient creatures ready to ship, this time to Germany. It was interesting to be dealing with larger animals and the monkey had to have a veterinary certificate of good health before the airline would accept it. We also stocked her crate with fresh bananas for the journey. She was already half tame and used to wearing a dog's collar, enjoying her perch in a leafy tree in front of the house. In the native markets there were piles of mummified monkey heads, as well as other unfortunate creatures, for sale as grisgris. I could not help thinking that someone in Europe would be delighted with this gentle creature as a pet and it would probably enjoy a far better life than at the hands of the market vendor.

Life improved enormously for us. The native market in Ouagadougou provided fresh meat at very reasonable prices and we were both becoming fit and strong once more. Karl was becoming well-known there as a hard bargainer and absolutely nobody was his match. One day he returned with an authentic fetish statue. It was about three feet in height, a female figure obviously of some vintage. We realized that this might be a very lucrative market. A customer in Vienna became very excited and we promptly shipped several similar statues and masks to him.

206

Meanwhile, Rudolf and Louise had taken advantage of another school recess and departed for a couple of weeks, exploring neighboring Mali. When they returned, they showed us several souvenir masks that they had bought. Beside the ones that Karl had found, there was no comparison. These were merely imitations, clumsily made to sell to tourists. Karl's were authentic and museum quality.

At this time Karl received a letter from England from Jane Harrison's mother. I had written to Jane, translating for Karl, having no idea that she had died. I had picked up the mail at the Ouagadougou post office while Karl remained at the airport, preparing a consignment of animals for their journey. The preparation of the shipment required great care and this was not a time to interrupt Karl with the sad news. With considerable skill Karl methodically ensured that every creature was made as comfortable as possible and had access to water. We shipped the smaller reptiles as soon as we caught them to avoid having to procure food for them all. They would receive a hearty meal of crickets and worms upon their arrival. Larger animals, such as the Nile monitors from the quarry, we kept longer. We were able to feed them with meat.

After considerable effort, we had become moderately friendly with the crusty and impatient airport official who was in charge of freight and the essential communications with Paris through Telex. We had photographed him in his uniform and taken him to nearby African bar for a couple of beers. It was always a hassle dealing with him until, with these little encouragements, we finally won him over.

Soon Karl was ready and we drove over to the airport freight building and, adorned with colorful freight labels, the boxes were loaded aboard.

Naturally Karl was very distressed when I translated the letter and the sorrow of Jane's mother was equally evident in the writing.

* * *

The next time we visited Kampala it was almost the close of the rainy season. The grass was still very high but now parched and golden. This time we spent more time with the chief of the village who proudly showed us about inside his very large castle-like house where the bats flew

207

about in the rafters of the musty, dark rooms. The chief told us that a good part of the house he had built himself and had plans for other alterations and repairs. He showed us the kitchen, which was a separate round house with a flat roof, very dark inside and with several adjoining rooms. In the roof was a hole which let in a ray of light, just enough for one of the chief's wives to be able to see to grind millet between flat stones and prepare sauces. Between each round room, there was a small round hole which meant, after climbing over a low wall, you had to bend yourself double to get through. All around the rooms, against the walls, hung nets full of dozens of calabash bowls of various sizes, some of them dyed crimson. It was extremely impressive and we had not seen such organization or structure in any other community. Everything was gracefully and even beautifully made while other villages, using all the same indigenous materials, by comparison were haphazard and seemed somehow temporary, like camping.

Returning to the chief's main house, we were met by a young Gurunsi tribesman who had business with the chief. They settled in a couple of chairs to conduct their affairs in their own language while we remained within earshot.

A very strange thing occurred. After numerous greetings and much hand shaking, the conversation flared into an argument. Instantly, as the pitch rose, both men reached out their hands and reverted to the formal ceremonial greeting, asking after each other's well-being and affairs. When heated words were once more exchanged, the pattern was repeated and they returned to amiable conversation.

Finally the chief said, "All right. That is good. You can find your wife and take her home."

More handshaking and cordial greeting and the young man departed.

It appeared that the chief's daughter was married to this man but she had run away from her new home. The chief and the young man had discussed and settled this sensitive matter without open hostility. I pondered on this for a while and it occurred to me that the worse thing imaginable in this hostile environment was a rift among the Gurunsi themselves. Historically, it was essential to remain on good terms with one another and retain a solidarity against the common enemies of other hostile tribes and the unpredictability of the climate that might in any season reduce them to destitution from which they were merely one harvest away. Community cohesion was essential for survival and a difference regarding a straying wife could not be allowed to flare up and disrupt the indispensable common good.

After the young man had departed, we drank Dolo with the chief. Dolo is beer made from fermented red millet and we noticed that the chief was fairly tipsy and he became progressively more so until, in his enthusiasm, he resolved to show us his armory. He owned an impressive and chiefly saber with a lion's tail drawn over the handle in addition to a shotgun and two other rifles, one of which was an American Army 303 which he said a missionary had given him.

"It is good for hunting elephants" he boasted.

But he really was a significant man. This Gurunsi village was situated in the midst of the forest where abundant wildlife yet remained. There were very real dangers and a hunter would have to be a brave and skillful man indeed.

Finally, he presented Rudolf's wife Louise with a lion's skull. He was obviously very taken with the white woman with her beautiful blond hair and had been solicitous and gracious towards her the whole time.

We wanted to visit the Volta Rouge again and asked the chief if he could lend us his donkeys to travel the few miles where we would then camp and return the next day. He was very pleased to do so and even agreed to let Louise borrow his own horse. He shouted orders to several of his sons who set about getting things organized for us. They brought two carts and hitched up the donkeys and finally saddled up the horse, which was a sinewy and tough bay but very slow and dogged. We hoped that it would be able to keep up with the donkeys. The bridle was incomplete by European standards. It consisted merely of two lengths of leather tied to an undersized straight snaffle bit which would have fitted one of the donkeys far more appropriately. It was bound securely to the animal's head with string. But it worked just fine for walking. The saddle was a tree of wood with scant leather only covering the seat itself. The reins were far too short, so Louise let them go altogether and the animal proved very amenable and followed on plodding slowly behind the donkeys.

Getting ready for the journey had taken far too long and the sun was already high in the sky before we finally set off even though we had gotten up an hour before dawn. I sat on the first cart with the luggage and one of the chief's sons while Rudolf and Karl rode on the second cart with another of the sons and a third young man followed on behind with Louise and the horse. I imagined the chief had given him strict instructions to look after her.

Several times on the way, we had to get off and help the donkeys over the elephant's footprints, which had been made in the rainy season when the track had been muddy but now were deep and as hard as cement. There were also four or five riverbeds to cross on the way which were now all dried out except for a slight trickle of water in one of them and they were no longer much of a hindrance. We simply all got off and pushed while the boys beat the hell out of the donkeys.

On the way we saw the droppings of monkeys, antelopes and elephants as well as where some elephants had passed through the long grass and trampled it flat.

Karl, with the alert eye of the naturalist, pointed out as we rested beneath the shade of a spreading tree that there were three cobras coiled in its branches. It made me appreciate the very real dangers of the bush that the Gurunsi encounter in the fields or the surrounding forest every day of their lives.

After about four hours, hot and parched, we arrived at the river and promptly plunged into the warm, refreshing water. The water was slow moving, muddy and very deep, up to our necks. Once Karl saw a baby crocodile come to the surface, but the noise we were making would keep the larger ones away. At least we hoped so! But something brushed against Rudolf's leg and we all quickly scampered to safety. The knowing Gurunsi men did not go down into the water.

Unfortunately, this beautiful area was plagued by flies, absolutely millions of them, which flew into our eyes, noses and mouths and buzzed the whole time about our ears. We built a huge bonfire aligned to the wind and covered it with green leaves so that the smoke would blow through our camp. But the flies were hardly disconcerted while we choked on the smoke.

Soon night fell and the flies fortunately disappeared, but then came the mosquitoes. The African boys built a large fire at one end of the camp and we made one at the other, in order to keep the wild animals away from the donkeys, the horse and ourselves.

We had washed and cleaned the tent throughly after the last camping trip and repaired some of the tears in the canvas. But, in the night, it was so cold that we all got up and built up the fires again to keep warm. Rudolf wanted to go and chop some more firewood, but a terrific roar from somewhere not far away in the bushes changed his mind for him and he spun around on his heel and returned to camp. The whole night long we heard wildcats spitting and lions snarling down by the river bank and a thousand other noises from wild creatures which convinced us to keep the fire going. Sleep was of little importance in comparison. The chief's sons remained with the donkeys and also kept the other fire going all night. This was as well. I am sure the chief would have been very perturbed if his fine old charger was eaten by a lion. But when we were warmed up again, we slept the couple of hours left until the morning and were on our way back to Kampala before it became really hot.

About halfway there, we came across a group of hunters with the skins of the animals they had poached on their heads. They were all heavily armed and looked a very formidable group indeed, but, seeing the cages on one of the carts, they assumed that we were also hunting and they were very friendly to us, even allowing us to photograph them with their trophies which in retrospect seemed imprudent of them.

At the chief's house again, we drank Dolo and then one of his wives brought in a meal of Fufu, which is boiled yams stamped with a mortar and served with a hot paprika sauce. It is absolutely one of the most delicious African dishes even though, second best was the peppery stews that tasted like goulash and could be purchased in the city at the little African cafés. Finally, early in the afternoon, we headed off back to Ouagadougou after Karl promised the chief that he would bring him a casting net next time we visited a few weeks later.

I could easily have spent much more time among the Gurunsi. They appeared to be a fascinating and cultured people and it would have been intriguing to remain close to their villages as we had done in other countries and learn more of their customs. Now forty years later, under the influence of an extensive tourist industry, I suspect that they present a very different face. But we certainly had good fortune getting to know the chief when we did and enjoying his sincere hospitality and generous good nature.

14. THE ELEPHANTS OF KABORÉ TAMBI

During our previous visit to Upper Volta, we had explored an area of the White Volta where there was an almost parched river bed, close to which we established our camp. Karl had gone exploring on his own, as was our custom in a new place, because we resolved never to leave the van unattended if we could possibly avoid doing so. But it became quickly apparent that this location was remarkable for its solitude. It was a far less populated area than the south of the country and we never had a single visitor.

I had left camp during the morning in order to set out a trap. I was feeling meat hungry. We had two roosters with us but we enjoyed the novelty of their crowing and we only finally dispatched them when we later arrived in Dahomey.

I set the gin-trap in a location where I imagined a small ground squirrel or rodent might pass by and then headed back to camp. I planned to leave the trap until evening when Karl would return from his afternoon excursion. When he returned he showed me an interesting fish that he had found by digging with his machete into the dry creek bed. It was a West African Lungfish (*Protopterus annectens*). During the dry season these creatures can survive in a burrow of hardened mud using a rudimentary lung.

While still in Austria, Karl had planned to export fish as well as reptiles and we had a box of strong plastic bags and an oxygen cylinder for this purpose. The bag is half filled with water while the remaining space is expanded with pure oxygen, thereby affording the survival of the fish for at least a few days. The animals would then be boxed and flown to Europe. After our difficulties in Mali regarding the diseased fish we had never returned to this idea. Exporting reptiles appeared to be a far easier concept. Tropical fish were so much more complicated than reptiles and there was a consistent danger of *Schistosomiasis*, from wading about in pond and lake water contaminated with the parasite. The effects of *snail fever*, as it is otherwise known, can become chronic, causing severe, internal organ damage. Karl had been lucky once but had since grown more cautious from the experience.

That evening I found that I had indeed caught a ground

squirrel and we ate it for our supper.

These excursions to the bush, far from the cities, were fascinating to us both and frequently resulted in the capture of some unusual creature. It was intriguing to discover some animal that we had otherwise only read about in natural history books. But it remained the **bush** nonetheless and a couple of times Karl had mishaps that would have landed us in serious difficulties. For this reason, we were cautious in every new situation and constantly alert to danger. Nothing was taken for granted. If we turned over some rocks to make a fire pit we always check underneath the rock for scorpions as a matter of course. We never left camp without our machetes and indeed slept with them beside us in the tent. In the event of any suspicious noise, we could be out in a moment, flashlight and machete in hand to face whatever danger may have arisen, be it animal or man.

Karl, on a quest for snakes, met our old friend *Psammophis sibilans*. This snake goes by many names but Karl identified it as a green grass or sand snake and that was sufficient authority for me. He found one holed up in a tree stump at the edge of a farmer's field. This wily creature proved to be elusive and refused to be caught. Karl had set up a net covering the entire stump so that the snake could find no way out. Then he agitated it with a stick. This is a practice he had developed that had proven very effective in the past. The snake would make its escape only to find itself entangled in the net. But the Psammophis is a notorious wriggler and this one, frantic to escape, bit Karl through the net.

Psammophis has significant poison glands that, fortunately, only produce a relatively mild venom. Additionally, it is back-fanged so the snake has to bite deeply into its prey in order to disable it. Nevertheless, we were in the bush, miles from civilization. Karl returned to camp mildly concerned and suggested I slice the wound with a razor blade and suck out the venom. I could see some marking on his wrist but, hovering uncertainly with the blade, we concluded that a slashed wrist may be far worse than the bite of the Psammophis. We left it alone and it became evident that the venom had failed to enter his blood stream.

Another near disaster involved a scorpion. We were seated by

214

the camp fire after our evening meal when Karl went to the van to retrieve something. He was wearing leather sandals. Suddenly, he felt a series of vigorous strikes against the leather. He stooped down, peering with the kerosene lantern, to see what it was and found a scorpion determinedly stabbing at the side of his sandal merely a breath away from the skin of his foot.

My own worst incident occurred in Dahomey when I was working on the van. I had crawled under the vehicle to make a simple adjustment when suddenly I felt a severe sting in my shoulder like that of a wasp but from some creature that I could not see in the grass. I thought little of it but within moments my hair started to itch alarmingly and I imagined ants crawling over my scalp. I dipped my head in a bucket of water but to no avail. And now my face began to swell and grow puffy. We had some antihistamine in our medical chest and I quickly filled a syringe and gave myself a shot. I immediately became very groggy and found that I had to lie down. Karl arrived shortly afterwards from his exploration of the area around our camp and found me amidst the various medicine bottles and capsules from our upside down medicine chest which I had frantically overturned trying to find the antihistamine and syringe. I remained dopey for a few hours but began to feel much relieved. I gave myself a second shot and, by the next day, I was fine. I never knew what had bitten me but such experiences as these caused us to be constantly wary and alert to possible danger.

* * *

In Ouagadougou, we became friends with a husband and wife from India. They were part of a business venture in Upper Volta, setting up a factory that would produce plastic bags. Prabodh was a fine man and I enjoyed speaking English with he and Deepthi, his wife. It was an unusual treat. Typically, I spoke German with Karl or French with everyone else except in Gambia and Ghana which are former British colonies where English was required. As the plastic bag factory became established, it amused us to see the street vendors now selling French loaves in plastic bags as if that somehow ensured their

215

cleanliness. In fact, the baker-boys merely threw them in the bags so that customers would think them more hygienic.

Deepthi was a beautiful and graceful woman and also a fabulous cook. If we happened to visit them when returning from the bush she would whip up something exotic and tasty in moments and present it to us while we were sitting there chatting.

We decided to invite our new friends and two of his Indian colleagues and their pretty daughter to a feast at Rudolf's house, in Ouagadougou. Rudolf had a large covered porch surrounded by raised flower beds that he carefully tended. He liked to entertain and agreed to the idea.

Karl bought a small pig. It never occurred to us that our guests were vegetarian and did not eat pork because we ate almost anything. Fortunately, there was enough other food and we enjoyed a pleasant evening in spite of this very significant social blunder.

A few days later I was at Prabodh's house. He was feeling unwell with malaria. He had asked if we had any citronella grass with which to make some tea and, as we had some growing in Rudolf's garden, I brought some over. Prabodh had tried to establish some himself in a planter but could not understand why it did not flourish. Typically, given sufficient water, everything grew rapidly in West Africa, including construction lumber. As he returned to the house, I noticed his dog approach the planter and chew on the citronella.

"Prabodh, it is your dog that is eating the lemon grass".

"What! You are the culprit!" He then proceeded to scold and berate the dog severely and, at length, in French, having purchased the animal locally from an African, as a guard dog. At the time this seemed perfectly reasonable to me that we spoke with each other in English but he addressed his dog in French. But, upon reflection, I realized that it was crazy. Surely, the dog only understood Mòoré.

* * *

Karl and I were in the bush south of Ouagadougou when we had a visitor. A well-dressed African approached and, in fluent French, requested assistance. The donkey cart that he owned had a flat tire and he

216

had no means of repairing it.

"Very well," we agreed. This man was unlike the wily city con men who constantly try to cheat and swindle. He merely needed some help and we were glad to assist. Upon later reflection, I realized that, in the isolated bush, as opposed to the city, this request for help was more an inclusion or acceptance into the native community and it was, by no means, always one-sided. We were often treated with genuine and gracious hospitality. If ever we visited a small village someone would inevitably bring us a calabash bowl of fresh cow's milk or perhaps offer to share their meal. In those situations there was no subterfuge or cunning whereby they hoped for more in return. It was merely the traditional convention of hospitality.

Soon our friend reappeared with a couple of boys who helped drag the cart to our camp. We must have given the wrong impression because when we had finished the job, the man fished into his pocket and retrieved a little purse and asked how much he owed us. Of course we did not take his money. We invited him to sit and we chatted for a while.

Simon was a school teacher and, as an educated man, he was well aware of the difference between the illiterate farmer of the bush and the modern well-informed mentality.

"If I approach that man over there working in the field and told him that people had achieved a moon landing and that several men had walked upon its surface he would think I am crazy!"

He spoke with a high squeaky voice that was unusual. The farmers spoke in a warm, dreamy way. Simon had a contagious humor and he was one of our African friends whose company I really enjoyed. One could simply sit and talk with him, enjoying his wry philosophy.

We stayed good friends with him and, on one occasion, we felled some dead branches for firewood and brought a load for him from the bush when he moved into Ouagadougou to teach at a school there. He complained of feeling middle class.

"The farmer has his land and his hut. He is poor but he makes ends meet in a variety of ways. I receive my small salary but I am always struggling to stay above water because I have no land for a garden and I must pay rent for my house in the city"

As usual, Simon also had an extended family to support.

217

We planned another trip to the Kaboré Tambi National Park. Karl wanted to give the Gurunsi chief the casting net that he had bought for him and we were determined to see elephants, if it was at all a possibility. Once again, Rudolf, Louise, Karl and I set off driving south towards the town of Pô near the Ghanaian border.

First we visited the chief and Karl presented him with the net. This was a splendid gift. He could send his sons to the river to catch fresh fish. Then the chief surprised us. He asked Karl how much the net had cost and seemed to imply that he wished to pay for it. This seemed very unusual considering his generosity towards us and it remained uncertain whether the chief was grasping and desirous of a more expensive gift or if he was sincerely generous and merely wanted to reimburse Karl. Karl graciously placed the net in the chief's hands and it appeared that the latter had been his motive and we parted on friendly terms.

We drove deeper into the forest along the sandy track leading into the interior. Suddenly we surprised a pair of antelope that scattered at our approach, dashing in alarm for cover with long leaping strides.

Soon we came to an area of meadow covered with rich green vegetation. Seventy yards away were two large buffalo grazing leisurely, unimpressed with the arrival of four humans and their annoyingly loud vehicle. Unlike the antelope, the buffalo did not scatter and, in fact, we had placed ourselves in considerable danger. Armed with a couple of machetes what did we imagine we would do if they got wind of us and charged our way. However, remaining close to our transport for a quick retreat if necessary, Karl managed to film them as they continued, apparently unperturbed, about their own business.

A little later a herd of huge horse antelope (*Hippotragus equinus*) scattered across the path ahead of us and we became vigilant, eager and excited to see more of these magnificent creatures. Sometimes a straggler or two would dart across the path trying to catch up with the rest of the herd and it is possible then to achieve a closer view.

We continued on our way, scanning the road ahead, alert to the possibility of more forest wildlife perhaps around the next corner or among the trees at the roadside. All at once we saw our first herd of elephants. It was a group of possibly six or seven with one massive matriarch who bellowed with alarm at our approach. These truly

218

magnificent creatures perhaps may only be fully appreciated for their power, largeness and colossal presence when experienced like this, in the wild. This was their habitat and they were free with no bars between ourselves and the herd. These were no unflappable, docile zoo animals but tons of raw power that became quickly disturbed and obviously agitated at our approach.

Nevertheless, we resolved to approach cautiously on foot so that Karl might catch the creatures on film. They were gathered in a group among some small trees, perhaps one hundred yards away. There were some young, the giant female and several other matrons. Karl managed to shoot some film but, as the distance between us and the matriarch narrowed, she turned, bellowed towards us and, with ears spread in alarm, she charged. A sapling in her way was crushed and thrown aside. The dusty ground churned to a cloud about her as she plowed furiously in our direction.

We had never run so fast in our lives. But, as we reached the vehicle, we realized that the chase was done and the herd had reassembled, determined to escape to the peace of the denser forest. I imagined, from our meeting with the poachers during the previous expedition into the forest, that the big game was easily spooked with good reason. Once again, it occurred to me that these light-hearted jaunts into the wilderness were ill advised without adequate preparation. I would have felt much better if we had had a gun.

During the afternoon, we saw more wildlife, including some baboon and I imagined that the renegade that we had hunted with the Mossi villagers, which now seemed so long ago, might have originated from this region.

The tropics do not have the gradual evening of the temperate zones of Europe and both sunrise and sunset are abrupt. We knew that it was getting late and we decided to leave the forest and make our way back to the city. Then suddenly, Karl spotted a low bush clustered with white Cattle Egrets (*Bubulcus ibis*). They were settling down to roost for the night. We approached the tree quietly on foot in the gathering dusk. The birds were making a melodic cooing noise, repeated softly over and over. It sounded like the French question, *ça va?* which means, "Are you O.K.?" Rudolf was approaching the tree from one side while Karl was already close and about to reach for a bird. Suddenly, Rudolf heard the call, *ça va* and, not thinking, he answered in French that he was fine. And the birds, suddenly alarmed, flew away!

We turned to leave, motoring steadily as the shadows lengthened and darkness crept closer. Suddenly, to the left of the track was another formidable herd of elephants. They were clustered together within fifty feet of us settled drowsily in the encroaching darkness, already tranquil and nodding.

Rudolf slowed the vehicle to a crawl and it was as if we were slowly creeping passed a cluster of enormous dusky buildings that loomed up from within the shadows. They grumbled in their half-sleep, perturbed at the disturbance but too drowsy to more than drag a mighty foot, flap an ear or swish a tail.

We were absolutely thrilled. This was a wonderful climax, not only to our long day in the forest but also of our West African journey. But now the time was approaching for our return to Europe and we were resolved to cross the Sahara.

15. LOOKING NORTHWARD

Our Volkswagen van was equipped with rows of cupboards on each side inside. The space on top of them and under the roof was where we stored the two bunks that could be attached, one above the other down the center. We had more equipment on the roof, including a huge glass bottle of preserving alcohol and some large, heavy-weight plastic water canisters as well as cages and nets and traps in the back of the vehicle. When the side door was open the kitchen area was revealed where we could prepare food and keep pots and pans. It was the ultimate camping van although spartan and without any luxury whatsoever.

In preparation for our homeward journey we resolved to sell the Volkswagen van. We stripped it entirely until it was once more an empty cargo vehicle. Karl was able to sell most of the things that we no longer required, including the bunks which went to a Catholic mission, the oxygen cylinder and our typewriter. He managed to find buyers for everything we possessed that was not essential.

We planned to restore the van to good working order and buy a Citroen for our journey home. We were able to have the crankshaft resurfaced and I rebuilt the engine so that it was tip-top once more. Karl quickly found a willing customer. Prabodh's Indian business partner needed the van for the plastic bag venture and they eagerly made an equitable deal.

In Ouagadougou, we remained with our friends Rudolf and Louise. They had ample room for our animal cages and even a garage without a door where I could work on the van engine before we sold it. This seemed to be a time when my skill as a self-taught mechanic paid off. One day a Lebanese shopkeeper came to me with a VW engine housing and various other larger parts, including a burlap bag full of the small and oily bits and pieces. Everything was thrown together. He had had a mechanic try to repair the engine and the job had never been completed. We agreed upon a price and I set to work. I cleaned all the parts thoroughly with kerosene, replaced the bearings and reassembled the engine in record time. It was a snap and it purred like a kitten. The shopkeeper was very pleased but one of his sons took it immediately

221

out into the bush and the fan belt broke. The engine can still run a short time as long as there is juice in the battery but the fan cooling the engine will no longer turn. The engine should have overheated, especially with the new bearings, but it didn't. I replaced the belt and a leaky seal and the delighted Lebanese gave us a colorful blanket from his store. He then asked me if I would work for him as a mechanic if he opened a garage in town. "But I am not a mechanic", I told him. And he went away, scratching his head in confusion.

The next VW belonged to an army officer with red hair. It was the first time I had seen a black man with red hair. We fixed his engine for a charge but he immediately sold the vehicle to another man who owned a bar. The van was used as a bush taxi and no care was taken to properly run-in the rebuilt engine. It was immediately put to grueling use and very soon it broke down once more with a seized up engine. The VW is air-cooled and suffers very badly in the blistering heat and dust of the African bush.

The last Volkswagen repair was a vehicle belonging to Rudolf and Louise. Naturally, we were glad to help but the vehicle was not in Ouagadougou. It had broken down in the bush somewhere and Rudolf had left it at a French agricultural station a day's journey away. This posed some difficulties. We had to take the replacement parts that we thought we needed along with us, as well as some tools, hoping that the research station would loan us the other more conventional wrenches. We set off by bush taxi, crammed inside with farmers and their wives returning from market with their bundles and livestock. By late afternoon we arrived and presented the French scientist in charge with our letter of introduction from Louise and he quickly welcomed us and offered to help in every way necessary.

The repair was quite straight forward and in no time the vehicle was ready for the return journey. Before we left the two Europeans at the station introduced us to their district. The station was occupied with developing varieties of peanut that might produce a higher yield while remaining resistant to disease. The project was a lengthy one but they seemed optimistic of significant results.

Before the main building was the skull of an elephant which still lay where the creature had been shot when it inadvertently wandered amongst the peanut fields and towards the residence. It had been there several years and was bleached chalk white by the elements. I removed a section of the huge molar teeth to keep as a memento.

The evening before our departure we were invited to join the Frenchmen to watch a film that they had made of African music and dancing. We had seen many of these celebrations and knew them to be both extremely repetitive and interminable. This must have shown in our faces and our host asked us pointedly if we found it tedious. We assured him that we enjoyed his film but, after half an hour, it became excruciating and we excused ourselves because of our early departure the following morning.

* * *

With our van off to its new home, we set about finding a new vehicle. Karl scoured the town and eventually found a Citroen van. That type of vehicle has a small two-cylinder engine in the front. It is extremely cheap to run with extraordinary gas mileage because of the basic nature of its construction.

We bought one that no longer ran and some Mossi men delivered it to us disassembled. Three men came in two vehicles towing the little van. One of the Africans was an enormous man, tall with thick knots of muscle all over his powerful body. The giant was nicknamed *The Car Jack*. We asked why, although we knew the answer already.

"Look here!" said one of his friends. And he yelled at the big man in Mòoré.

With the greatest of ease, the huge fellow reached down under the side of one of the vehicles and lifted it right off the ground. This would be a useful companion to take on a trip into the bush! It is true that the Citroen is a lightweight vehicle compared to most cars but it was an impressive feat. I could scarcely begin to lift even one corner although later we found that with a length of construction lumber as a lever and the aid of a sturdy block as a fulcrum, we had an expedient method of raising a corner of the vehicle to change a flat tire. Thus we applied simple technology to the situation because we lacked a giant of

223

our own. It was so much quicker and easier than using a conventional car jack, particularly as we had a great many punctures on our journey from Ouagadougou to Niamey, the capital of Niger.

The first thing I did was to completely strip the engine and body down to individual parts and go over everything to see what we needed to put it back into reliable working order for our return trip. We bought new cylinders and bearings and added an oil bath air filter that had once been used on a truck. In addition, we made a simple hand operated system so that we could work the accelerator externally. The doors we strapped to the roof so that, should the vehicle begin to slide and drift on a loose surface, we could both jump out while it was still moving and push and drive at the same time. This often spared us much toil and the tedious task of digging out the wheels while manhandling the vehicle to firmer ground.

Soon it was ready. With our possessions reduced to a minimum, there was little extemporaneous baggage of any kind so that we had ample space for water and fuel. Along the side of the Citroen, we secured two lengths of steel boards and a shovel that was essential equipment for every traveler in the desert regions. Even the powerful trucks had to use steel boards from time to time when they became stuck in the wind blown sand.

16. THE SAHARA DESERT

We had made some good friends in Ouagadougou and enjoyed the local people enormously. I think Karl considered staying there much longer and greatly expanding the animal catching business. But we had done very well during the previous several months and we resolved to continue north, visiting three more African countries while crossing the Sahara.

Before we left, however, we were surprised by an unexpected visit. One afternoon, a car drove up and a Frenchman approached the house. It was the man from Lomé who had the animal export business. He was touring with his parents who were visiting from France and had heard that we had missed him in Lomé and had decided to return the courtesy. He had found out where we were from the Austrian school. He was much like Karl although a decade or so older. He was a powerful, extremely confident man and infinitely knowledgeable about the fauna of West Africa. He promised Karl that he could have most of the royal pythons that we had seen at his compound in Lomé and I was certain that Karl was reflecting upon the situation and wondering if a detour south to Toga could somehow be made practical. We enjoyed speaking with him and meeting his parents. He told us of his wife in Lomé who had remained behind and was running things there.

"My wife has even less fear than I," he boasted. "She once put her hand down a pangolin burrow and just pulled the thing out by the tail!"

We had never seen the scaly ant eater but had sometimes discovered the burrows in the neighborhood of termite hills.

We said goodbye to the Frenchman and set about the final preparations for our trip. There were some items that we considered souvenirs that we did not wish to relinquish. These consisted of some animals skins, including the baboon and my cobra skin from Gambia. Also a number of attractive and valuable masks and figures as well as a musical instrument that Karl had bought from a Mossi griot. The young man was a court musician of the king, the Mogho Naba. The *kora* consists of a skin covered calabash as a sound box from which extends a wooden neck like a mandolin. The several strings are horsehair. Our young friend came by one afternoon and struck up a conversation. He played some songs that were droning chants accompanied by a plucking of the strings. We offered him some refreshment and he quickly became light headed from the beer and agreed to sell Karl the instrument. This was a shame and he regretted it later because it meant he had to fabricate a new one.

I made a large wooden crate for these remaining treasures and we shipped them back to Karl's home in Austria. Now we were ready for our northern journey.

If the land is dry and poor in Upper Volta, two thirds of Niger is desert with much of the northeastern part of the country uninhabitable. The remaining third of the country is savanna, suitable mainly for raising livestock and limited agriculture. Niger, like Upper Volta, is landlocked, bordered in the north by Libya, Chad to the east, Nigeria in the south, Benin and Upper Volta in the southwest, Mali in the west and Algeria in the northwest. It is surrounded by these seven other countries and in the north-central region by the volcanic Air Massif mountain range, attaining heights of up to 5,900 ft.

Our chosen route through the desert was the Hoggar. We would leave Ouagadougou and head east towards FadaN'Gourma, cross the border there into Niger at Kantchari, continue to Agadez via Tahoua while gratefully avoiding Nigeria at the southern border. We would cross into Algeria at IN Guezzam, heading north to the Oasis at Tamanrasset and then to Tunisia and the Mediterranean. This is a journey of approximately three thousand miles from Ouagadougou, mostly through the desert.

What a string of exotic sounding names! And, although nothing was to be easy about this trip, it was fascinating to be traveling through these extraordinary regions of Africa.

The first stage of our journey was not particularly difficult but we had added to our difficulties in two significant ways. We had allowed our Upper Volta visas to expire. And we saved money by buying used tires for our Citroen.

We had a friend who was a government minister working in Ouagadougou. We called him *grand frère* as did his cousin Michel who was a close and very good friend of ours. Michel Tapsoba had studied auto mechanics in Austria and spoke fluent German. Upon his return, he had found employment teaching mechanics at the Austrian school in the city. There, with four other former students who had also studied in Austria, he was able to establish a VW repair shop at the school. But later their position was superseded by Europeans.

We had attended Michel's wedding and had joined him and his friends in various other celebrations and parties.

Grand frère was very amicable and introduced us to the officer in charge of visas but, instead of being helpful, this individual screamed all kinds of abuse, trying to intimidate extra money out of us. We had had too many experiences of this kind of thing and, of course, we refused. However, we still needed visas to leave the country.

Karl put a brilliant if dubious scheme into operation. He went to the police station and reported the theft of our passports. The officer in charge gave us a piece of paper as a temporary substitute for the passports with which we could cross the border.

The road was pretty good for a short while but it soon became a two-way dirt track. Choking dust clouds of red powder accompanied every vehicle as it sped by. When we passed a truck or bush taxi the way forward was temporarily entirely obscured.

The jarring, shaking punishment of the washboard surface continued hour after hour. Fortunately, the Citroen rode the bumps like a little boat over the waves and the experience was quite different from the Volkswagen.

At the border, we sheepishly presented our slip of paper to the officer in charge and crossed into Niger without any further difficulty.

But the road became terrible and now the tires started to cause trouble. We had one flat after another. We would lurch off onto the side of the road, lever the car into the air with our block and the length of timber, remove the wheel and get to work. It was very difficult to repair a car tire using tire levers in the dust and heat at the side of the road but we had to remove the tire and repaired the inner tubes over and over again. We had so many punctures that the threads of the nuts holding the wheels on became damaged and were only able to attach the first four of the five securing nuts, then only three on a couple of the wheels. I have never changed and repaired tires so many times in my entire life. We would drive just twenty or thirty miles and a tire would burst again.

The washboard roads were occasionally resurfaced to a moderate flatness by towing a series a huge metal brushes behind a tractor. The bristles of the brushes would eventually break off and remain scattered in the way, mile after mile, along the track. It was these little tacks that pierced our worn tires.

Eventually, we arrived at a mission station run by American evangelists. They were very kind to us and allowed us to camp in their compound while we set about making repairs because we were also having trouble with the brakes. During the course of the week some other travelers in two Citroens came heading along the same road in the direction of Niamey. Their vehicles were much newer and their tires were in good condition. They very kindly lent us one of their several spare tires so that we could continue our trip. We promised to return it when we arrived in Niamey.

Pretty soon we were on the road again and this time things were better as the road improved and we arrived in Niamey without too many more difficulties. We drove into town realizing that we needed to reorganize and become thoroughly prepared for the desert part of the journey. We needed to remove the wheels and have new bolts welded on. We needed new tires and brake cylinders and, most of all, somewhere to work on the Citroen and prepare for the next stage of the expedition.

As we drove through town, we saw a European lady in the garden in front of her house. She and her husband were from France and involved in one of the many aid programs trying to alleviate the destitution of the native people impoverished by the terrible five-year drought.

The French lady very kindly allowed us to camp in her garden and even told us to use their swimming pool.

That evening, she and her husband invited us to join them for dinner and, towards the end of the meal, the French lady asked me if I could ride a horse. I told her that I could.

"Well, take mine out for a ride tomorrow. It needs exercise!"

So before dawn the next morning the watchman came to me

with the horse already saddled up and ready to go. But the animal was nervous. I headed for a quiet track down by the river but it seemed the horse was on high alert the whole time. I calmed it as much as I could until we came across a couple of young men selling bread at the corner on the street. They started yelling and begging in the usual city fashion and I cursed and insulted them back but suddenly the horse decided it was time to go. It pulled back its head and, in a furious panic, bolted off down the road and swerved along the track, which was fortunately the direction that I had intended to go.

After a while I was able to bring it under control and we continued our morning exercise with a dignified walk. The next day Karl took it for a ride and it seemed to respect scarcely better.

Within a week or so (nothing happens fast in Africa) we were ready to continue our journey. The van had new tires and repaired brakes. We had bought a large quantity of canned food as well as a box of dates. But before setting out, we decided that we would drive out of town and spend a week exploring along the river for a few miles.

We were probably twenty miles from the city when, to our surprise, we saw a sign at the side of the road that said, "Campground". This was the very first time in all our travels that we had seen such a place. We had always camped out in the bush. There weren't any official campgrounds as far as we knew. We decided that these people must be Europeans.

We headed down the track and soon came to a clearing with a number of small tin-roofed buildings accompanied by picnic tables and other facilities arranged in perfect order and tidiness. Sure enough, two young men from Germany ran this place.

They had crossed the desert from north to south along the way that we were soon to be headed. They had two vehicles, a German four-wheel drive army truck and a Volkswagen van. Predictably, their VW engine had seized up in the desert and one of them had rebuilt it inside the van during a sandstorm. They were interesting characters and we spent the afternoon and evening with them, talking and drinking beer.

Both of these men had served in the German army where military service was compulsory just as it was in Austria. One of them had been a truck driver and he began to relate the odd phenomenon of driving in a convoy.

"The leading truck heads out driving close to the speed limit. The second follows but has to catch up and drives a little faster. The third now has to drive faster still in order to maintain the convoy. If you are last in line you have to drive like a fury to keep up."

I have repeated this story many times. I have even explained it to a mathematician. Invariably, they maintain that it is not possible. If the vehicles travel at the same speed they will remain evenly spaced. But here was a soldier who had actually experienced the phenomenon. While abstractly his take is easily faulted, in practice what he said occurred consistently. His friend confirmed it.

At dusk another guest arrived, also a German called Alto. Several African companions accompanied him. Alto had been a travel guide, taking tourists on treks into the Northern Sahara. Unfortunately, he had become lost on one such trip and, during the ensuing panic, one of his passengers had died of a heart attack from the heat and stress. They had found their way back but Alto had a lawsuit looming over him and was prudently avoiding civilization, hiding out in Niger.

Soon it was dark and one of the Germans decided that he wanted to get a mosquito net, swim across the river and sleep on an island some distance from the bank. I told him that I would swim over also and he ran to find two mosquito nets.

His friend said, "This is the sort of clearly thought out plan that occurs to people who drink too much beer!" And he managed to dissuade us from our reckless nocturnal adventure.

Back in Niamey we were greeted with quite a surprise. There were soldiers at all the crossroads and a roadblock across the road leading back into town. It is alarming to be confronted by hostile, heavily armed soldiers but, in Africa, there is another element that made me very nervous. It was the casual way they carried their rifles. They were carelessly slung across their shoulders or hooked under the arm, pointing dangerously in all directions while the men stood around chatting and even laughing. We asked them what was going on and one of the men said ominously, "Coup d'Etat".

This was our second in Africa. The first time was in Dahomey where there had been an assassination attempt on the life of President Mathieu Kerekou. That had upset the president very much and his typical vitriolic anti-European radio broadcasts had become even worse than before. We also had heard that a Frenchman had been involved in the plot and that made matters even worse. People were beaten up in the streets, stores looted and cars smashed. Niger, on top of all its troubles from the drought, was now going through the same thing.

Later in the afternoon the few cars gathered at the roadblock were allowed to proceed. We headed back into town to see our French friends who told us that the government had indeed been taken over by the army. President Hamani Diori was overthrown and his wife, who shot at one of the soldiers, had been killed. This was April 1974. The French couple had heard gunfire and sirens all night long. It was a very abrupt change of the administration and we took it to be a clear sign that we should be on our way.

The evening before our departure Karl and I visited a small bar that was merely the back room and courtyard of an adobe hut. We seated ourselves on a bench at a long table and ordered two beers. There were several Africans in the room but, because of the shadows, they were unaware that we were white.

All at once the African man next to me leaned over and spoke in English.

"I was in the British Army during the war," he confided. "I have my papers here to prove it".

He reached into his robe and produced his identity papers, along with a reference from his commanding officer. The paper was a verification of his honesty. No mean achievement in West Africa.

It stated, "I am very pleased with this man. He is reliable and doesn't steal or drink".

It was nice to sit and talk with him in a normal way, with only quiet conversation going on all around and no other disturbance.

I wished my Nigerian friend a good night and Karl and I returned to our camp.

The following morning, on our way across town heading for the road to Agadez, we stopped at a little African eatery that we had visited a few times before. They served the most delicious white yams.

These yams are enormous roots, weighing as much as twenty pounds. They are boiled until soft and then pounded into a firm paste by two women, each working a long wooden pestle. There were several women running the place and the yams were stamped fresh for each person's meal and served with a hot peppery fish sauce. It was delicious.

In spite of the unfortunate business while I was horseback riding, the people of Niamey were really very nice. The several times that we had eaten at the café we were treated with the same indifference as anyone else and no one tried to cheat us.

I attributed the civility of the people of Niamey to the metropolitan nature of the city. We had been to other cities where we were jeered at and taunted as we walked down the street. It seemed like a national sport that often made us furious. In one city, a bunch of kids even began throwing stones at us. But we never really had any trouble from the middle-aged or older people except, on that one occasion, in Dahomey when a villager had attacked us. But he was incensed because of the negative propaganda against whites that he had heard on the radio. This was very unusual and quite contrary to conventional custom and hospitality.

Apart from the Europeans in Niamey, there were refugees from different African cultures because of the famine. We saw Peuls, easy to recognize because of the elaborate hair of the women and the countless silver coins that they wear as a symbol of the wealth and status of their husbands. They have the same pleasing characteristics typical of Ethiopians: beautiful oval faces and defined features.

There were many Tuareg tribesmen, riding high and proud on their camels and I even saw a couple of young Fulani men wearing swords while casually walking down the street. They looked very poised and confidently marshal and were indeed authentic warriors. I thought I had stepped back into the middle ages or during the time of the Crusades. Years later, I came across a book of old black and white photographs from before the First World War. One of the pictures showed a mounted tribesman in Mali dressed in quilted cloth armor and wearing a helmet. He carried a spear and a sword and even his horse had a quilted blanket for protection in battle. It was very easy to

232

make a comparison to the European medieval knight. The speculation was that this was indeed a historical throwback from the time of the Crusades when the tribesmen had imitated the arms and armor of the invading armies.

Our plan was to travel the six hundred miles to Agadez and hopefully meet up with some other travelers heading north for the crossing to the oasis of Tamanrasset. This was smart. Between Agadez and Tamanrasset there is only desert, without either gas or water. Traveling with others is essential.

We hoped to see some wildlife on the way as there was said to be giraffe in the area around Niamey. In fact, there was a paddock in the center of the city where a solitary giraffe was kept. This whetted our interest to see them in the wild. We drove out of town some distance where we were told that we might see giraffes but, unfortunately, that day we were unlucky and it was time to journey on.

The journey to Agadez took us through the drought-stricken Sahel zone where the nomadic tribes had suffered appallingly during the recent years, losing most of their livestock. They were reduced to destitution. There were enormous camps established for them offering food and shelter. We spoke to a number of people involved in the relief work and heard many different opinions. It was suggested that, as there had always been droughts, it was, in fact, the relative prosperity, better health care and western medicine that had caused an increase in population and the consequent overgrazing of the sparse vegetation by their livestock. When the rains did not come what grass there was became quickly devoured. In the camps, the people lost all heart and hope, the men sat about and waited forlornly, the young women turned to prostitution while the boys begged and stole.

It was appalling to see the enormous piles, one mound after another, of bleached animal bones as we drove along the track and to hear the groups of devastated people at the roadside yelling out to us, hoping for a handout.

The journey was pretty difficult. The paved road ended quickly and soon there was only a sandy track into which we frequently sank up to the axles. We had removed the doors of the Citroen and tied them to the roof. If the wheels began to sink into the burning hot sand, we could sometimes jump out quickly and push the van through a soft area. Our device that adapted the gas pedal so that it could be operated by hand, while pushing the vehicle at the same time, worked splendidly. This saved us a lot of digging out. But the sand was patchy: soft here and then suddenly firm again. In spite of our clever maneuver, jumping out while the vehicle was still running, we had to dig away the soft sand many, many times and lay down metal boards so that we could get the tires to grip and reach the harder surface. It sometimes helped to speed and traverse a soft spot using the momentum. With luck, we sometimes avoided some of the tedious digging. There was one stretch where we stopped time after time. It was predictable that, no sooner were we free, then we became bogged down once more in the talcum-fine dust. The entire journey through the desert was an experience in endurance but this particular stretch from Niamey to Agadez was insufferable. We struggled mile after tedious mile, day after day. Karl and I were so exhausted that tempers flared and we almost came to blows with each other.

Karl was standing in the door frame on his side of the vehicle while I drove. We rotated driving each day and today happened to be my turn at the wheel. It was sometimes possible to see the patches of lighter colored, finer sand and avoid them. As Karl saw an apparent soft spot, he would indicate it to me by waving his arm in that direction. It seemed to work but I could not always tell exactly what direction he was pointing and, sure enough, we suddenly sank down yet again into a nasty stretch of soft sand.

Karl was furious and started yelling and cussing. We were both worn out. I went for him. We locked into a deadly grip, hands around each others' throats and started to snarl furiously at one another.

While Karl had started the whole thing, he did not see it that way and yelled something to the effect: "If you fight me, you'll make the mistake of your life!"

The soundness of his reasoning was self-evident and it breached the fury of the moment. It made glaring sense, in spite of our rage. We had to work together whatever might happen or we were done for. I released him and he let go of my throat and we just walked away. If you lose your temper in the Sahara, you lose everything.

234

Calm once more, we quietly dug the van out and drove to some firm ground where we cooked our canned food and found a suitable place off the track to make camp for the night. Strangely, during this part of the journey, we never saw a single other vehicle. Not even one. This made it even more dangerous. There was no help if needed and no civilization for hundreds of miles. We might just as well have been entirely alone in the world.

The days passed, sometimes without event, but frequently it was a struggle that required enormous staying power. When Karl was driving and the way was smooth and steady I simply closed my eyes and half-slept, conserving energy for the next day. We spoke very little and this became our practice during the rest of the trip. The air was as dry as parchment and the sun merciless. There was simply no strength to spare. Our faces were abraded from the blowing sand as we had removed the doors out of necessity. Quickly our lips became chapped and bleeding. We had a linen sheet that we tore into lengths like wide bandages and, with these, we bound our faces in the manner of the Tuareg. I found that by moistening the cloth around the mouth with spit the splitting and cracking and consequent discomfort was considerably reduced. Mercifully, the nights were cooler and we revived sufficiently to prepare our evening meal and check the vehicle, replenishing the oil in the air filter and making sure we were ready for the next day. Finally, thoroughly exhausted, we made it to Agadez, the oldest town in Niger and the gateway to the Sahara proper.

We found the campground that was a well known rendezvous where travelers beginning the Tamanrasset stage of the journey could meet up and travel in convoy. It was a compound built of red and yellow adobe brick and we paid just a small amount to camp there and use the bucket showers. You had to fill a bucket at the well then pour the water into another that was hung upon a beam. The bucket on the beam had a shower sprinkler attached to it. You pulled a chain and enjoyed a quick cold splash. It was very welcome and pleasantly refreshing.

At first, we were the only travelers there and enjoyed a few days' respite. As usual, there were things that needed attention in order to be prepared for the long trip ahead through the desert, void of oases or habitation, until Tamanrasset. We had extra cans of gasoline as well as all the water that we could carry. We still had plenty of canned fish as well as the dates and a few other provisions.

Our first arrivals were three young Japanese men with a four wheel drive Toyota Land Cruiser. We made friends right away. They were great guys and we were delighted to travel with them. Their Toyota could drive through anything and we were hoping for a quick crossing. They were mountain climbers and had traveled to Kenya and were now on their return journey to North Africa and then home by sea. They all spoke a little English and we got on just fine. We were thinking of setting off with just the Japanese men as companions but later that day another traveler arrived. He was an Arab who had a repair garage in Kano, Nigeria and was also headed back to North Africa. Unfortunately, he drove a Volkswagen van and we were very apprehensive about traveling with him because of our own experience with the VW. Neither of us liked this sullen man very much but the Japanese seemed willing and we finally agreed to travel on altogether the next morning.

We set out as soon as everyone was ready and headed north on the long desert road. In fact, the road was merely a direction through the sand marked every few miles by oil drums filled with rocks. We only saw four or five other vehicles on the road each day, most of which were trucks carrying whatever could be sold in the south together with a few passengers. Some of the trucks carried firewood. It seemed an enormous distance to travel with just a load of wood! It also now seemed strange that we had seen no other travelers along the stretch from Niamey to Agadez but suddenly there were several vehicles each day. Then it occurred to me that they were all headed not to Niamey but Kano, Nigeria which was the typical route for travelers using the Hoggar route. From Kano, they could travel west to Niamey by a different route and avoid altogether the dreadful track that we had traveled.

The first few days were fairly uneventful with us slowly and steadily traveling in convoy with only a few occasions when we became stuck in the sand. The Japanese men were very generous and willingly towed either us or the Arab out of the soft sand several times each day so that we were quickly on our way again without the incessant labor of digging out the wheels.

The Arab was a rude and gross individual and our opinion of him did not improve. There was nothing pleasant in his character. In the evenings, he sat with us and cussed and grumbled. He complained on every subject.

"Ah, the Bridge … I do not like the Bridge. In Nigeria, they think they are mightier than us …" And then he would spit. He did not realize that I was *"Bridge"* or British, thinking that both Karl and I were Austrian or perhaps Australian. He was not quite sure of the distinction. The Japanese mountaineers disliked him also. But we were nevertheless stuck with him.

We were about half way to Tamanrasset when suddenly there was another problem with him. His van engine seized up. Luckily, he was a mechanic and he began stripping the motor down to do repairs. It is true that you cannot get far in Africa unless you can fix your own vehicle but a complete overhaul would take a lot of time. We did not wish to wait around in the desert. We discussed the problem with the Japanese. We were already proceeding slower than they had expected because of the many times we were getting stuck in the sand. They agreed that we should continue on as best we could while they would stay with the Arab until his VW was running again. They could easily catch us up once they got going.

Karl and I set off. It was his day to drive. When he drove I again relaxed as completely as I could, conserving my energy for the next day's travel. Without doors, the wind-whipped sand was constant and blistering but the face bandages we had fabricated worked remarkably well. We looked very strange: our door-less Citroen, motoring steadily across the vast desert, our faces swathed like a couple of mummies.

We made quite good progress and only got stuck in the sand once or twice that day.

As we drove along Karl noticed that the road was curving consistently in a steady arc and he suggested that we could save many miles by cutting "across country" off the track and meeting it again later as it continued to curve. This seemed a reasonable idea so we set

237

off across the dunes. A few times we had to jump out and push with the engine still running in the manner that we had developed to a fine art but we were never thoroughly stuck in the sand.

However, it was taking a long time to get back to the track. There was absolutely no sign of the oil drum markers on any horizon anywhere we looked. We had no idea if, by this time, we were ourselves traveling in a circle and would miss the way entirely. There was also the distressing possibility that we had already crossed the track between the oil drums which could have been obscured from view by the terrain. And all the time the shifting sands and the brisk wind were concealing our tracks behind us. It also occurred to me that we might miss the Japanese and the Arab as they tried to catch up with us and they might instead pass us by completely.

But I did not say a word. We had made it through so many hazards that I had grown to trust that we would always come through. Then suddenly, over the next rise, appeared the track with the oil barrel markers!

"That was a close call!" Karl said, with relief. Clearly, the same apprehensive thoughts had crossed his mind, too. We descended the rise and rejoined the proper track.

While the journey was grueling, it would be a mistake to imagine that it was merely physical endurance and that we failed to be impressed by the majesty of the Sahara. The sculpted dunes towering above us, orange like fire in the fierce sunlight, wind carved and shaped into magnificent writhing ridges and rippling away towards the horizon. The spectacular colors, grays and blues and stark white. And the shadows cast, lurking between the ridges or thrown in long splashes by the retreating sun. It was both majestic and intimidating at the same time.

The next day, towards evening, the rest of the party caught up with us. The Japanese had the Arab in tow. He had traveled a few miles with his repaired engine but it had broken down yet again.

We had just set up camp when we noticed two vehicles heading south down the track. They were brand new Land Rovers and we were green with envy. One of them was large, like a passenger truck, while the leader was the conventional size. The vehicles stopped and several

238

young men jumped out and we chatted amiably with them for a while. They were all students from an English university on a desert trek during their vacation time.

The Land Rovers were very well equipped. Obviously, they were well financed. The entire trip from Tunis to Kano in Nigeria can be made in two weeks or less with a Land Rover. Our own total travel time from Ouagadougou to Tunis was to last almost three months. There were ten people in the Land Rovers including several very pretty girls. We invited them all to camp near us for the night so that we could talk some more. But the drivers said that they wanted to travel a little further on before stopping. I noticed that the passengers were all very silent. The girls wore sullen, worn expressions of strain and fatigue. They were spending day after day sitting in the back of the Land Rovers with nothing to do, no tasks or responsibilities. They were just passengers. There was no distraction, only the endless sand and nothing to do but sit. It is well known that people new to the desert or wilderness begin to unravel. I had a friend who, as a young man, drove overland from England to India four times. On the last trip, he agreed to take a small party with him and he equipped an old ambulance for that purpose.

He noticed that, during the long journey, the passengers with nothing to do experienced a certain madness. They became unreasonable and would fight and argue and even burst into tears for no reason. It looked to me as if the pretty girls in the back of the Land Rover were experiencing the early stages of a similar phenomenon.

We, again, pressed them to stay but they insisted on continuing. It probably would have done them all a lot of good to have stopped and talked a little, sharing a cup of coffee before they set off once again. Strangely, we noticed that they made their private camp just a few miles further down the track from us. We could see them there from our camp. This made the Arab bitter and he began grumbling and cursing about the "Bridge" aloofness. But, in reality, the young men we spoke with seemed merely bewildered and perhaps even a little shy. They had suddenly traveled out here, fresh from college and civilization, full of excitement and adventure. And here they were now, in the middle of a vast endless nowhere, entirely on their own with only their wits to rely on and saddled with a bunch of despondent passengers. They seemed overwhelmed, exhausted and they appeared to have already reached that threshold where people become unreasonably irritated with one another. The last thing they wanted was to sit around in the middle of the desert with an assortment of strangers of whom only one spoke their language. But they should have. Remaining insular, they would miss the authentic Africa of which fellow-travelers through the desert were an interesting part.

The next couple of days were relatively uneventful and we soon arrived in Tamanrasset, the Japanese with the Arab in tow. There we parted company with the Arab as he set out to find some way to repair his Volkswagen. He grunted a "Goodbye" and we were glad to see the back of him.

At Tamanrasset, we were able to replenish our water and fuel and prepare for the next stage of the journey onwards to In Salah, a distance of just over four hundred miles.

It would be true to say that our trip might have been easier if we would have had a vehicle such as the English students with their Land Rover. But we did not have that kind of funding. We had each scraped and saved for over a year and a half before we set out on our journey. And, while still in Austria making preparations, we had also worked hard and saved every penny we could.

Shipping animals back to Europe had proved to be a precarious business for most of the three years we spent in Africa. It was only in Ouagadougou that we started to make some significant income from our variety of schemes and enterprises. A Land Rover would have been nice but it was quite out of the question.

There were many interesting and exciting adventures on the desert part of our journey beyond digging our Citroen out of the sand and attending to various mechanical failures. Even in the Sahara, Karl was busy catching animals. We made our camp late one afternoon after a particularly tiring day motoring in the heat and struggling to make good time. Several times along the way we had come across abandoned vehicles. There was usually not a bolt or a screw left on them that was any use and the remaining steel was wind-whipped and burnished. Any part that could be unbolted was removed and gone. They were merely chassis skeletons, steadily being further worn away by the relentless wind driven sand. It may take a hundred years but one day all that steel would be reduced to powder and lost forever among the dunes.

We made our camp next to the shell of an unrecognizable car and rigged up the canvas flysheet to allow some shelter from the remaining afternoon sun.

Karl wandered over to the wreck and pulled away a sheet of metal that had once been the hood. To his astonishment, there was a poisonous snake under it. It was some kind of adder that he deftly transferred it to a cloth bag and tied securely. We had a number of creatures in the back of the vehicle by this time, including at least one python that we had brought from Upper Volta. Other dangerous snakes were bagged up and kept in a cage.

Another time, we stopped, for some reason or other, beside the track and Karl noticed the spoor of a monitor lizard and set off in pursuit. The likelihood of him catching up with the creature was remote. But he did. He was following the tracks when suddenly, there before him, was the lizard. It turned and hissed at him but Karl gripped it by the back of the head and lower body and brought it back to camp. It was probably eighteen inches long, golden brown and writhing with all its strength. It joined the other creatures in the back of the Citroen.

We encountered other more traditional wanderers of the desert beyond the few trucks heading south. One day a Tuareg, swathed in black, sitting high on his camel, rode out of the swirling wind. He asked us in French for water using just that one word, "de l'eau."

This was not a good sign. Of all people in the world, the Tuareg knew the exact location of water in the desert. It is, after all, their own back yard and their lives depended upon such knowledge. We were well aware that he did not want water but, at the very least, hoped for some sort of handout. We were also concerned that he may not have been alone. It made no sense. He must have seen us approaching from afar and ridden to intercept us. In all likelihood it was his and the intent of the as yet invisible companions to rob us. We waved him off aggressively and continued on our way.

It is because of dangers such as these that it was wiser to drive in convoy with other travelers. The Agadez to Tamanrasset section was the longest and loneliest stretch without towns or oasis along the way. But we enjoyed the continued companionship of our Japanese friends and I suspect that they appreciated the shrewd and mildly cynical manner in which we viewed things, an approach that we had painstakingly acquired through our many direct experiences in West Africa.

Between Tamanrasset and In Salah, we had some more mechanical troubles. The suspension system on the front of the Citroen broke away from the chassis and sheared the bolts securing it clear through. We had bounced over a particularly nasty trough in the road. There was a loud crack and the front wheel disappeared into the wheel housing so that we could neither move forward nor backwards.

It was very hot and dusty and there was nowhere to do a proper repair except in the blistering sun. I wanted to improvise and rope the beam that we used as a lever to change tires under the vehicle. I thought that, if we could insert the beam beneath the front axle system and bind it securely, we could at least continue until we found a place where we could work more easily or perhaps even reach In Salah and do a proper repair.

But Karl saw things differently and again we almost lost our tempers with one another. The Japanese were very distressed to see us arguing. But they had only been on the road a couple of months and drove a vehicle built for this terrain. By comparison, we were exhausted.

I decided to acquiesce and do the repairs where we were and, carefully, I removed the two broken bolts. Luckily, the heads had sheered off and I was able to grip the stems and unscrew them. Unfortunately, we only had one bolt that would fit and that was too short to grip the chassis significantly.

As we were considering what to do next, a huge diesel truck drove by and, seeing that we were in difficulties, the African driver stopped. He was a nice guy and showed real concern for our situation. He let me look through his toolbox to see if I could find a bolt that would fit. He had all kinds of junk in the box, including wire and nails and rusty bits of metal, as well as bolts of all sizes and shapes. He clearly needed this stuff in case he broke down himself and had to improvise a repair. I had a similar box myself. A number of the trucks we saw crossing the desert were old and dilapidated and gave the impression that they limped from one town or oasis to the next, held together with wire and good luck.

But there was no bolt in his box that would work for our problem. Either they were too short or too long or had the wrong thread. It looked as if we would have to improvise a repair with the beam and rope after all.

I put his things back into the box and closed the lid hasp, securing it with the bolt that he had for the purpose.

Suddenly I began to laugh! The bolt used to hold the toolbox closed was the exact one that fitted our broken axle. It was incredible good fortune and our new friend was as delighted as we were. He wished us "Bon Voyage!", waving happily as he drove off down the track on his way south. To secure the axle was now easy and, in no time, we continued on our way.

A day or two later, we had another interesting experience. We came across the wreck of a Citroen. As usual, there was nothing left to salvage except, by luck, the springs were still attached. I was able to remove those crucial bolts to use as spares and even replace the entire front axle system with this abandoned one which was in better condition that our own.

We were now in far better shape but we were still in for one final calamity. On the outskirts of In Salah, the spring suspension broke altogether. You cannot drive the Citroen without that suspension spring. The springs lie horizontally along the sides of the vehicle and hold the wheels down and in place. If they fail than the wheels cannot rotate.

Karl and two of the Japanese decided to drive into town and try to get the part welded. I would stay with the vehicle and our other friend and guard the camp. We sat in the shade of the tarp in front of a small table that we had set up and we waited. It was going to take some time and the heat was intolerable.

A fly settled on the table and I swatted and, by luck, killed it. Another landed and the Japanese man squashed it. Sometimes it was possible to catch them by hand, coming from behind so that, as they took off, you could whisk them up. We also hit them with our shoes.

By the time the others returned with the repaired spring we had between us squashed almost one hundred flies. It was a novel new way of measuring time.

In In Salah, we had a farewell feast with our good-natured Japanese friends. We were extremely grateful to them for their many kindnesses, in particular for dragging us innumerable times through patches of soft sand. We were headed for Tunisia and would follow the same route as them but they now needed to travel faster. Our broken down old car was slowing them down. Out of gratitude, we paid for a fine lunch of couscous and stewed lamb, washed down with cold beer and we bade them farewell.

Before we continued on our own way, however, we met some other travelers who were headed south. They were a young man from France and his pretty girlfriend and they were traveling alone. They had a Citroen car like the one we had found wrecked a few days earlier. I chatted with the young man and he proudly showed me the innovations he had made to his vehicle. He had added extra springs to the suspension and other small improvements. But I knew from our experience that these alterations were not going to help him very much.

I asked him where he was going and he replied, "Around the world!"

"And how long will that take?" I asked.

"All our lives if necessary!" he replied, enthusiastically.

He showed me a simple map that he had painted on the hood of his car, indicating the capital cities of the world connected by thick black lines of paint. His girlfriend was very lovely, dressed nicely and she even had painted fingernails. I wished, with all my heart, that they were traveling with some companions or with other vehicles as we had done. We tried to persuade the young man to go in convoy through the desert and we even invited them to camp with us for safety that night. But he would not hear of it and drove off a short distance to make camp just beyond the town. We watched them and they looked charmingly domestic as they set up their site along the roadside, the pretty girl arranging things nicely for their evening meal. What would they do if our Tuareg on his camel descended suddenly from the dunes and begged them for water? And, equally ominously, if they broke down, what then?

A few days later, we camped near the dunes on the soft sand near the road when, to our surprise, three small boys and a young Arab girl turned up at our camp. They settled in, squatting on their haunches and just watched us. We had no idea where they had come from but there must have been a nomad camp nearby, perhaps just over the next dune.

The children stayed around the camp, watching for a little while until we finally drove them off. But we were very alert. We could hear the hideous growling of the camels in the night and we were aware of people close by. We secured the Citroen and then we each settled down for the night at different places in the dunes, some distance away from the vehicle so that we could easily detect anyone approaching.

We had become alert like this after camping for so long in the bush. This hyper-vigilance remained with me months after my return to England. Back in Austria, I also noticed that Karl still went to sleep at night with a flashlight beside his bed. This time nothing happened and the next morning very early we continued on our way towards El Golea and further to Ghardaia.

We were now quite far north, still traveling the sand blown tracks through the Sahara. We had become increasingly adept at jumping out of the van at the first sign of soft sand. Suddenly, ahead of us, we saw something very surprising and very welcome. It was an asphalt road. It was new and the tar was fresh, coal black and smoothly rolled. Naturally, the moment we saw the road the van began to sink into the soft sand as if determined to make one last attempt to claim us.

We jumped out, locked the gas pedal and pushed and lifted for all we were worth. Still we sunk into the sand but we were moving closer and closer to the road until, with one last superhuman effort, the Citroen rose up out of the sand onto the freshly tarred surface. There was a workman attending to some machines and he gaped at us in astonishment as if to say "Where the hell did you come from?"

Now we had no more mechanical problems and there was no

more sinking into the sand. It was the easy life, sailing along the beautiful new road. But our mishaps were not quite over. As we drove on, a truck came in the opposite direction, heading south. As it sped by, it flung a rock from the road surface and smashed our windshield into a thousand tiny pieces. We pulled over and cleaned up the broken glass. We had traveled all this way and now this. As we cleaned up the shattered glass I became aware of our peculiar appearance. The Citroen was battered and dented and without doors or windshield. We had a goat's skin of water tied to the side and all kinds of baggage secured to the roof. Inside the vehicle were cans and cans of water and gas as well as cages of reptiles. And we both looked ragged and exhausted, swathed in our makeshift headgear with cracked and bloody lips and sun bleached hair. No wonder the road worker had stared at us. We could hardly have looked worse if we had traveled the desert on foot.

As soon as we could, we bought a replacement windshield at one of the small towns on the way. I installed it and already our overall appearance improved significantly. We replaced the doors and now began to look almost civilized as we dispensed with the headdresses in order to avoid drawing attention.

Pretty soon we reached the border between Algeria and Tunis. The Tunisian guard would not take the CFA francs we had with us to pay for our visas. He would only accept dollars or dinars. We argued the point with him for a while but it was no use. He would not let us cross the border. We did have some Austrian schillings. These the guard said could be changed at a hotel near the border. One of us could leave and do that while the other would have to wait. Karl drove off to the hotel to change the money and managed to do so without difficulty. We paid for our visas, had our passports stamped and were on our way once more. We decided to head for Tunis right away and rest a little before crossing to Sicily.

Along the way, we noticed how the color of the desert had changed and now was a rosy pink. We stopped and looked closely and saw the most astonishing crystal formations clustered like flowers. There were the famous desert roses and, as we journeyed on, we saw Tunisians selling them from roadside tables.

We found a grassy, vacant building lot where we stopped to rest and eat. As we were relaxing, a young black boy came up and rudely started yelling and begging for a handout. We sent him on his way but he turned and started throwing rocks at us, whereupon Karl gave him a sound kick in the backside for his trouble. But some Arab men had seen what was going on and they came over, furious with us.

"How could you do that to a kid?" one man yelled.

Karl yelled back that he was throwing rocks at us. But the men were very angry and we realized that we were no longer in lawless Africa but on the doorstep of Europe. Here we must not take matters into our own hands.

I spoke quietly with the men, telling them of our long trip through the desert.

"We are not at all pleased to be treated like this," I said, as I quietly turned away. To this day, I have no idea why this worked but the men left and later, when we saw them on the veranda of a café, they waved at us in a friendly manner as we drove by. Perhaps they had concluded that the kid had deserved a kick in the pants.

I really liked the Tunisian people. They were without exception, friendly and kind. We camped for a while near the beach, resting and preparing for our re-entry into Europe and easily made friends with the people we came to know. One family we met was particularly kind. The mother, enveloped in her black gown, gave me the ring from her finger. It was a brass ring with the shape of the Eiffel Tower set into a black background. I kept it for years but, unfortunately, I have since lost it.

We spent a couple of weeks camped on the beach until we were ready to take the ferry over to Sicily. We knew that we would need car insurance in Italy and, at Palermo, we found a company selling the necessary minimum coverage and then we headed toward the ferry that would take us across the Straits of Messina to the Italian mainland.

We motored along fairly slowly because the Citroen would no longer travel at usual speed. The engine had become worn by the sand and we had lost compression. We were beneath a road bridge near the port of Palermo when suddenly a police car cut us off and made us stop. The two young officers got out and began yelling at us.

247

One of them snarled, "You two! I am going to throw you in jail!"

But we had experienced this kind of intimidation a dozen times before. We showed them our insurance and engaged them in as little conversation as possible. They tried to threaten us again but soon realized that they would get no money out of us. We had become infinitely hardened to this kind of extortion. They saw the beaten up vehicle, noticed our rough appearance and stubborn faces and realized that they had met their match. They got back into their police car and sped off down the road, furiously.

* * *

This concludes the story of our Africa adventure. Without mishap, we drove through Italy and into Austria, stopping first in Innsbruck and then staying a couple of weeks with Karl's father in Styria. He had been incredibly helpful and supportive of us during our journey and he welcomed us back enthusiastically, having followed the entire adventure through our letters. It was strange to see him again after three years. He did not quite know what to think of his son nor did he realize the skills, resourcefulness and confidence that Karl had developed.

Karl sold the remaining animals to a pet shop in Graz, gave a couple of newspapers an outline of our story and began thinking about a return visit to Africa. We parted company at the Graz railway station, and, although initially I exchanged a couple of letters with Karl's father, Karl and I did not stay in touch. I have no idea what he did with his life after our journey or if he indeed returned to Africa. But I suspect he pursued an adventurous and fascinating life in some exotic country.

When I returned to England I was astonished how easy life was in comparison. I compared the stress and strain of even one day living rough in the bush with the ease of quiet civilization and realized just how significant our journey had been. For a while I had to check myself, over-reacting to any small sound or sudden movement and, of course, it became immediately apparent that the machete had to go.

POSTSCRIPT

Upon my return from Austria, I worked in Plymouth, England on the restoration of a three-masted schooner at Milbay Docks. Shipwrights, specialists in the craft, who would move from one such job to the next, all over the country, surrounded me. The entire deck of the ship was replaced with Iroko, African teak four inches thick. I enjoyed doing the caulking, wedging oakum into the cracks and pouring hot tar into the seams. Below decks an artisan has set up his lathe and was busy making belaying pins of Iroko, deadeyes and bullseyes from lignum vitae. Yet another craftsman was carving an eagle for the figurehead while someone else was making furniture. The ship was being refurbished into a floating restaurant.

This wonderful experience, more or less, shaped my future. I was determined to work in wood and, some years later, I had the good fortune to attend Emerson College, in England on a scholarship, studying sculpture. It was an excellent program with the students spending the entire day, every day, in the studio working with clay or carving wood and stone. Later, I worked as a theater properties artisan at the world-renowned Oregon Shakespeare Festival in Ashland, Oregon, U.S.A. The furniture we made in the prop shop had to be even better constructed than usual and stronger so that it could be moved about and stored after each show. The versatility I developed while working in theater and with theater designers was phenomenal.

Eventually, I left the theater in order to establish, with my wife Ellen, our own furniture-making business which has been a great success and a source of enormous pleasure over the years.

What a far cry this is from the wilds of Africa, which has continued to haunt my memory over the decades. It is for this reason that I have revisited the subject, reworking my original notes in order to expand the narrative with greater detail and historical significance. But the story remains as authentic as it happened.

I have been able to locate Karl Bischof in recent years. Unlike myself, he continued in a more exotic direction, developing a significant business exporting tropical fish from distant places.